To Claire,

Happy Christmas, hope you like my photographs and enjoy the views of the Dorset Coast.

Maybe you could visit some when you are there.

THE DORSET COAST

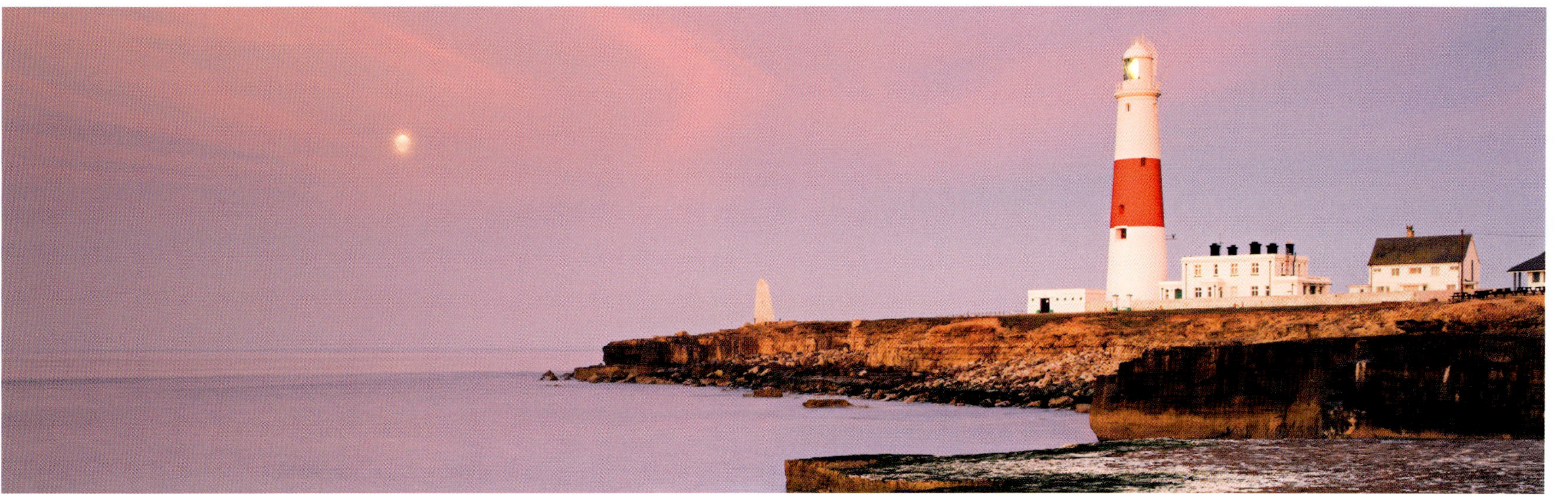

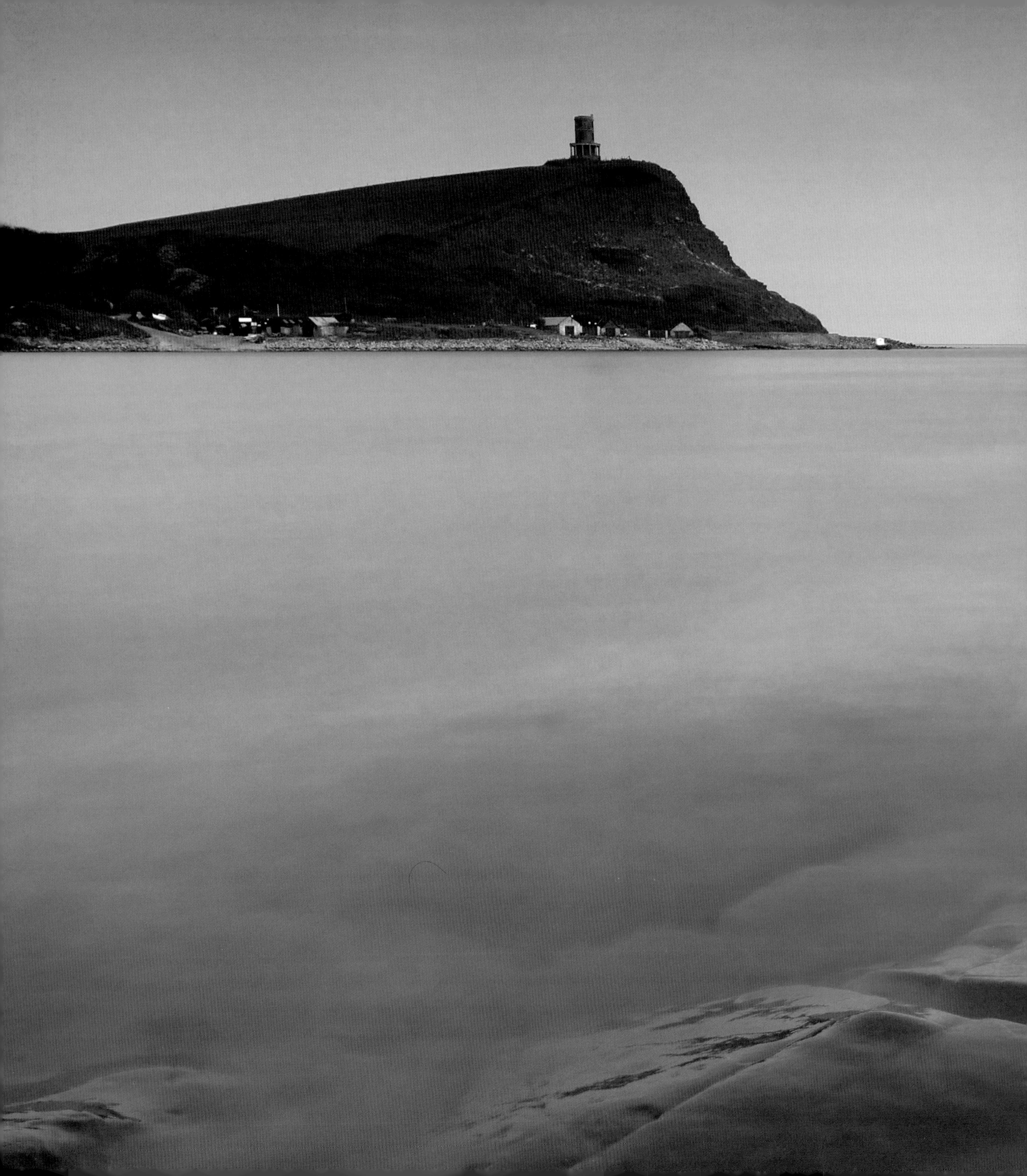

THE DORSET COAST

Adam Burton

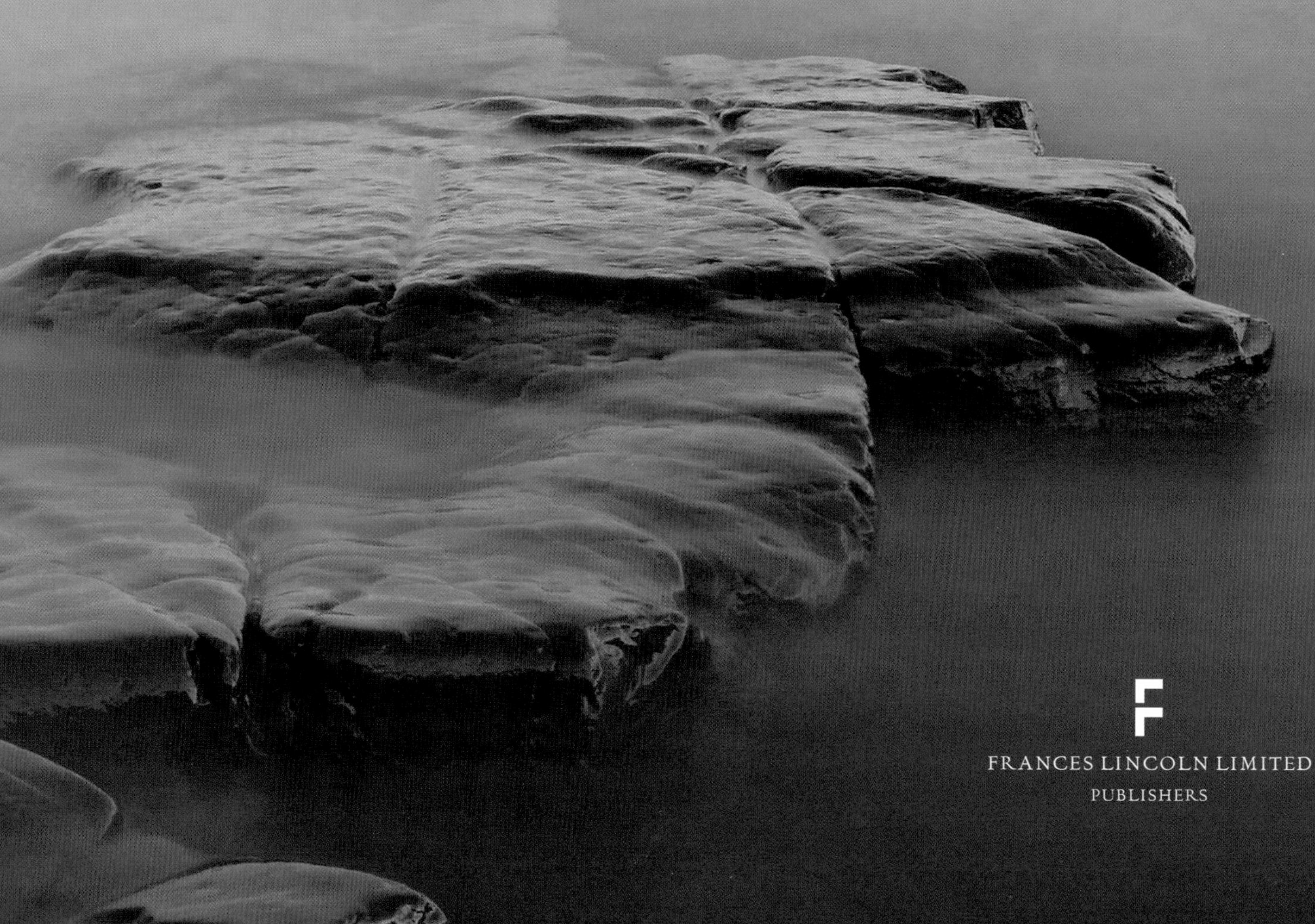

FRANCES LINCOLN LIMITED
PUBLISHERS

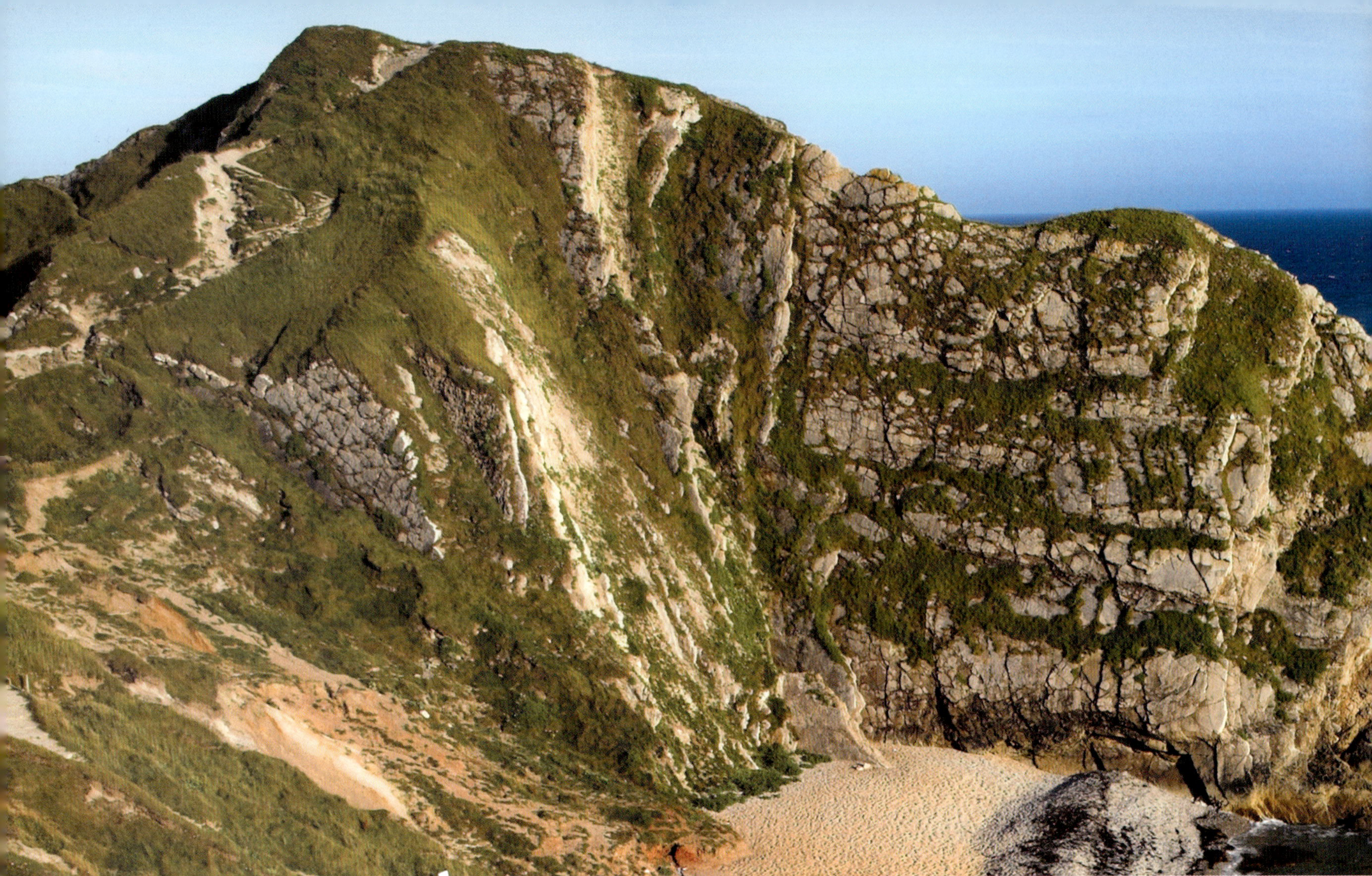

Frances Lincoln Ltd
4 Torriano Mews
Torriano Avenue
London NW5 2RZ
www.franceslincoln.com

For Beth, thank you for all your love
and support

The Dorset Coast
Copyright © Frances Lincoln Ltd 2008
Text and photographs copyright © Adam Burton 2008
First Frances Lincoln edition 2008
Designed by Ian Hunt

British Library Cataloguing-in-Publication data
A catalogue record for this book is available from the British Library.

ISBN 13: 978-0-7112-2919-8
ISBN 10: 0-7112-2919-8

Printed and bound in Singapore

9 8 7 6 5 4 3 2 1

PHOTOGRAPHIC ACKNOWLEDGEMENTS

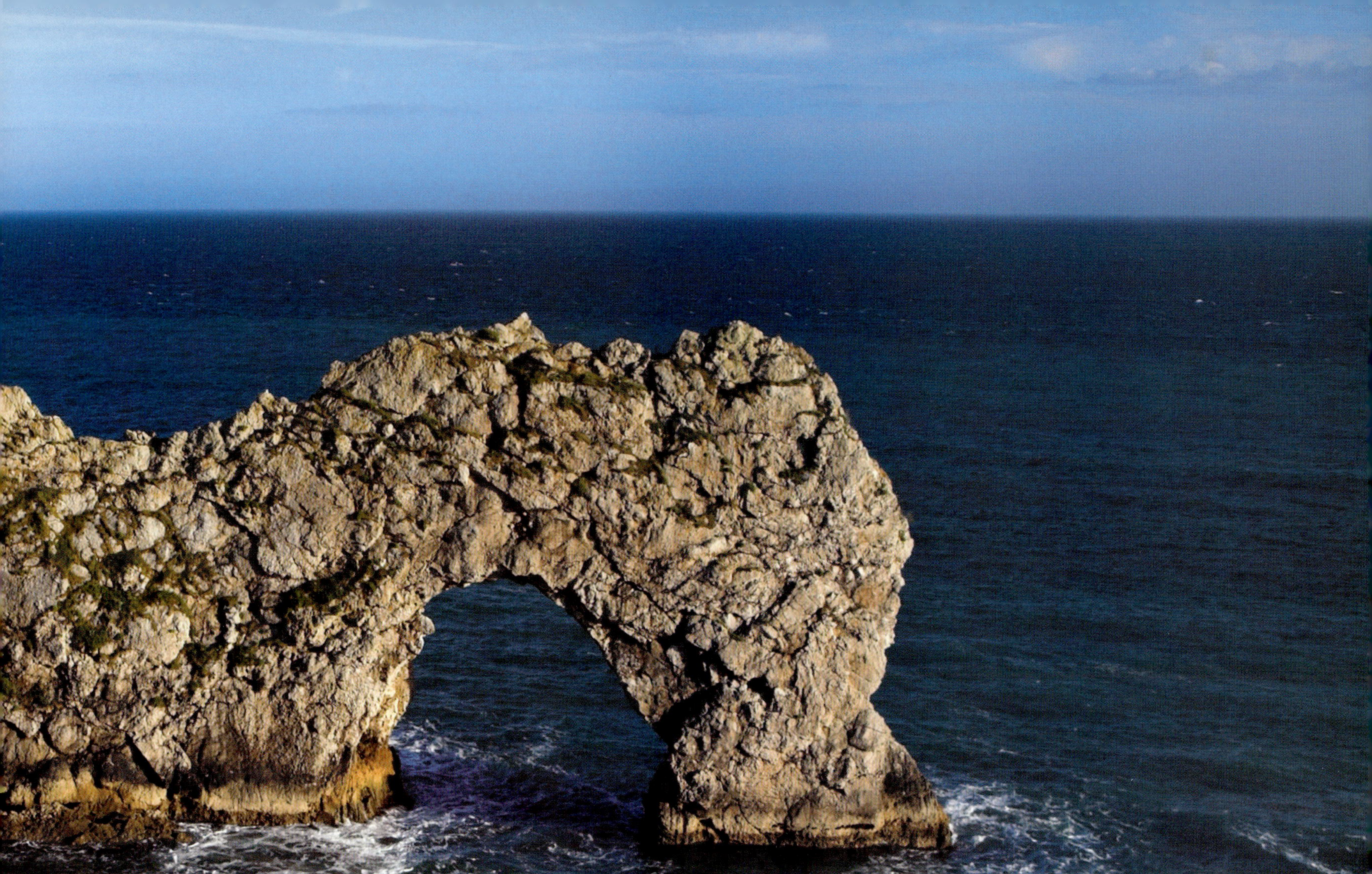

An unmistakable icon of the Dorset coast, and possibly the best known rock arch in England, Durdle Door provides an inspirational destination to all who visit. The arch is equally spectacular to behold whether viewed from the clifftops or on the beach below.

A pink pastel dawn presides over an unusually serene Portland Bill. The full moon will shortly fade when greeted with the first glimpse of the sun on this warm summer's day.

Whether arriving by land or sea, Clavell Tower provides an instantly recognisable landmark for visitors to this stretch of the Dorset coast. Built by Reverend John Richards Clavell of the Smedmore Estate, the tower, which is essentially a folly, has stood on this site since 1830. However, in recent years concern that cliff erosion may destroy the tower has led to it being dismantled and rebuilt some 80 feet from the cliff edge.

CONTENTS

INTRODUCTION

With a history stretching as far back as 300 million years, the Dorset coastline commands respect from all who come to see it. In return it rewards visitors with some of the most magnificent coastline in Britain.

This stretch of coast, familiar to many for its golden sandy beaches and seaside towns, has a well-earned reputation as one of England's most popular coastal holiday destinations. But that is not what this book is about. This pictorial view of Dorset passes briefly over the seaside resorts and instead concentrates on the natural wonder of the Dorset coast, a place of staggering beauty and variety which boasts some of the most spectacular and recognisable natural landmarks anywhere in Britain.

My own appreciation of the Dorset coast has developed in parallel with my photography. From the moment I picked up my first SLR camera, I headed to the coast to learn first-hand how to accurately record on film the beauty of this area. Five years later, I still find myself returning with the same level of eagerness, albeit now with a digital camera and hopefully greater experience.

Photography provides me with the perfect excuse to leave behind the hustle and bustle of everyday life and escape to the coast. I have been fortunate to have explored and photographed much of the Dorset coastline, and never tire of finding new locations or rediscovering the more familiar. What makes the Dorset coast so special for me is its diversity; geologically speaking, it is made up of many rock types providing very different subjects to visit and photograph. Some of those subjects are instantly recognisable and make popular locations such as Lulworth Cove and Durdle Door, but there are just as many relatively undiscovered yet equally spectacular places such as Worbarrow and Mupe Bays.

While the well-known sights make for awe-inspiring visits, it is often these less popular bays that I find more rewarding to visit. On a hot summer's day one could be forgiven for thinking that all of the Dorset coast is as busy as the beach at Bournemouth, but a wander through some coastal footpaths in the Purbecks will change this view forever.

Throughout this book I aim to share with you my impressions of this coastline. You will accompany me as I visit these locations at the times most special to me: usually dawn and dusk when they are at their quietest and most magical. Of course, no photograph can recreate the feeling of being at any of these locations. So I hope that after browsing the photographs in this book you might feel inspired to discover or revisit some special places to wander along this magnificent coastline.

A brief guide to the Dorset coast

Mudeford to Poole

For many this stretch of coastline will prove the most familiar. This is an area of golden sandy beaches and holiday towns, most notably Bournemouth with its two pleasure piers. Our journey begins at Mudeford near Christchurch, just outside the western outskirts of the New Forest National Park. On the thin sandbar that forms the entrance to Christchurch Harbour, beach huts are big business, changing hands for as much as £100,000 each.

Moving around the ancient hillfort headland at Hengistbury Head, the coastline arcs westwards in a continuous golden beach to Sandbanks, nearly ten miles away. The beaches of Southbourne, Boscombe and Bournemouth are all popular summer locations offering sand and safe bathing while positioned close to the many hotels of Bournemouth.

At the entrance to Poole Harbour is Sandbanks, a small yet very exclusive strip of land fronted by one of the most popular beaches along the coast. The single road leading in and out of Sandbanks is known as 'Millionaires' Row', and for good reason: this small strip of land is listed as having the fourth highest land value anywhere in the world.

Isle of Purbeck

A short ferry ride from Sandbanks lies Studland Bay. Owned by the National Trust, the bay contains several award-winning beaches as well as the Trust's only naturist beach. Despite its proximity to the crowded Sandbanks, Studland is a world away in all other respects. It marks the first section of the coast on the Isle of Purbeck:

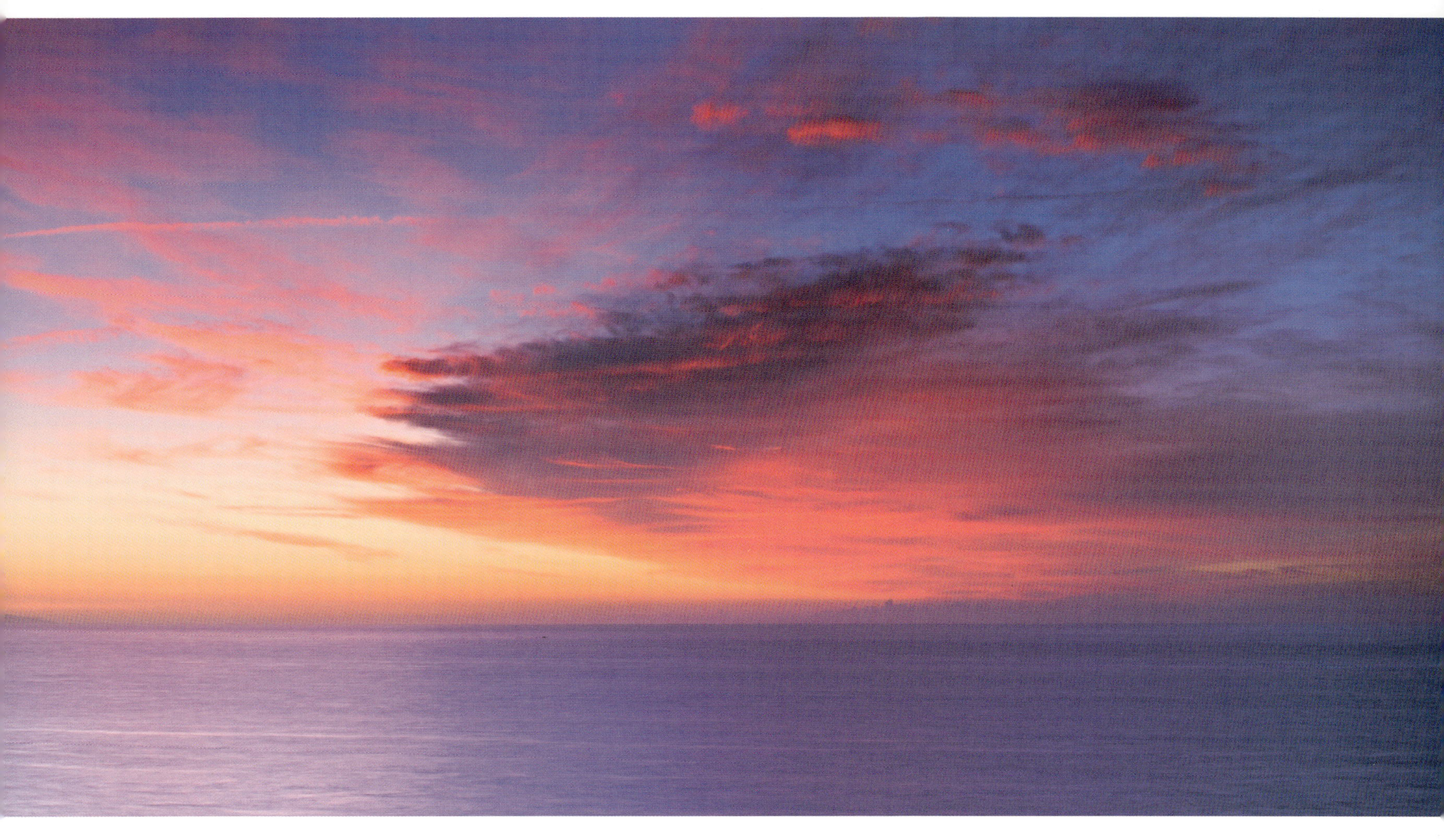

in reality not an island at all but rather a promontory. From this point onwards, the sense of a holiday resort diminishes as the big towns are replaced by small villages and touristy beaches become rocky coves.

Studland provides a starting point for the famous South West Coast Path, Britain's longest long-distance footpath, which runs over 630 miles around the coast of Dorset, Devon and Cornwall before ending in the Somerset town of Minehead. This is not a trail to be attempted by the faint-hearted; it has been estimated that the total height gained from walking up all the cliffs throughout this journey is around four times the height of Mount Everest!

Just around the corner from Studland's beaches, Handfast Point marks the start of the Jurassic Coast World Heritage Site. This elevated headland is dotted with many white chalk sea stacks, known collectively as Old Harry Rocks. It provides a fitting start to the wonderfully rugged Jurassic coast, an area world famous for its geological features.

A fiery sunset can often be enjoyed by walkers along the South West Coast Path.

Moving south around Ballard Down, the seaside town of Swanage provides one further glimpse of a holiday resort (albeit on a much smaller scale than Bournemouth) before the natural wonder of the Purbeck coast takes hold. Over the next ten miles no roads come close to providing access to the coast, resulting in miles of open countryside and relatively undiscovered clifftops. There are few opportunities here to come down to sea level, and when they appear they are rocky and very small. Yet this means that those making a trip to locations such as Dancing Ledge, Winspit and Seacombe often find they have the whole cove to themselves.

After rounding St Aldhelm's Head the coastline stetches briefly north-west until it reaches Kimmeridge Bay. Thanks to road access and a clifftop carpark Kimmeridge is always a popular location, but not for the conventional beach goer. There is no sand here, but in

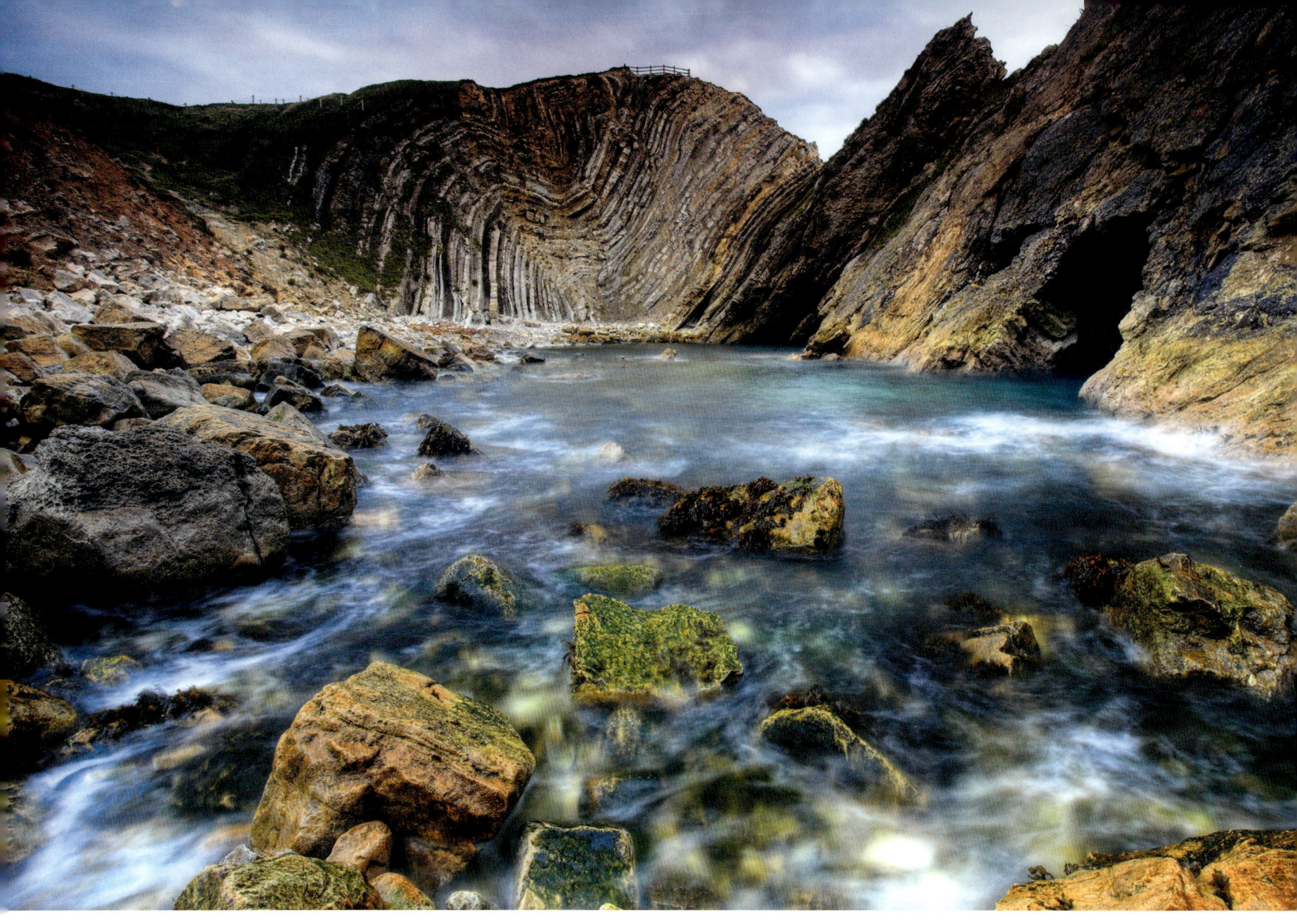

its place a rocky bay bursting with geological interest. Intriguing rock formations take on the appearance of dinosaur skin, many interspersed with rockpools at low tide. The cliffs are constantly eroding, offering the many fossil hunters the chance of discovering fossilised remains of creatures that survived here 70 million years ago. In fact, you don't have to look too hard to find the patterns of fossilised ammonites in the rock beds all around the bay.

Worbarrow to Osmington Mills

In the Second World War, the War Office occupied Tyneham village and its surrounding lands for military purposes. Despite this initially being a temporary measure, the land is still in the ownership of the Ministry of Defence. Due to this occupation, the countryside and coast of this area have remained free from development, and restricted access has resulted in many people being unaware of the splendour this stretch of coast has to offer. Worbarrow Bay, accessed via a footpath from the now ruined village of Tyneham, is an unexpected highlight of the Dorset coast. The sweeping bay backed by huge cliffs is beautiful to behold, surely one of the finest bays in England.

The cliffs above Worbarrow provide a challenging walk to Lulworth, via the incredibly rugged Mupe Rocks. For those wishing an easier method of reaching Lulworth, roads lead directly into the village only a short walk away from the world famous circular

Lulworth Cove. If the geology at the cove isn't commanding enough, a brief walk along the cliffs will provide a bird's-eye view down into Stair Hole where the beginnings of a new Lulworth Cove are available to witness first-hand.

Not far over the clifftops is Durdle Door, another icon of the Dorset landscape. This huge sea arch separates two beautiful sweeping bays, either of which is a pleasure to walk upon. Durdle Door provides an unforgettable experience to all who make the steep descent down to the beach.

Portland and Chesil Beach

Moving further west the coast passes the busy seaside town of Weymouth before venturing south to the Isle of Portland. Standing on high cliffs at its northern end, Portland gradually sinks towards the sea as it runs southwards. Along this route, evidence is all around of quarrying which took place in the nineteenth century. Portland stone has long been in great demand. Some of the most exceptional buildings in London have been built using it, most notably Buckingham Palace and St Paul's Cathedral.

At the very southern tip of the island, Portland Bill marks the lowest point of the island, where the limestone ledges sink beneath the ocean. This is also the southernmost tip of Dorset, stretching far south into the English Channel and making an ideal location for a lighthouse. The famous red and white lighthouse that stands on the headland can be seen as a tiny flash of light from as far away as Kimmeridge on the mainland. This is the third lighthouse to stand at Portland Bill.

The coastline now continues northwards along West Weares, where rocky debris litters the base of huge limestone cliffs. These cliffs abruptly end at the town of Fortuneswell, and are replaced by the incredible Chesil Beach. In geological terms Chesil Beach is a tombolo: a spit connecting mainland Dorset with the Isle of Portland. The best place to appreciate the enormous shingle bank is from Portland Heights, the highest point on the island. From here, spectacular views can be observed of Chesil Beach stretching for 18 miles north-west.

For much of its length Chesil Beach is accompanied by water on either side. A lagoon named The Fleet runs alongside the shingle, separating it from the land. The Fleet is a haven for many wading birds including a huge swan population at nearby Abbotsbury Swannery. It wasn't always so peaceful; in the Second World War this stretch of water was used as a testing site for the bouncing bomb.

Burton Bradstock to Lyme Regis

At its western end Chesil Beach plays second fiddle to two sets of beautiful cliffs. Burton Cliff and its neighbour East Cliff are unmistakable for their unusual colour and shape. Being composed of soft sandstone, the cliffs are prone to continuous and rapid erosion, yet in appearance they remain towering vertical pillars which from a distance resemble a massive man-made wall. Throughout the winter, when the late afternoon sun sets over the sea, both cliff faces turn a striking golden colour in the low sunlight.

Passing the small holiday town of West Bay, the pebbly beaches of Eype and Seatown feature as a backdrop to Golden Cap, the south coast's highest cliff. Owned by the National Trust, Golden Cap rises 191 metres above sea level. Its height and distinctive flat top make it an easily identifiable landmark from many miles away.

Continuing westwards, the town of Lyme Regis marks the border of Dorset with Devon. A fossil hunting hotspot, the beaches around Lyme Regis are rich in ammonites as well as larger fossils. This area became famous for fossil collecting in the early nineteenth century when Mary Anning made several important finds, including the first ever full skeletons of both an Ichthyosaur and a Plesiosaur, prehistoric marine reptiles from the Jurassic period.

Without exception, the most famous structure in Lyme Regis is its harbour wall. Known as The Cobb, this sea defence has been a major influence in the fortunes of Lyme Regis for many hundreds of years, helping the small village to prosper into a once major port.

Yet another instantly recognisable landmark amongst so many others on this beautiful stretch of coastline, it provides a fitting end to this photographic guide to the Dorset coast.

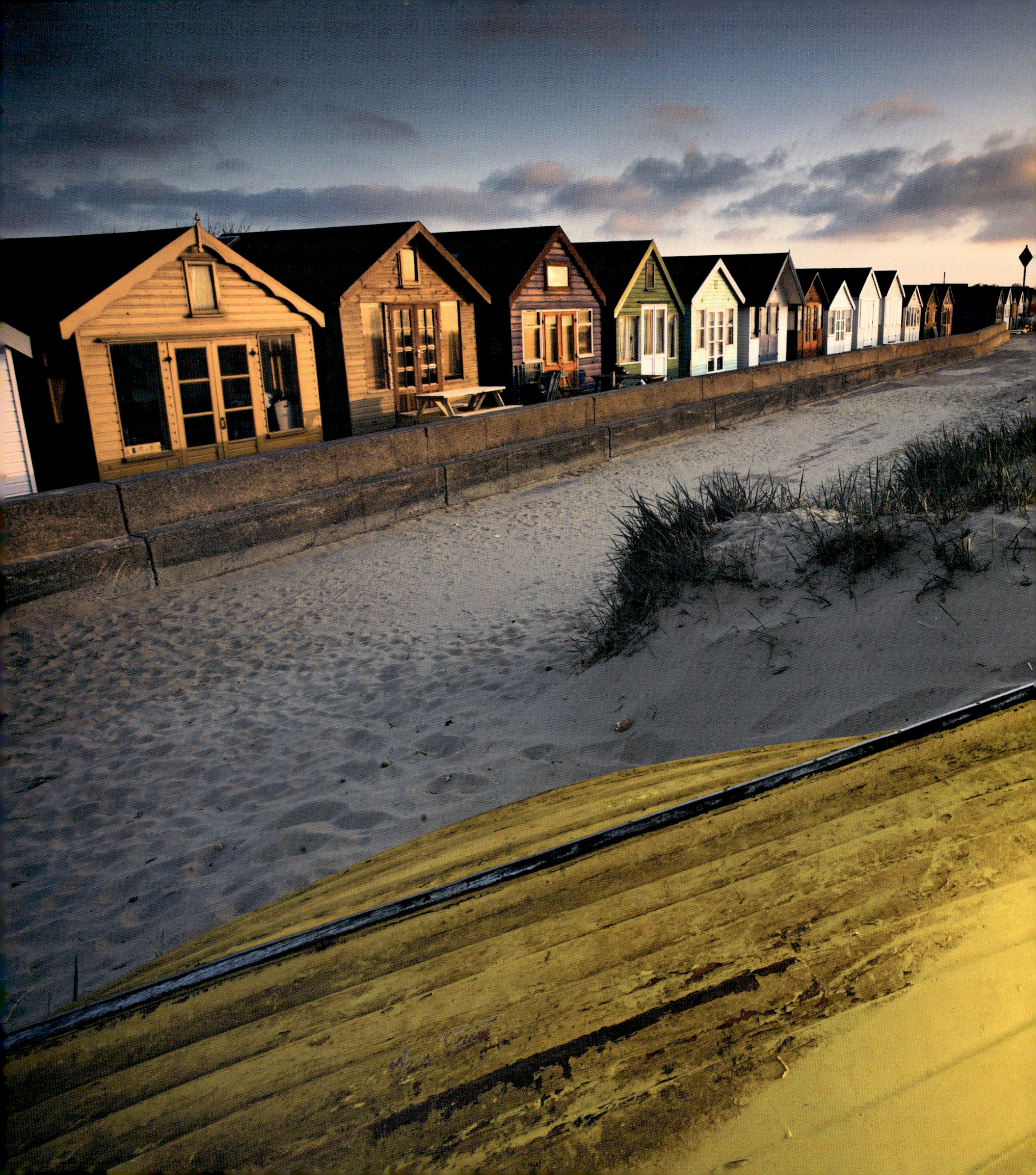

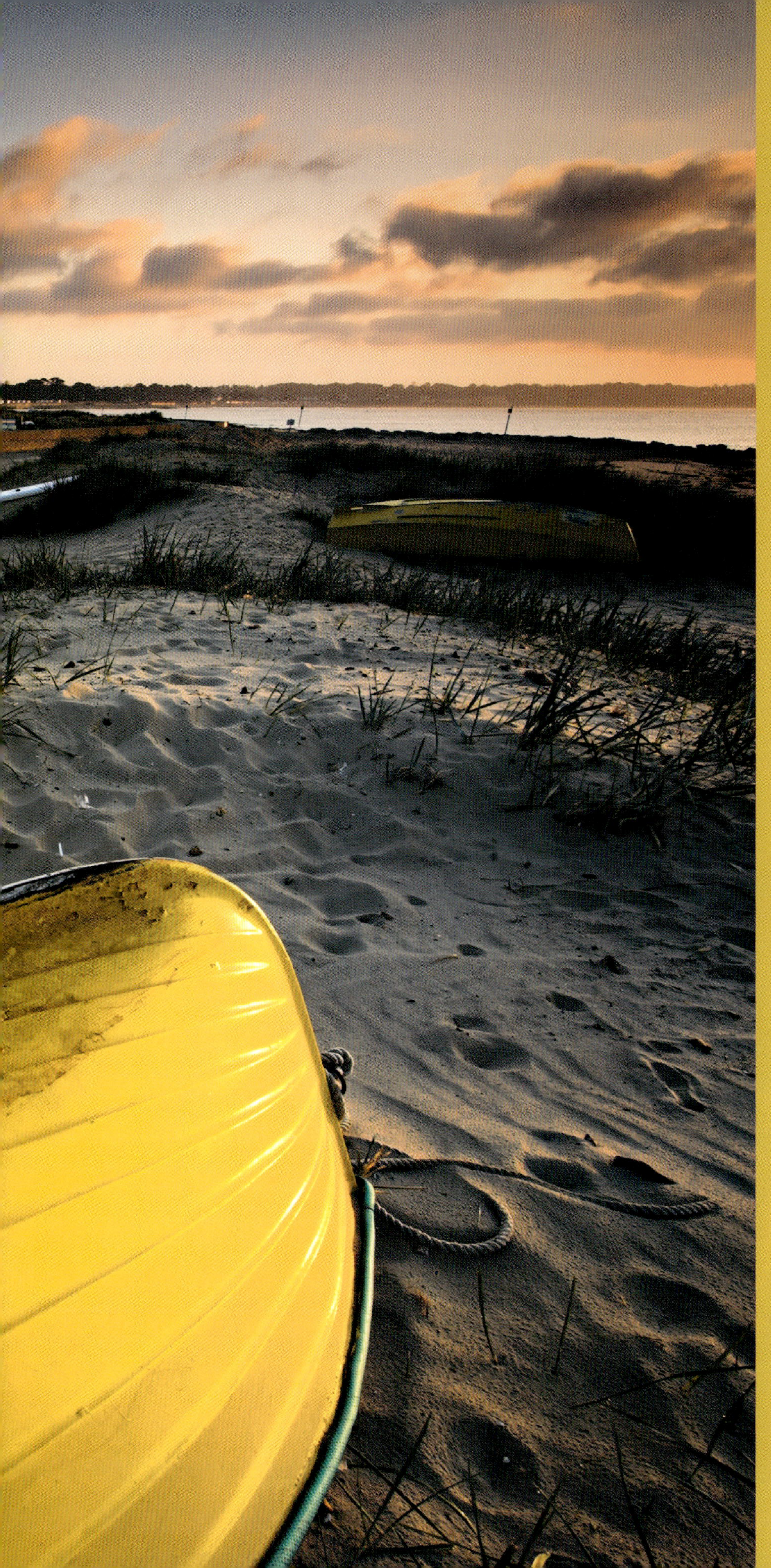

Mudeford to Poole

The first rays of a new summer day glow on the upturned boats and beachfront huts on Mudeford Spit. In beach hut terms this little stretch of sand is the equivalent of its high-flying neighbour Sandbanks. While Sandbanks may have some of the most expensive real estate in the world, Mudeford matches with record-breaking beach huts, many of which have sold for more than £100,000.

Mudeford

The coastline of Hengistbury Head suffers particularly badly from coastal erosion. To reduce the damage caused by the sea, this rock groyne was built along Mudeford Spit in the late twentieth century. Now weathered by the sea, the rocks are covered in eye-catching green seaweed, making slippery yet colourful structures that provide a more natural appearance than their wooden counterparts.

A beautiful sunrise emerges over Christchurch Bay.

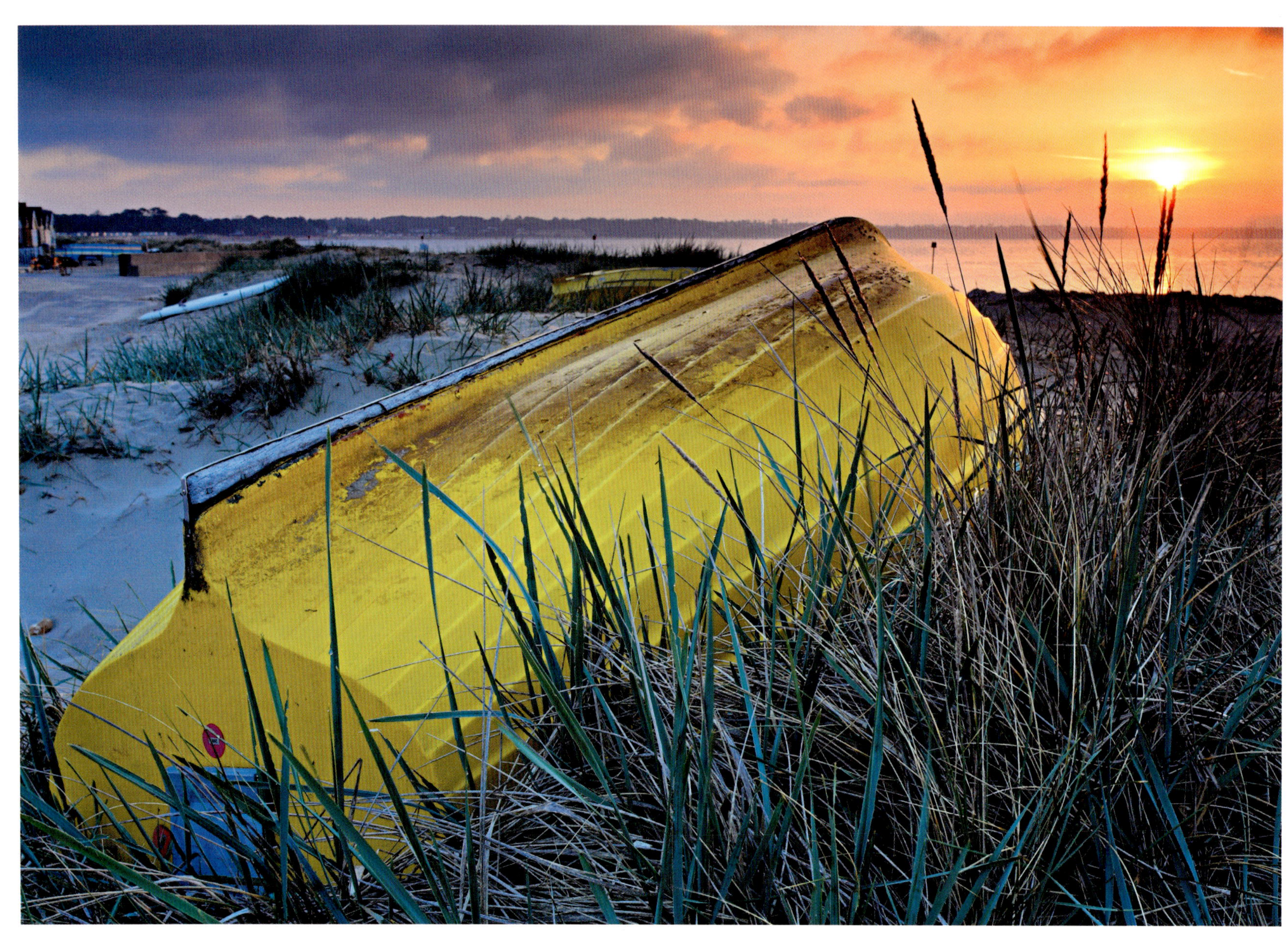

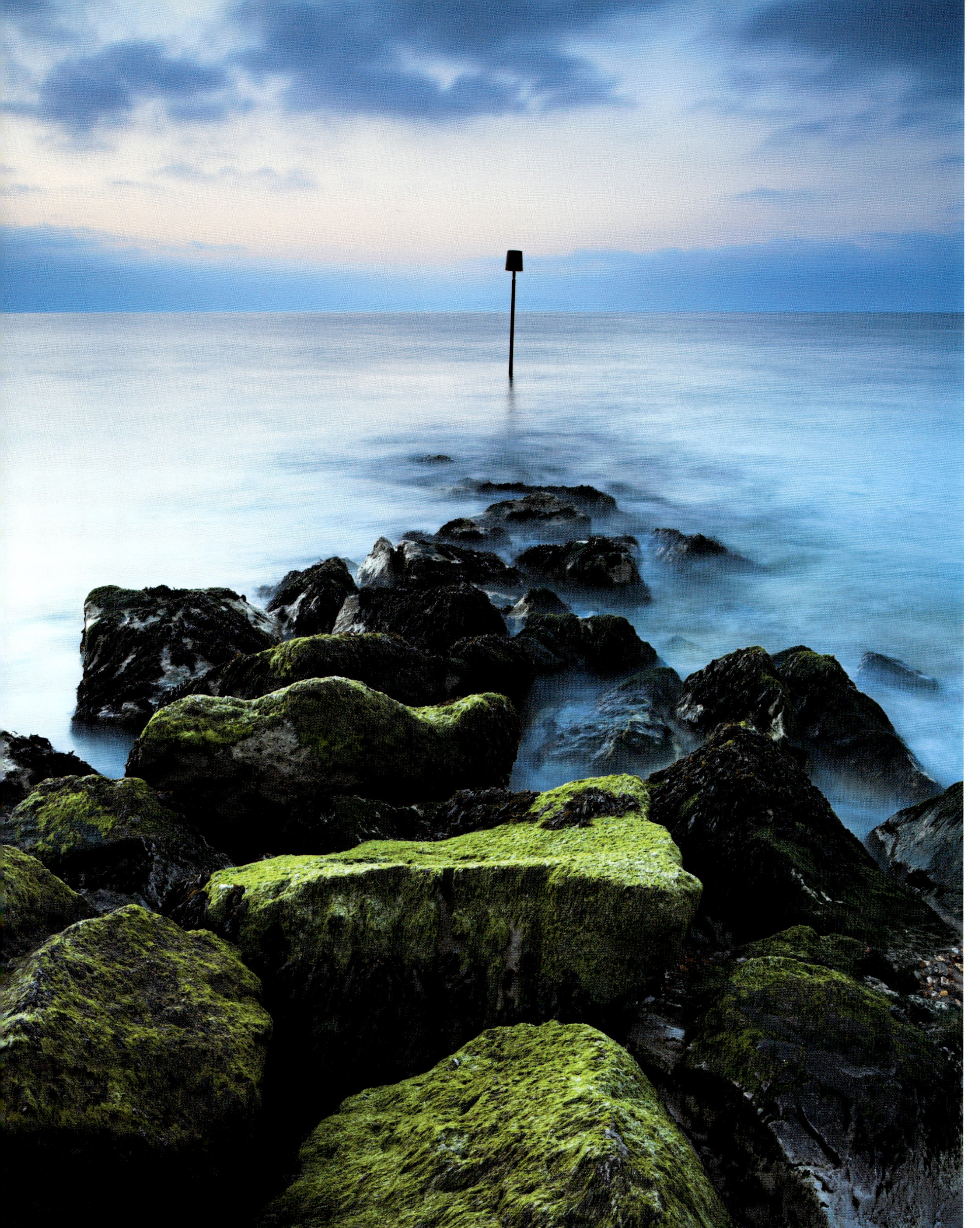

Hengistbury Head

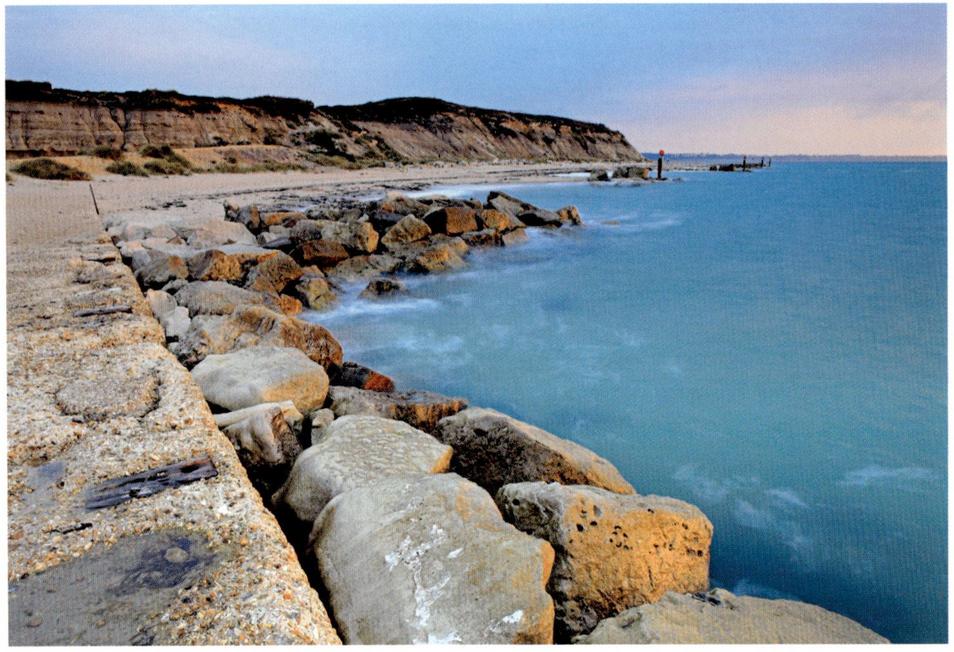

Named after the Jutish king Hengest, Hengistbury Head has witnessed a long history of human occupation. Offering a natural defensive position on a clifftop promontory, it is no wonder there is evidence of settlement throughout the Stone Age, Bronze Age and Iron Age. The clifftops now provide a nature reserve which boasts a quarter of Britain's native plant species.

The winter sun rises over the distant Isle of Wight. Just visible on the horizon are the famous chalk pinnacles collectively known as the Needles which form the island's westerly tip.

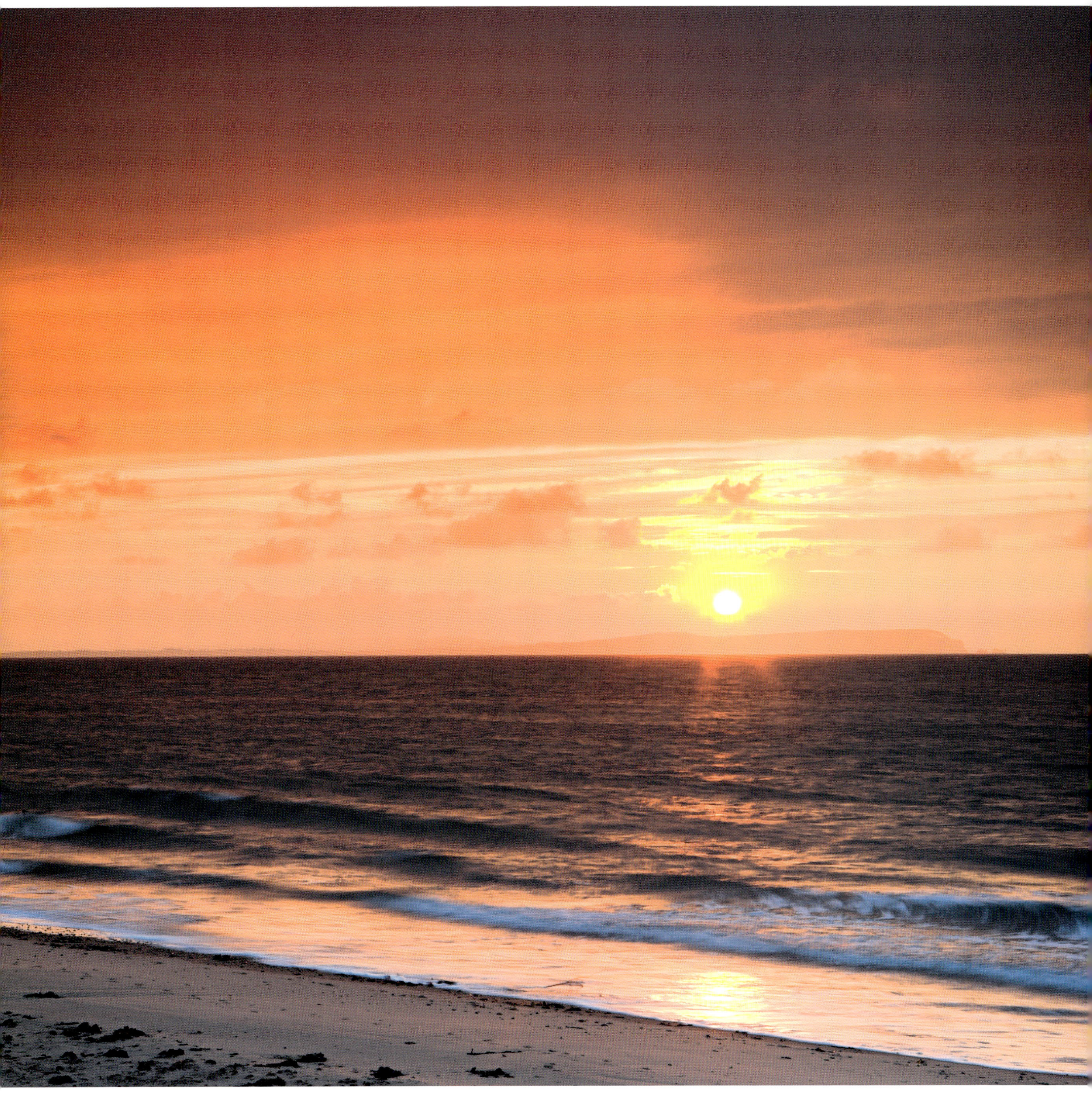

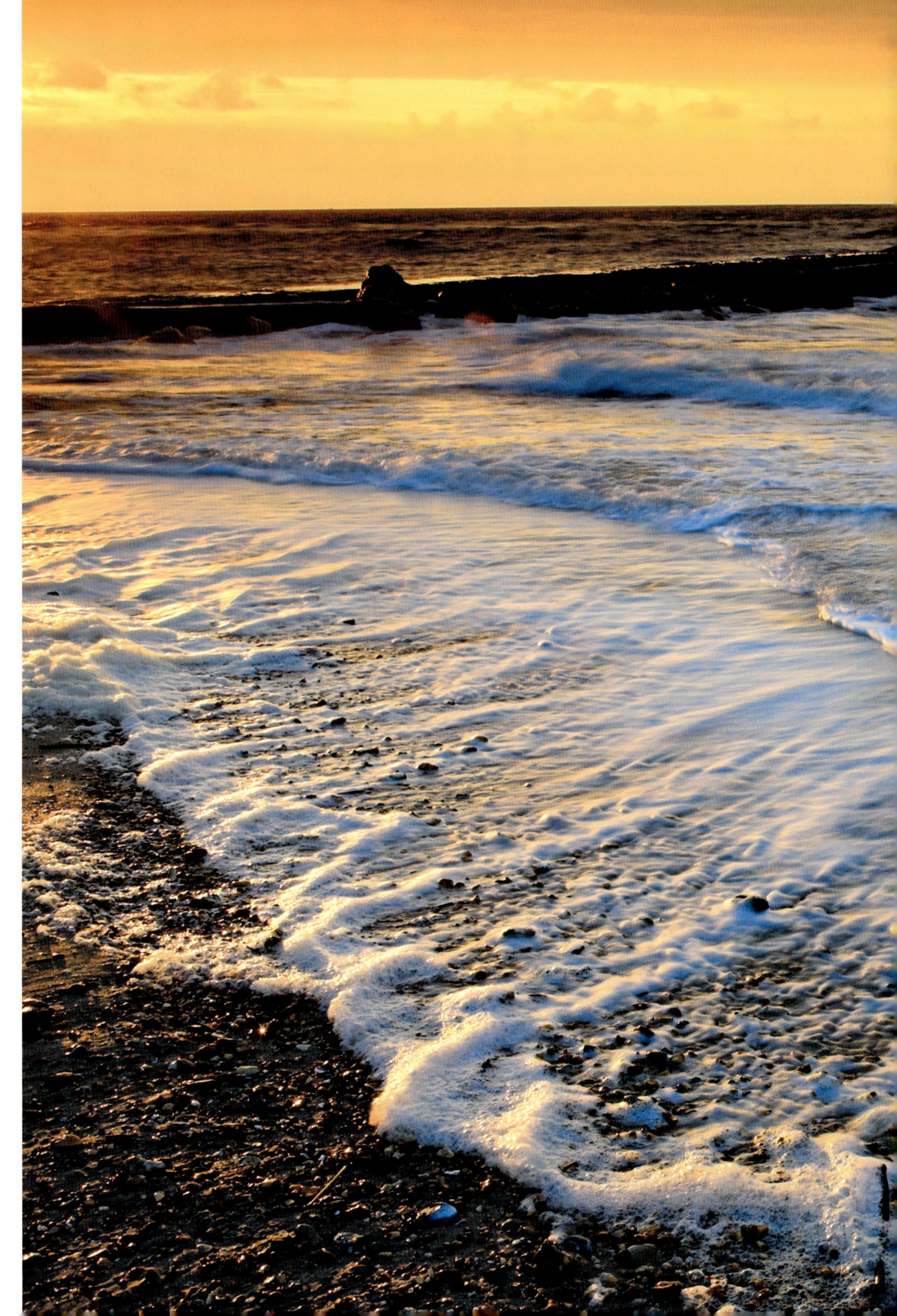

At 215 metres in length, the Long Groyne more than earns its title. This huge concrete barrier, far longer than any more recent additions, was created in 1938 to manage erosion of the Hengistbury Head cliffs. The project was very successful; as a direct result of the Long Groyne's position, sediment has been trapped causing the beach to widen and so offer more protection to the cliffs.

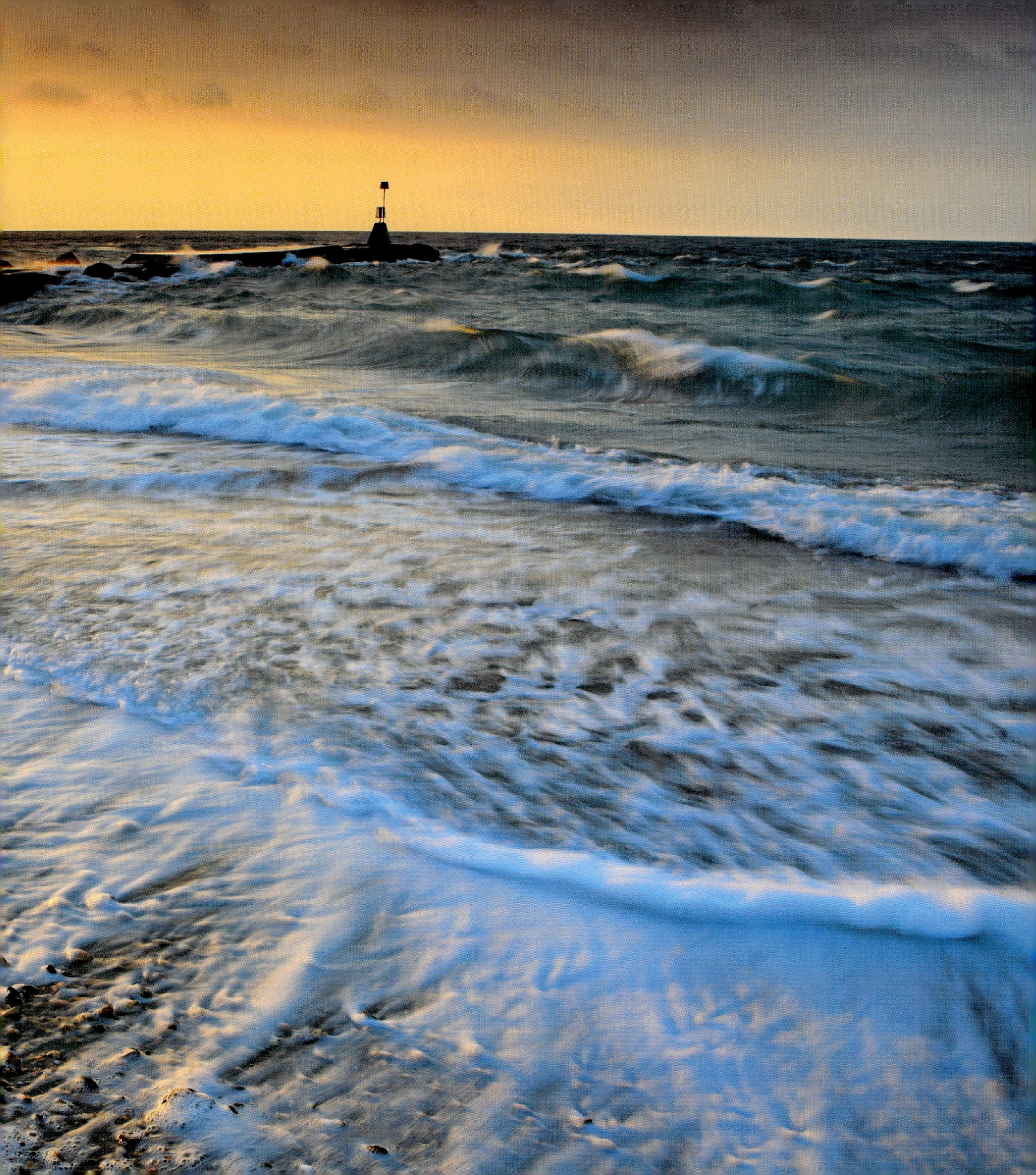

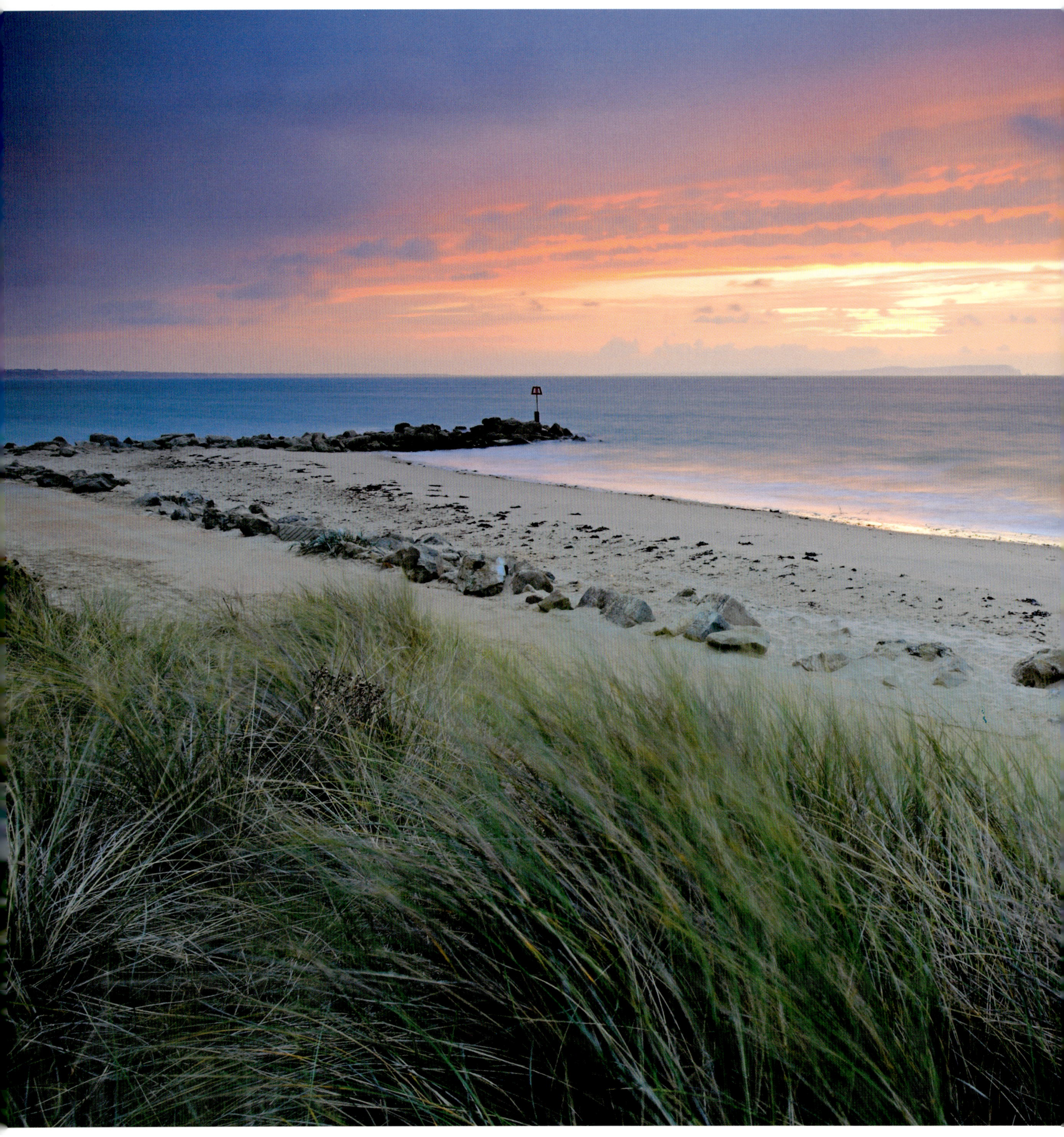

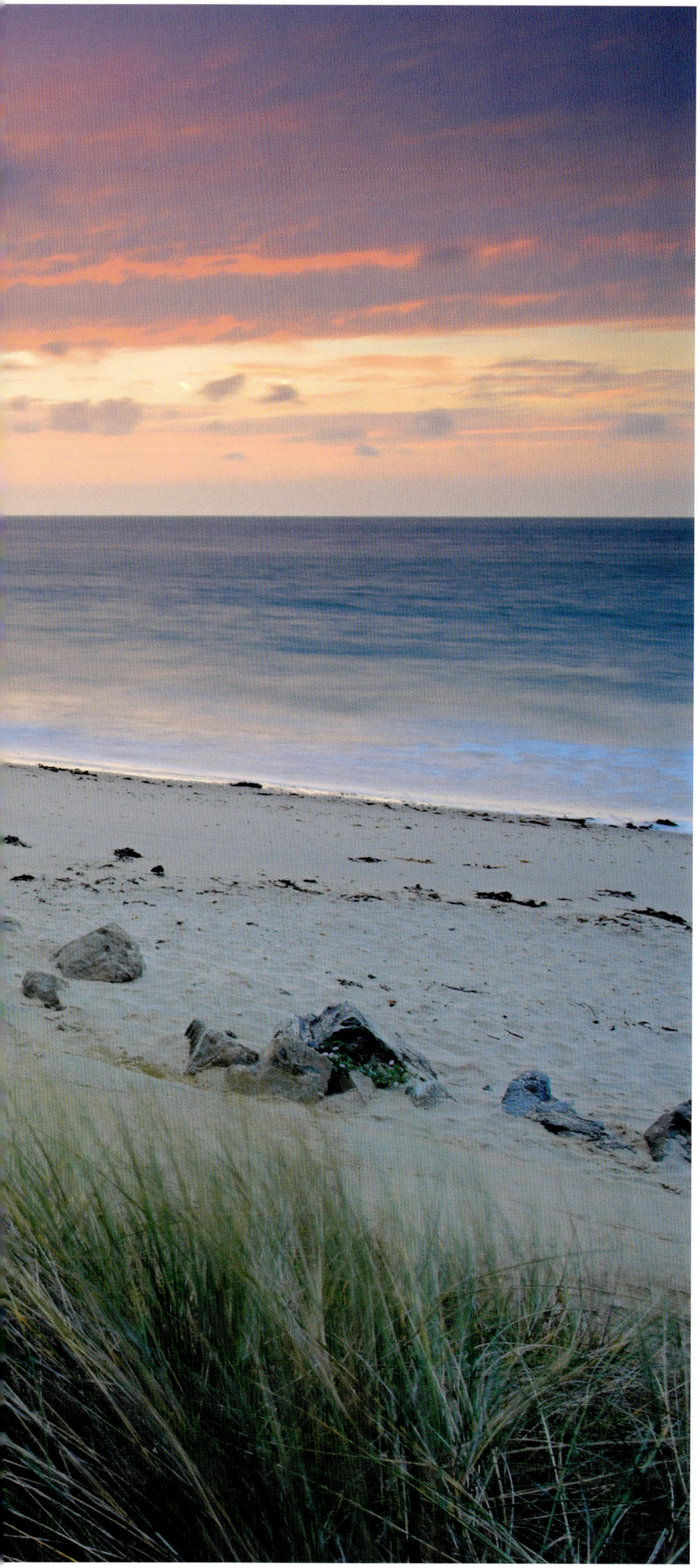

The sandy beachfronts on the
eastern side of Hengistbury Head
enjoy expansive views across
Christchurch Bay.

A lone yacht enjoys the solitude of
Christchurch Bay at first light.

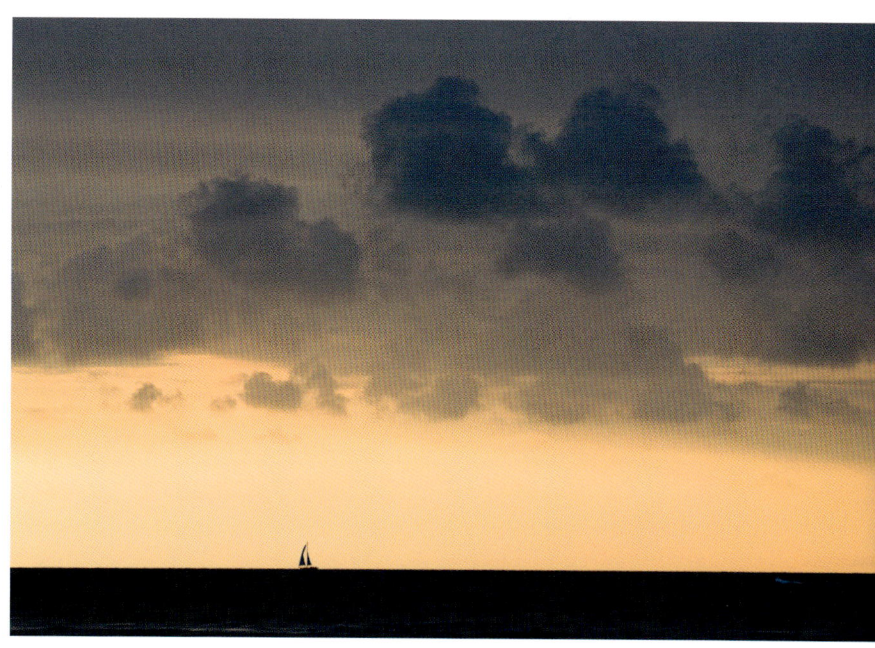

Southbourne

A stormy grey afternoon beside the
wooden groynes at Southbourne.

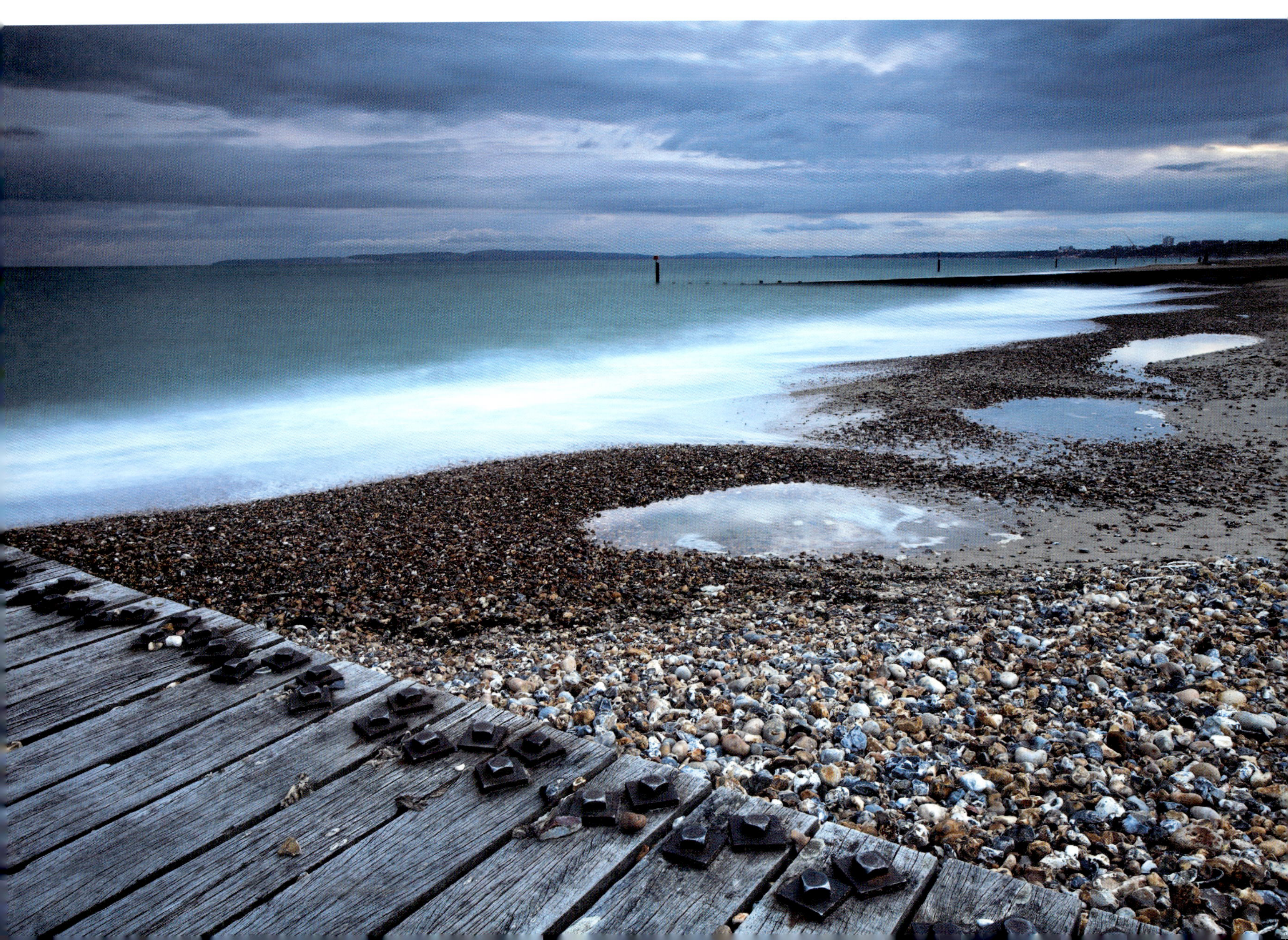

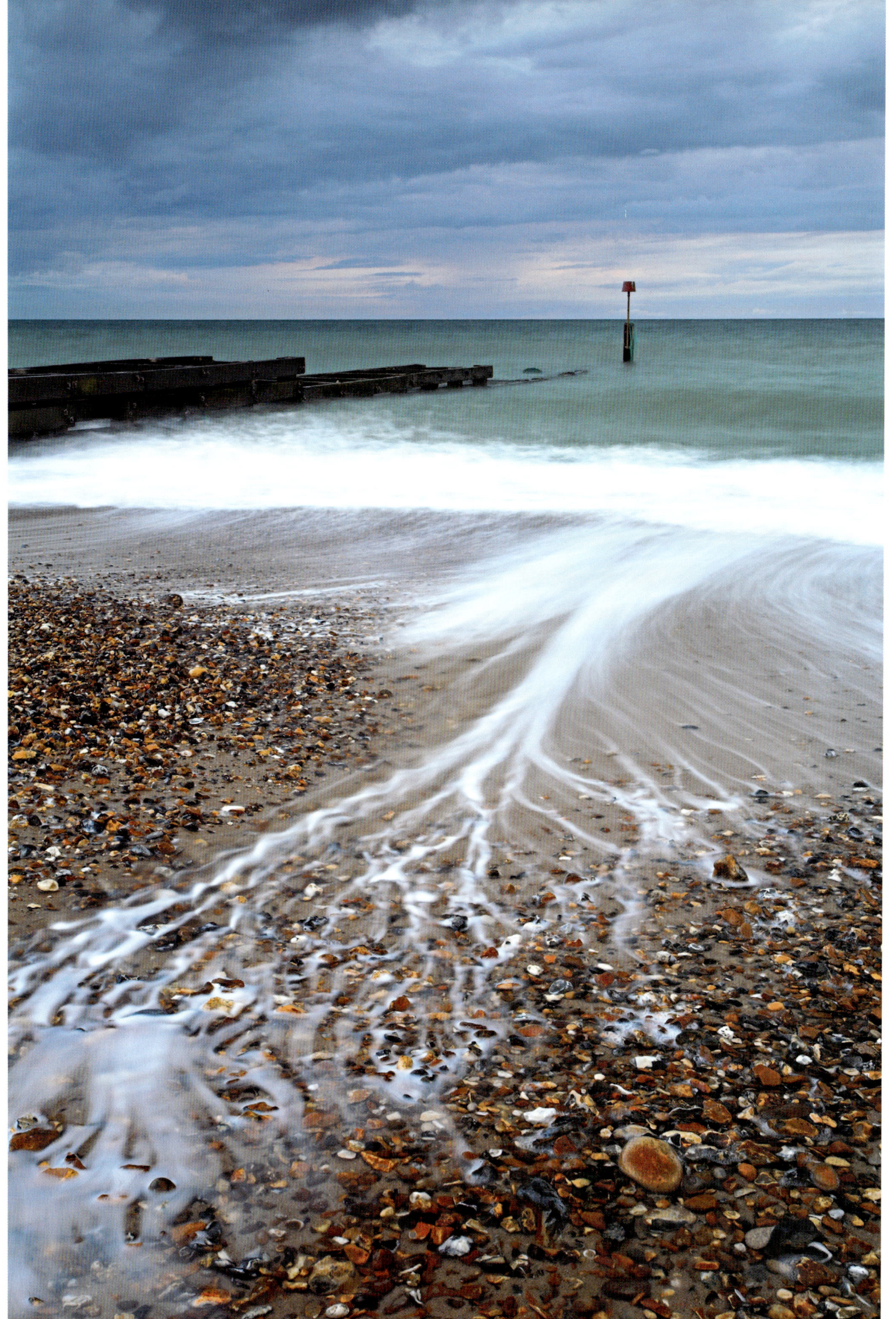

Boscombe Beach

Nearing the end of a sunny December day, the popular sandy beach at Boscombe is completely deserted. Shallow pools of water remain from the retreating tide, capturing the intense colours of the sunset above.

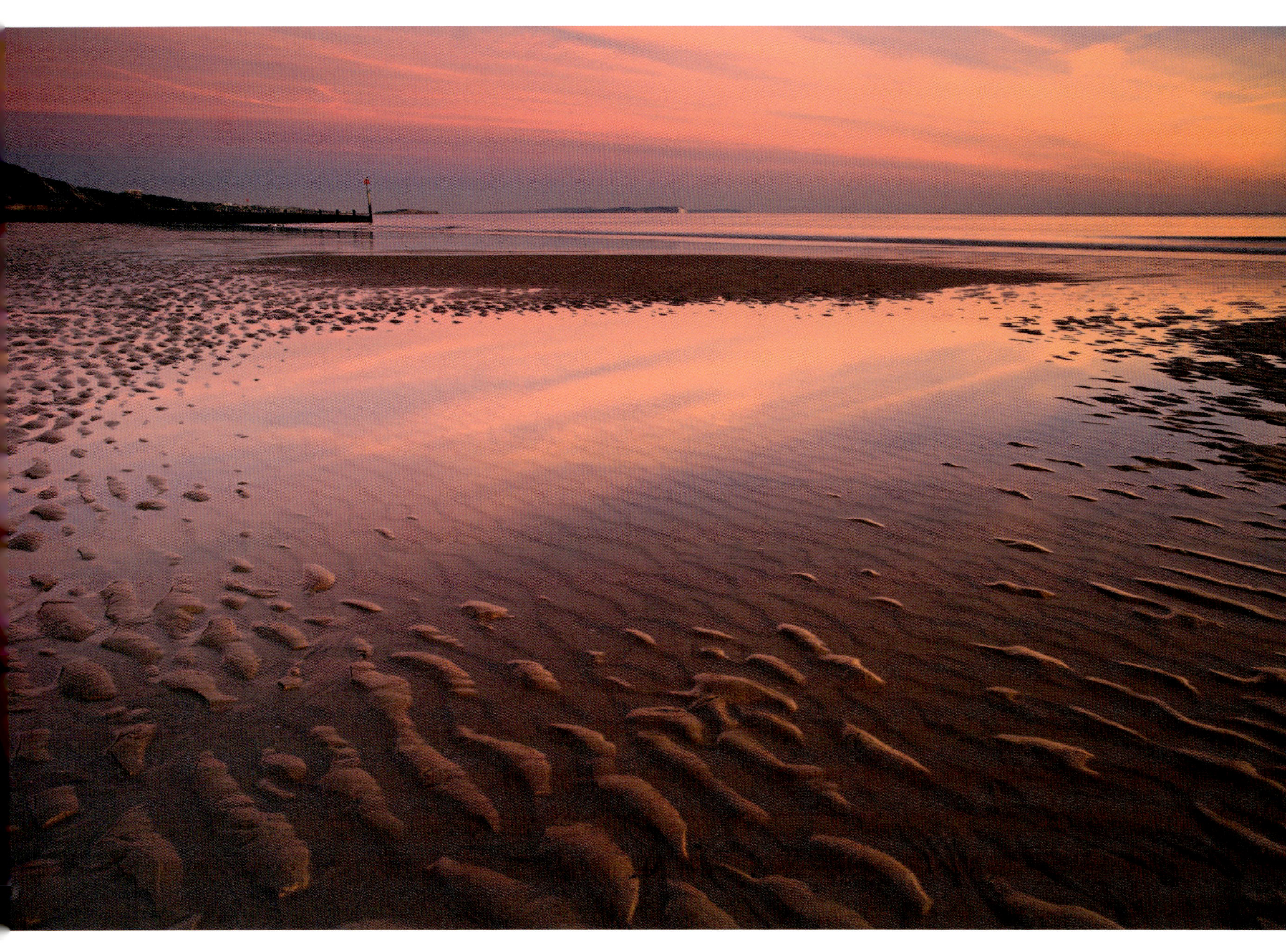

As British as the Punch and Judy show, beach huts are ever present features at many Dorset seaside resorts. These Bournemouth huts are barely large enough to provide shelter for two people, yet they remain popular with both locals and tourists, providing spectacular views and convenient access to the beach.

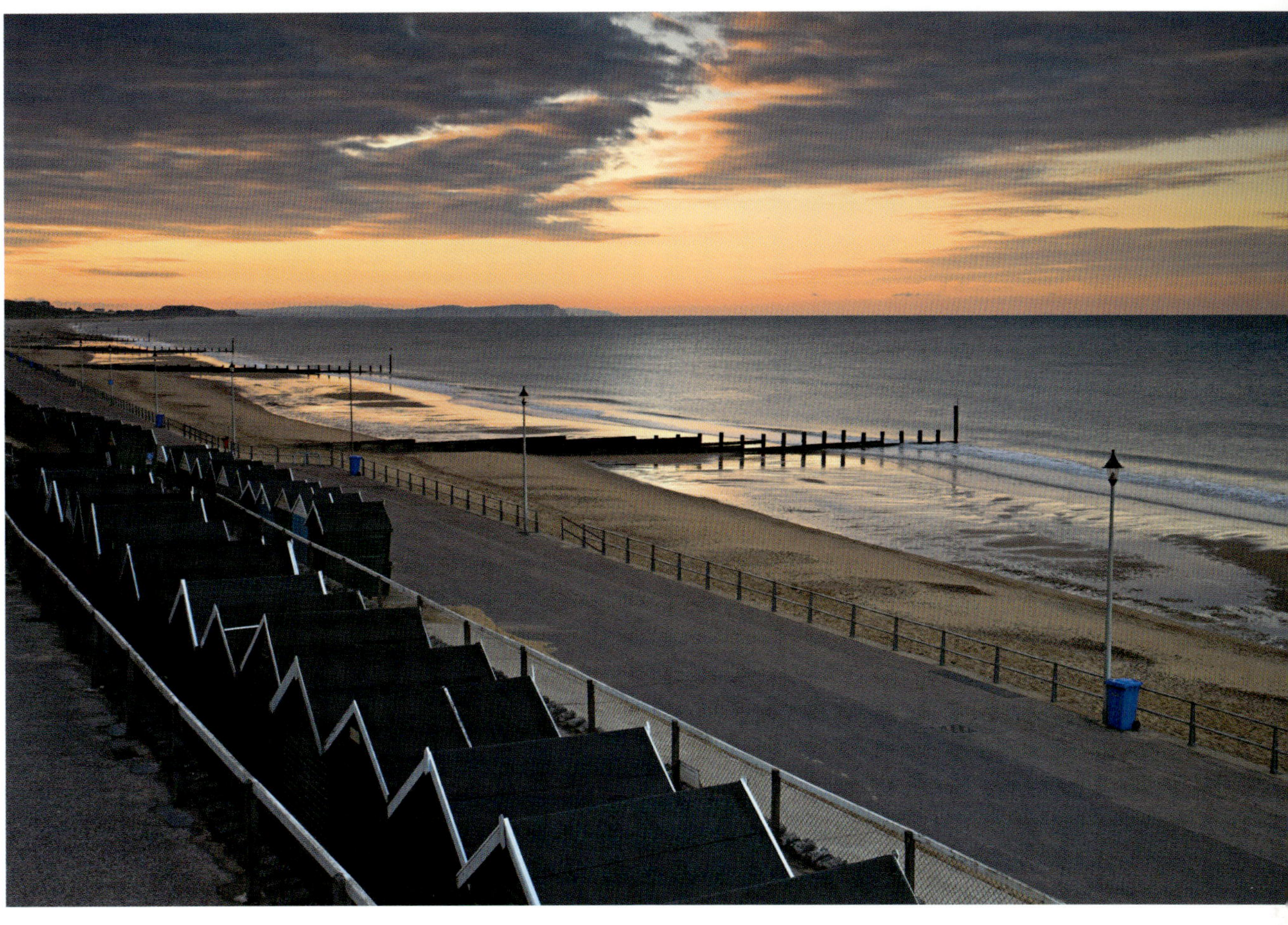

This crescent-shaped collection of shells and pebbles has been created by the movement of the waves lapping onto the beach. Without the wooden groynes that feature all along this sandy coast, the pebbles, shells and sand would be eroded away in stormy weather. Luckily these groynes provide not only effective sea defences but equally effective subjects for coastal photographers.

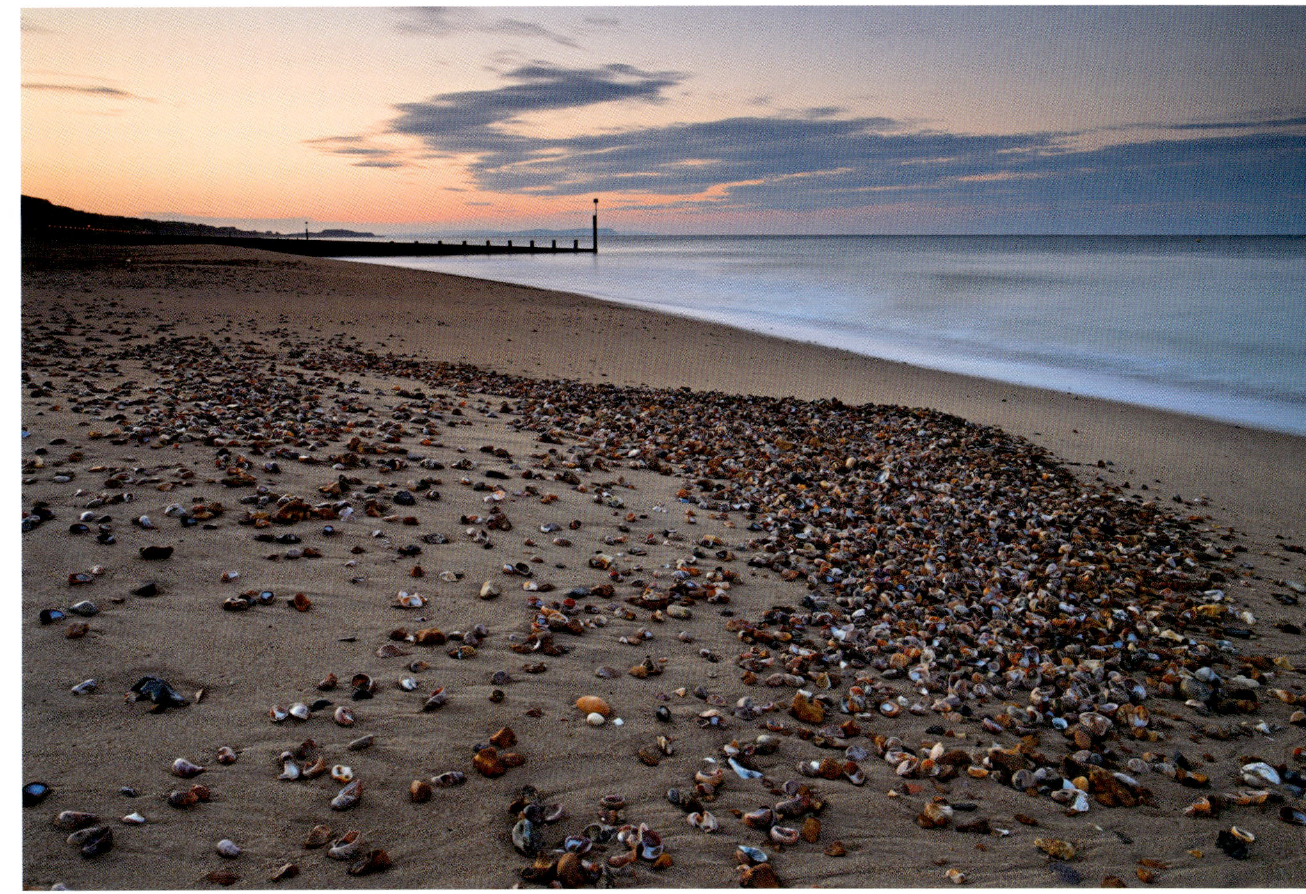

Bournemouth Pier

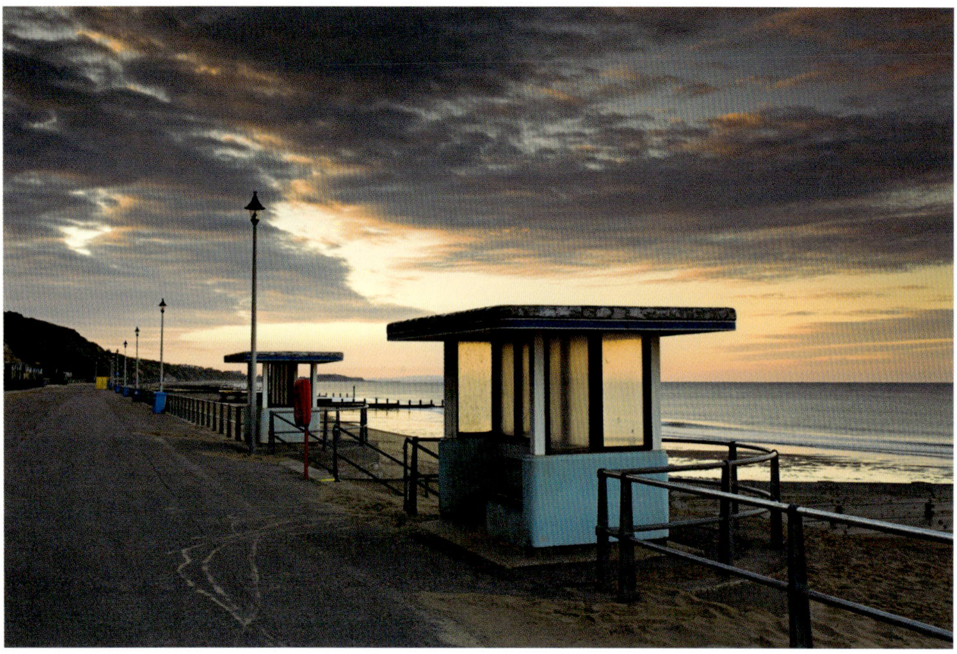

With Undercliff Drive deserted at this early hour, the distinctive shelters are the only witnesses to the fantastic golden sunrise.

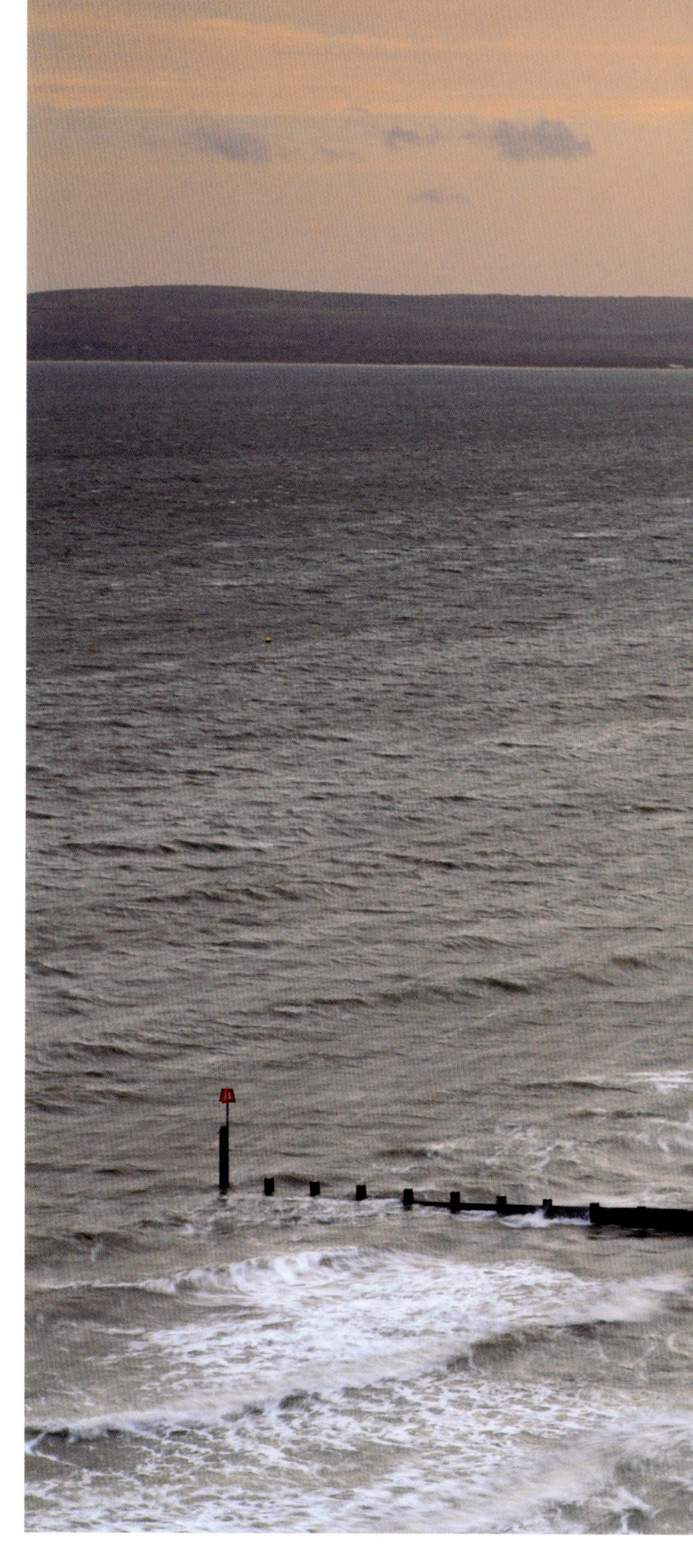

A stormy afternoon on the clifftops above Bournemouth Pier. In such conditions, both Bournemouth and nearby Boscombe Pier can offer ideal opportunities for surfers.

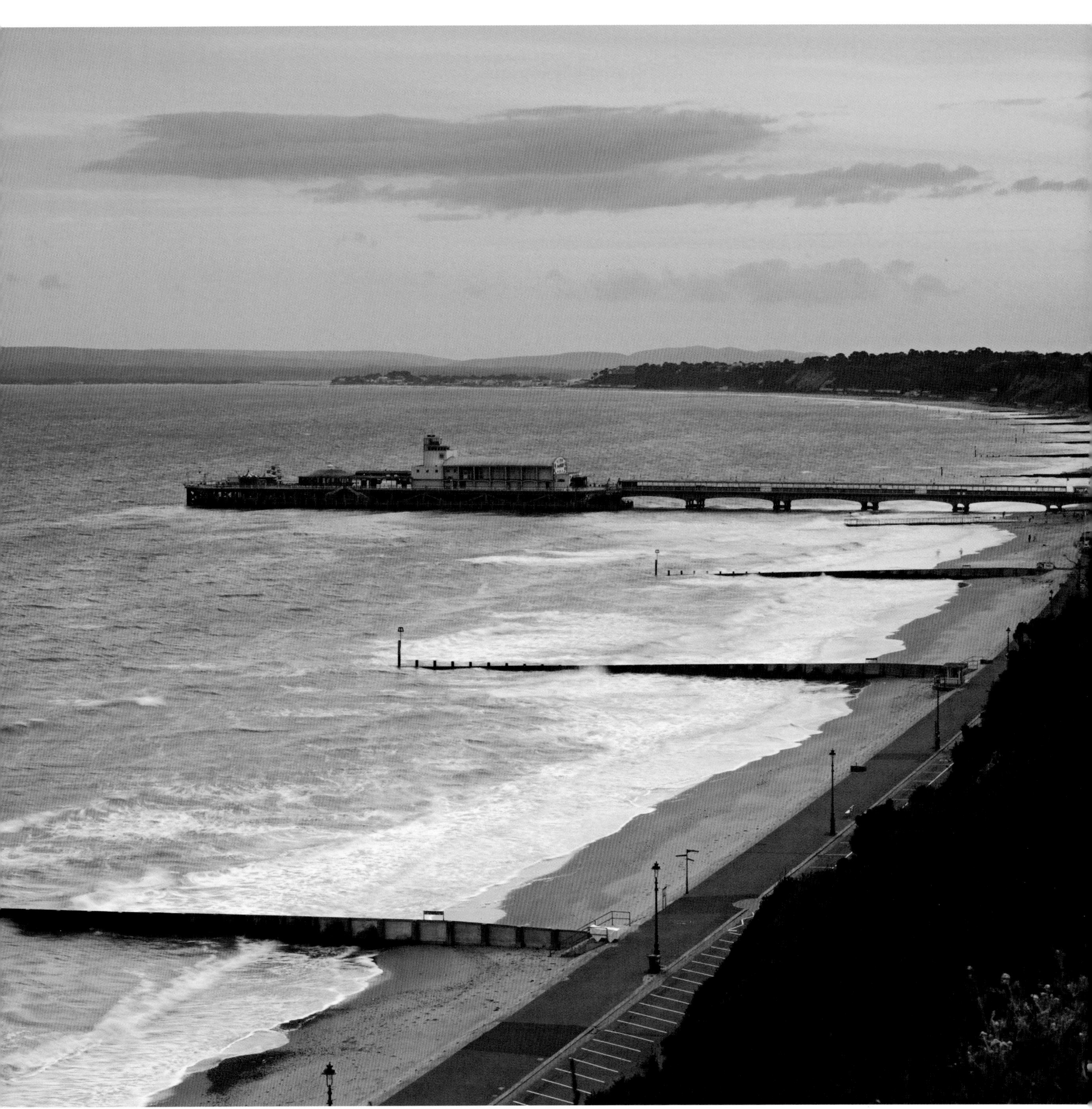

The third permanent pier to be
built on this site, the present
Bournemouth Pier was opened on
11 August 1880 by the Lord Mayor
of London. At a cost of £2,600 the
pier was initially 838 feet in length,
subsequently extended to more
than 1,000 feet.

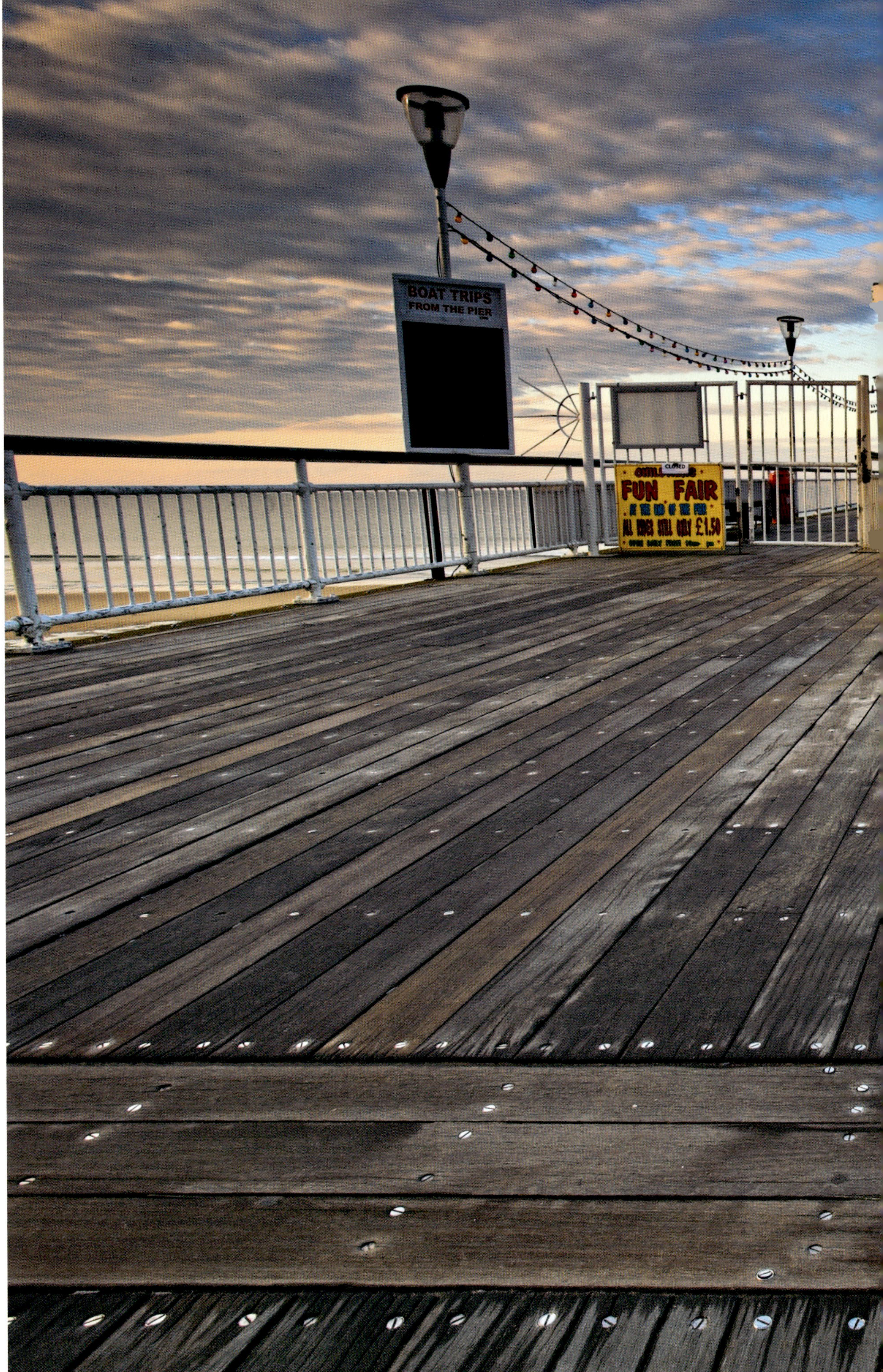

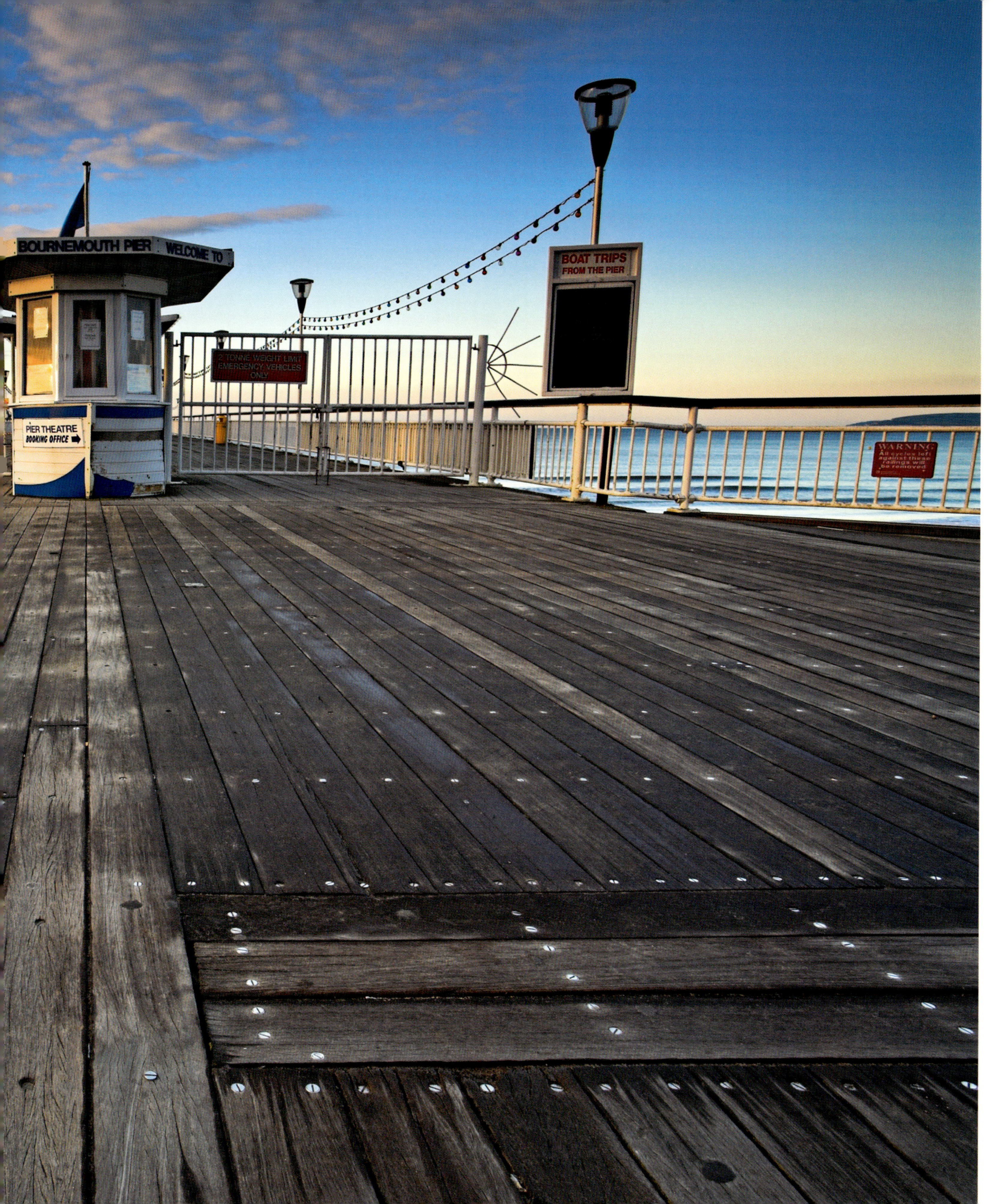

WELCOME TO
BOURNEMOUTH PIER
PIER THEATRE
BOOKING OFFICE
2 TONNE WEIGHT LIMIT
EMERGENCY VEHICLES
ONLY
BOAT TRIPS
FROM THE PIER
WARNING
All cycles left
against these
railings will
be removed

Sandbanks

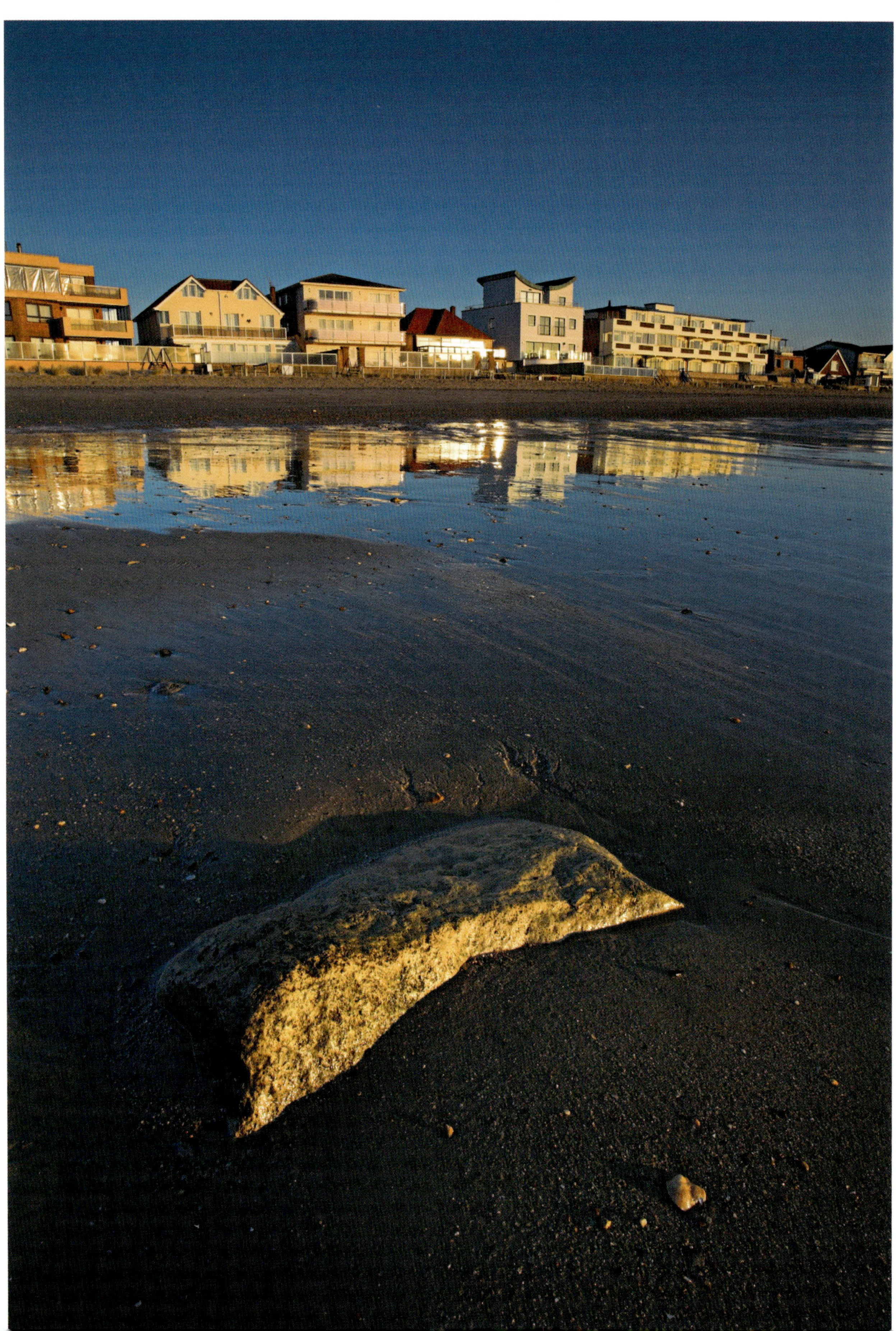

This small strip of land at the entrance to Poole Harbour lays claim to be one of the most expensive areas to own property anywhere in the world. As one would expect, properties on the beachfront command the very highest prices. On a glorious morning of sunshine one could be forgiven for thinking the houses were built of pure gold.

Poole

Home to the prestigious motor yacht manufacturer Sunseeker, Poole Quay has more than its fair share of luxury boats. In the quiet moments after sunrise, the warm pink sunlight provides a perfect showcase for the pristine yachts.

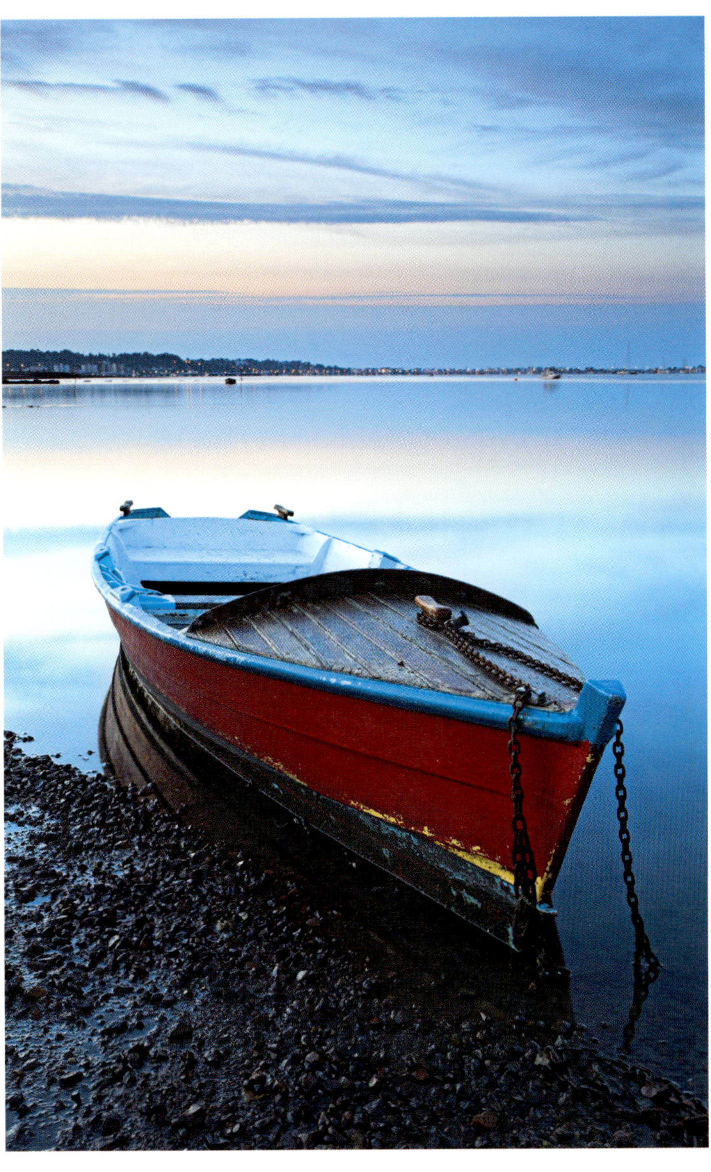

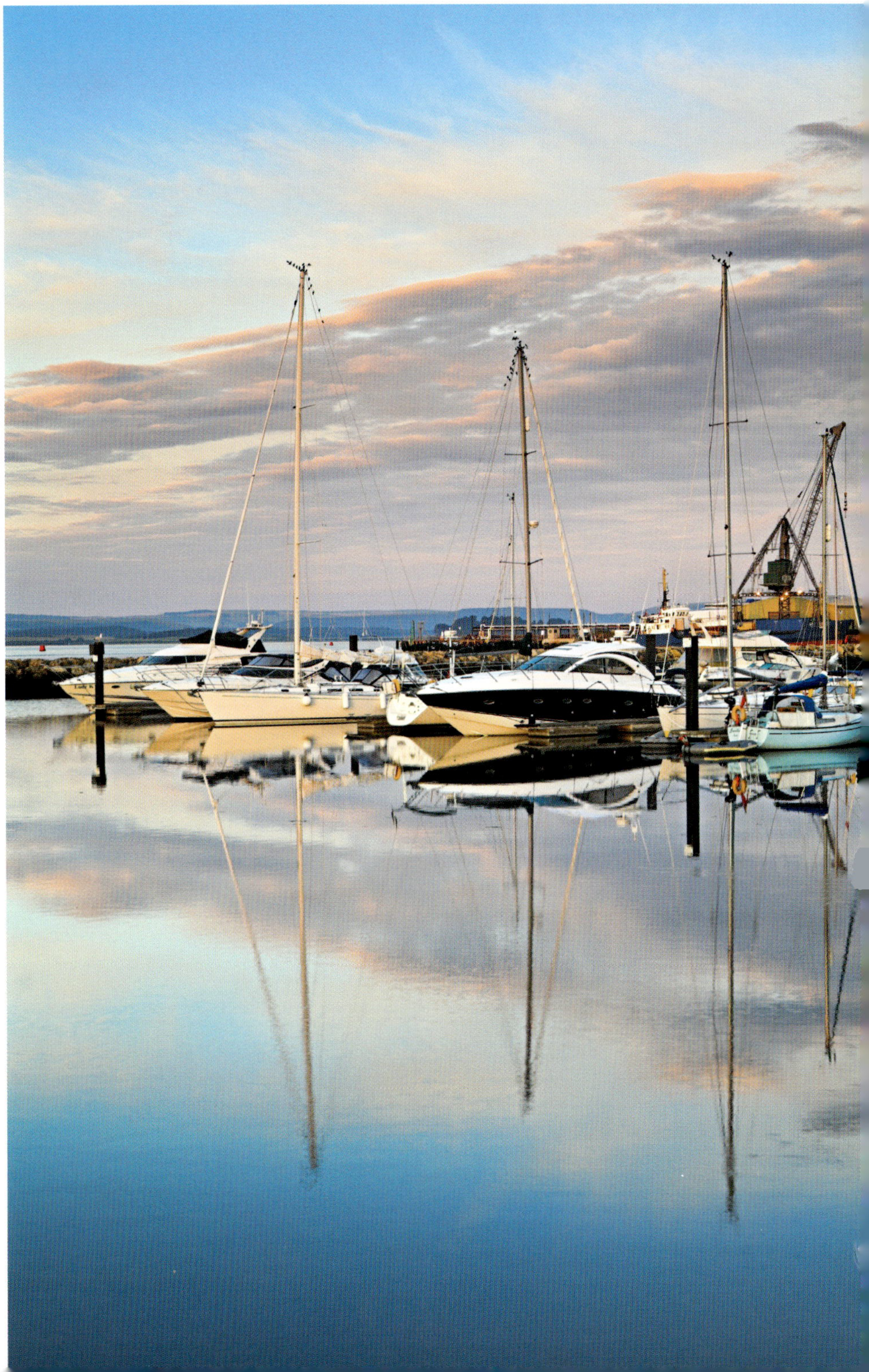

Predawn light on a silent and still Poole Harbour. Soon the ferries, motor yachts and fishing vessels will bustle the harbour into life, but for now the only movement is the gentle swaying motion of the tethered boats.

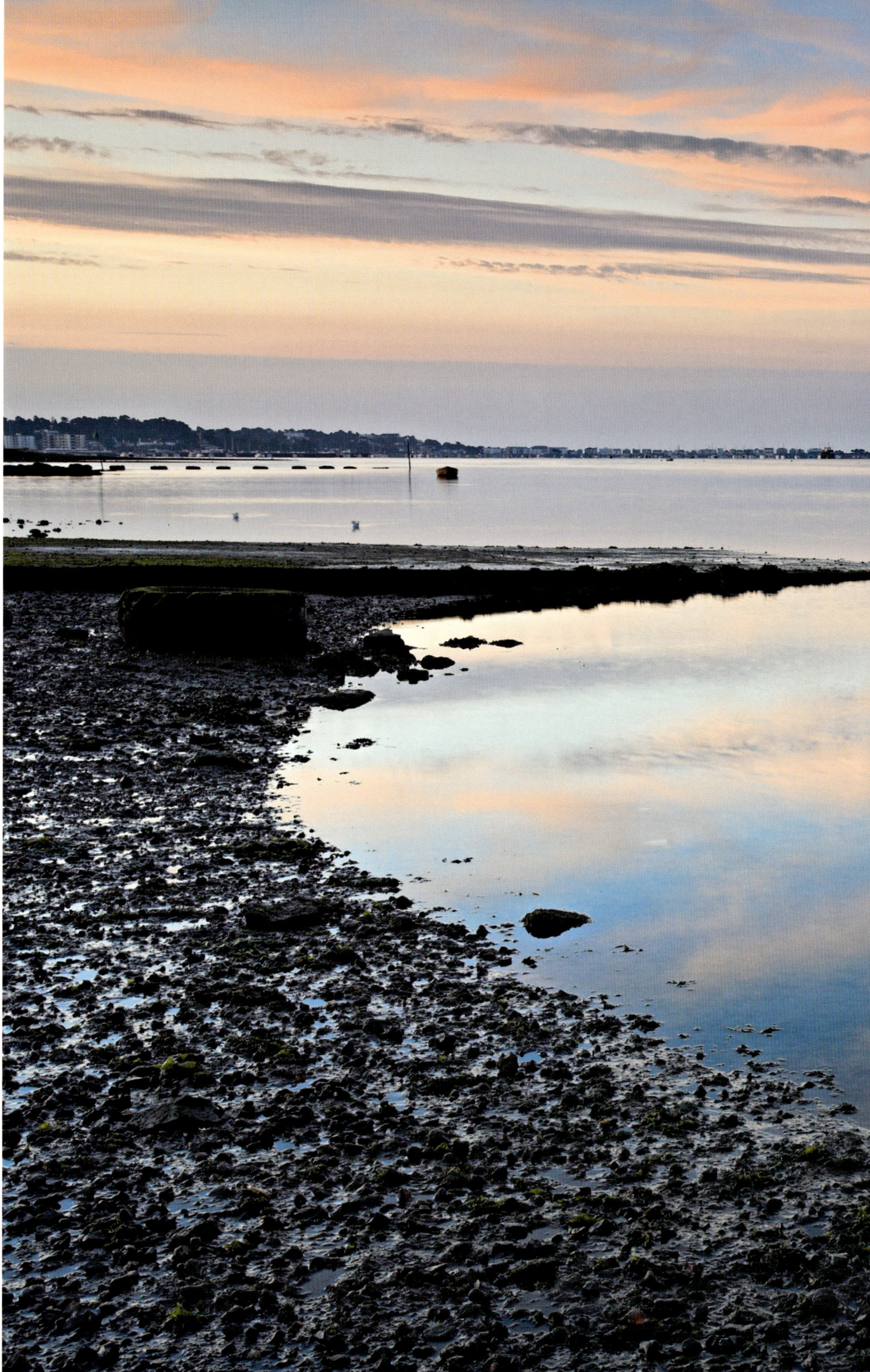

A perfect summer sunrise casts pink clouds amongst the blue sky, their reflections captured in the mirror-like water.

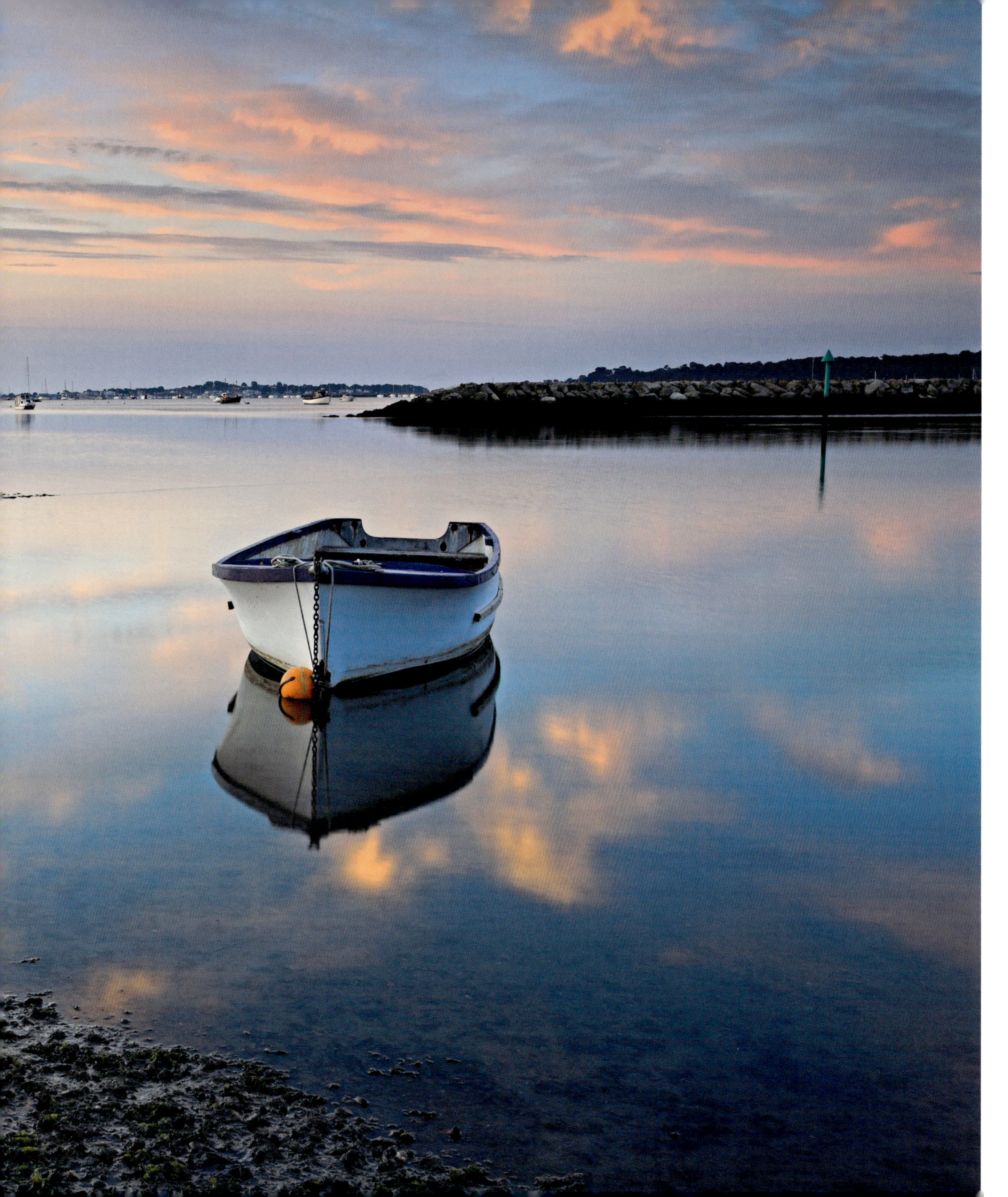

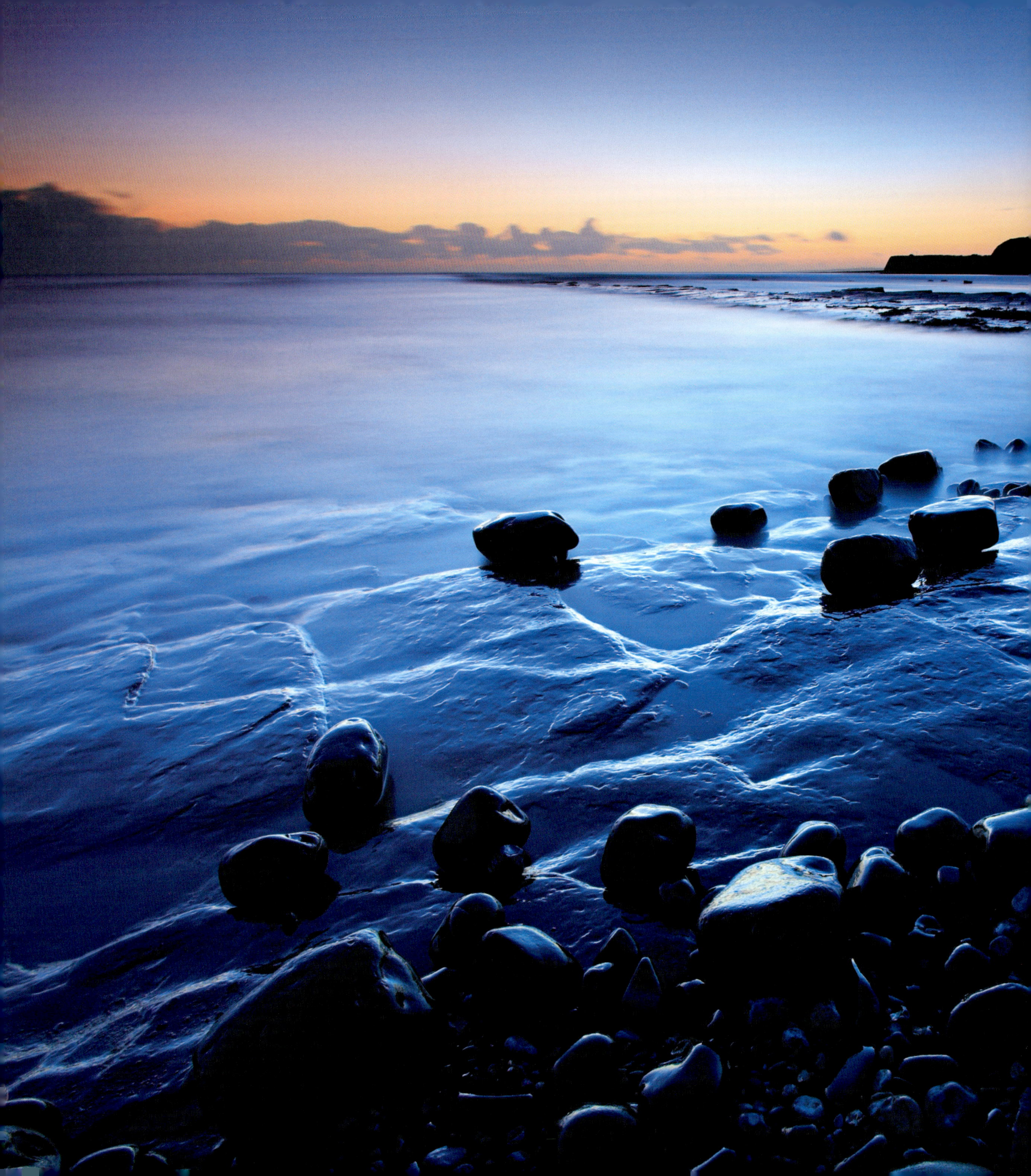

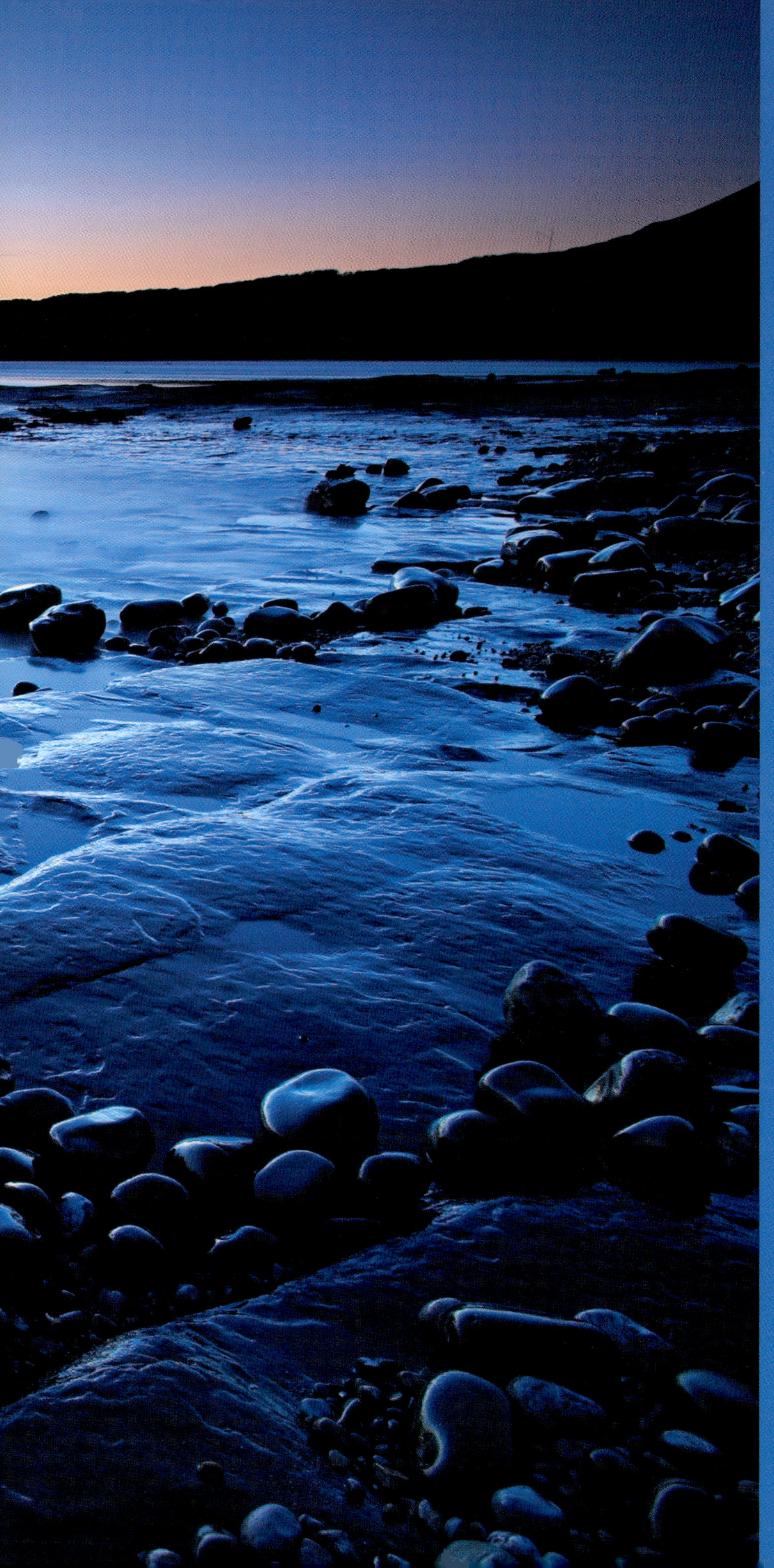

Isle of Purbeck

The many small boulders at Kimmeridge are constantly moved by tidal action, meaning that this shoreline can never look the same twice!

Studland

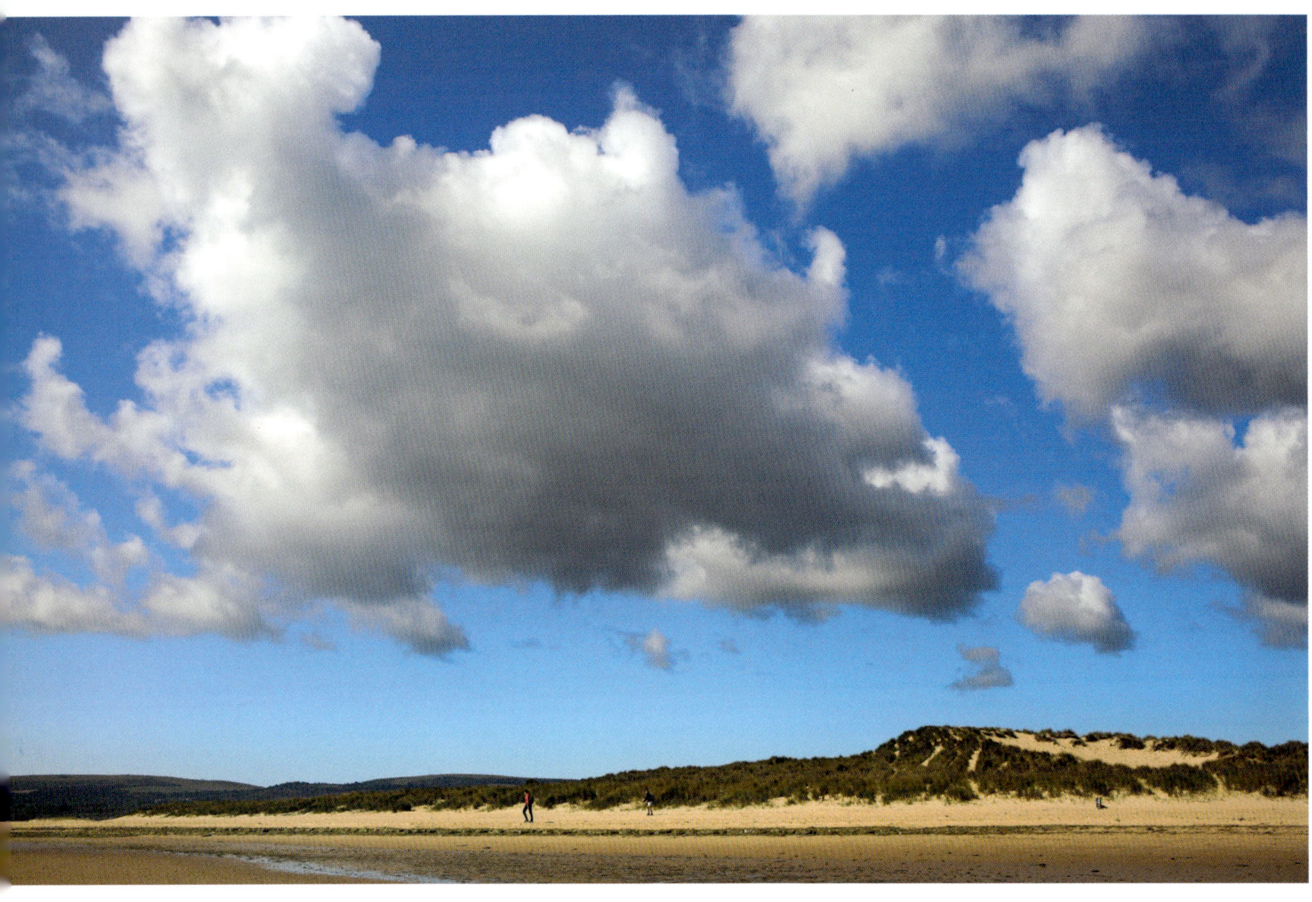

Cumulus clouds form above Studland Bay's extensive sand dune network on a hot summer's day.

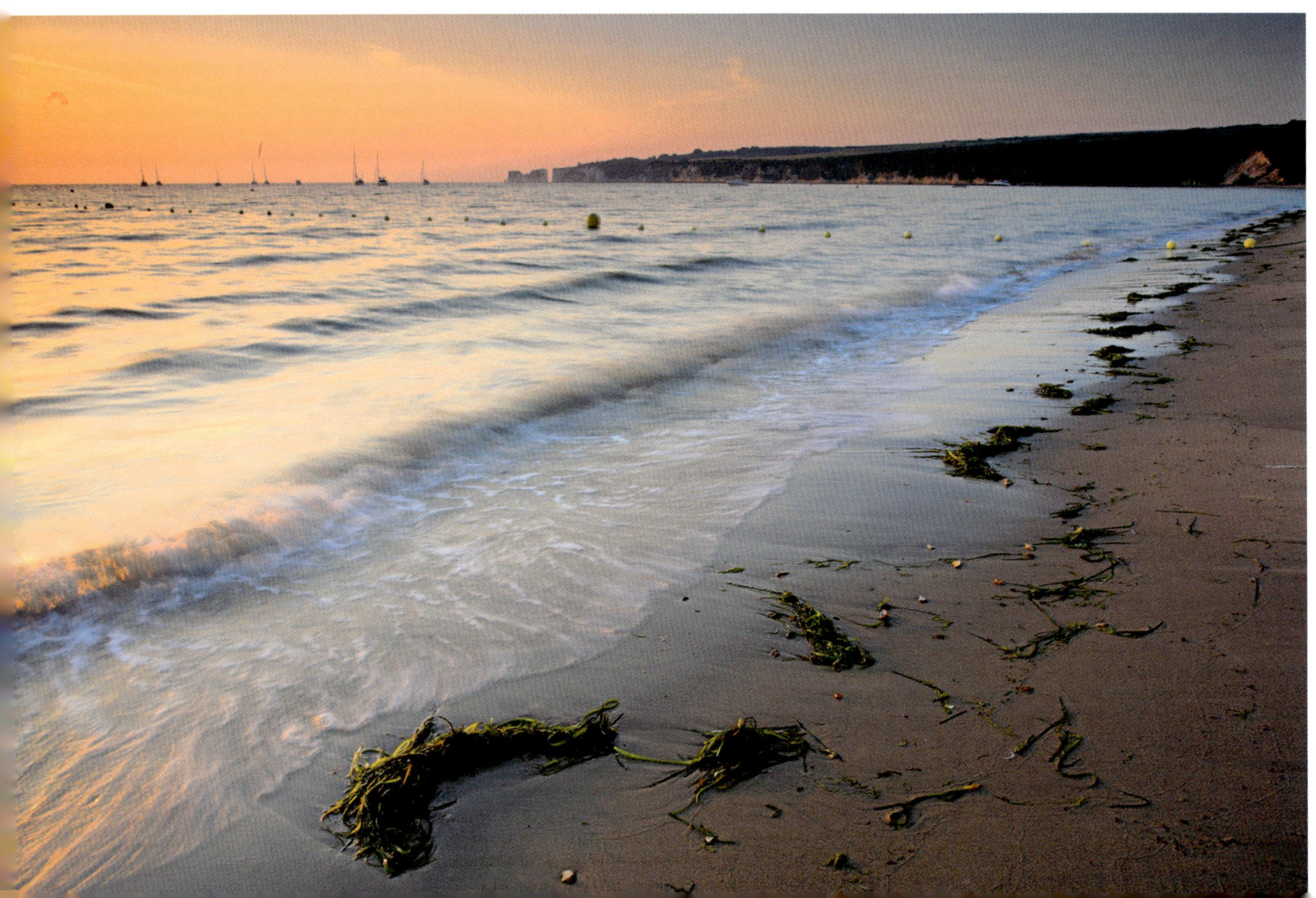

Seaweed washed up on the sandy South Beach in Studland Bay. On the distant headland the famous Old Harry chalk sea stacks are clearly visible. These mark the beginning of the Jurassic Coast World Heritage Site.

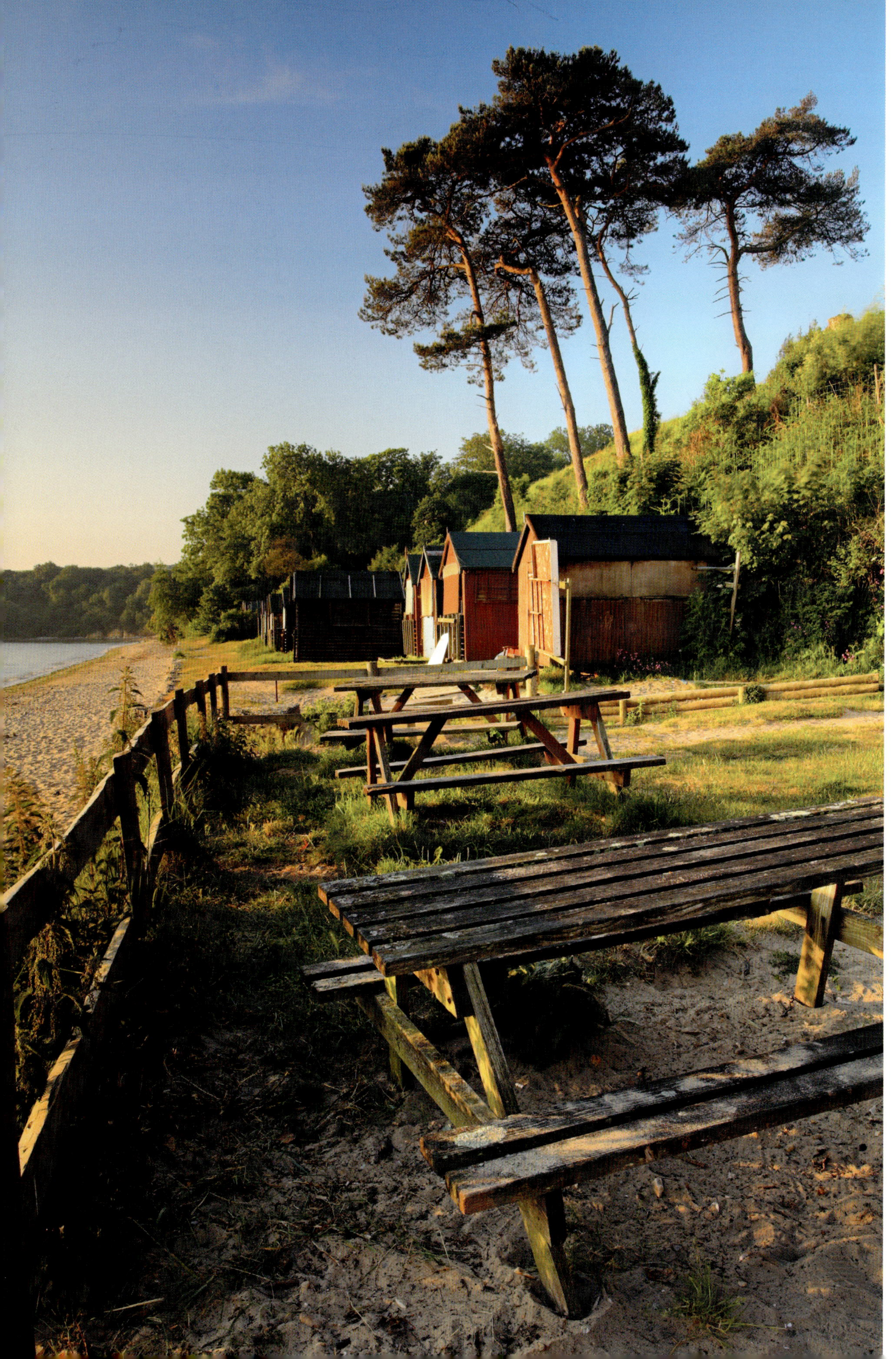

Beach huts and picnic benches
near Joe's Café on Studland's
South Beach.

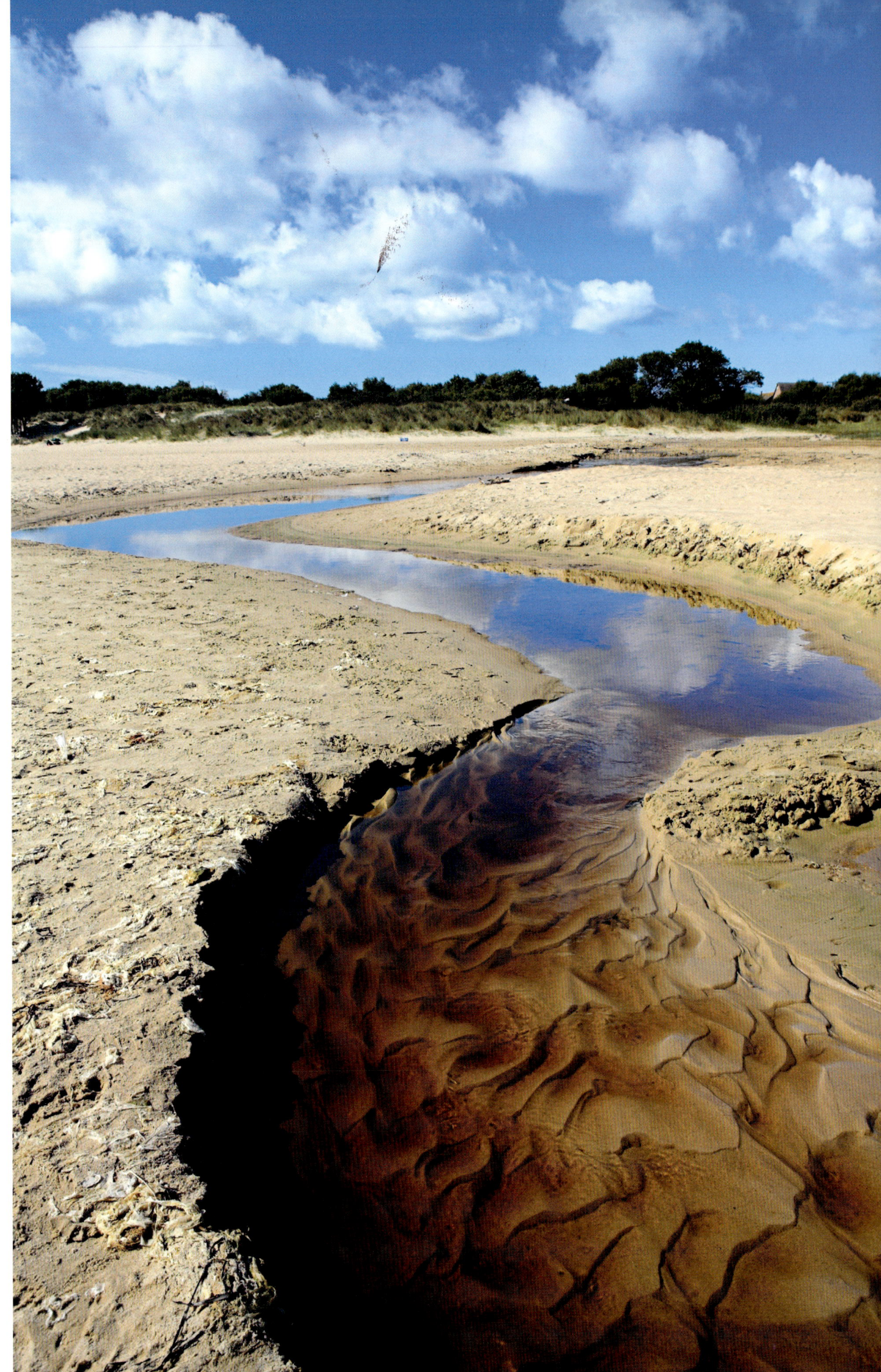

A small stream winds through Shell Bay on Studland's north shore. The brown water colour results from the leaching of tannins from the decaying leaves of riverside plants.

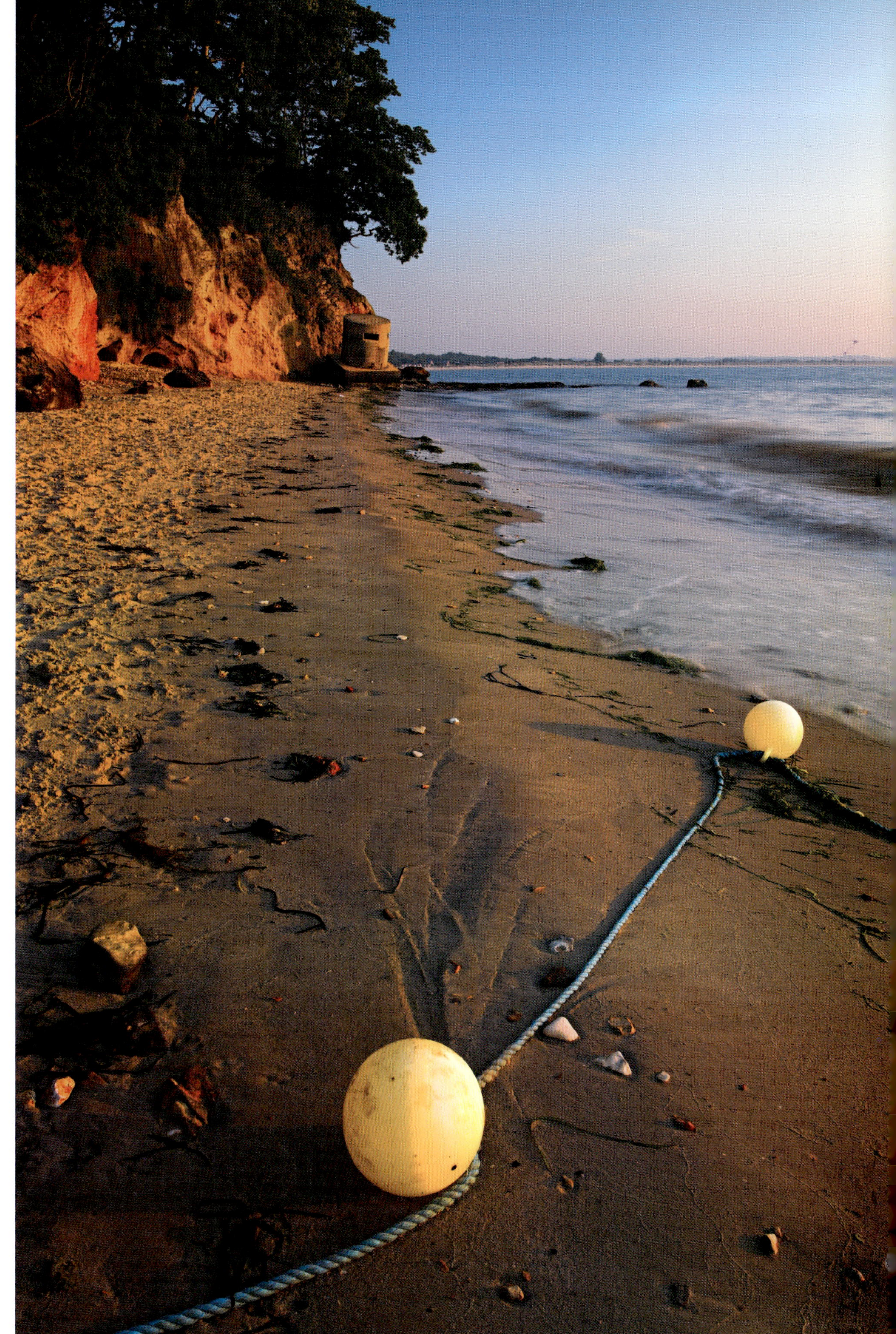

The vibrant red sandstone cliffs to be found at Redend Point are fascinating to behold, their intense colour unmatched on this stretch of coast. At the base of the rocks a pillbox rests at a jaunty angle. Once perched on the clifftop, this Second World War relic is now a victim of coastal erosion.

Old Harry Rocks

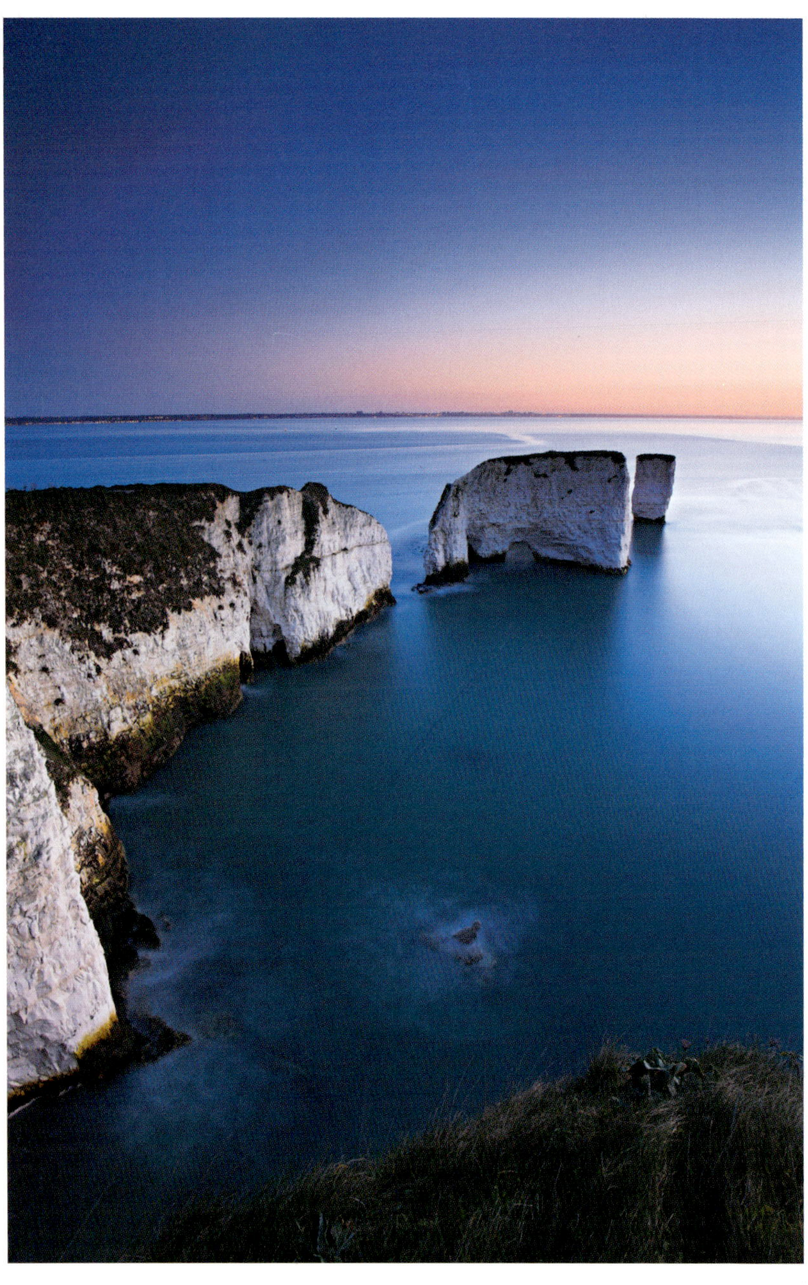

On a clear day the Needles on the Isle of Wight are usually visible from the cliffs by Old Harry Rocks. Both incredible sights are made of chalk and only a few thousand years ago were connected together. Over the years the constant sea erosion has created the beautiful sea arches and stacks we see today.

There are a few possible origins to the unusual name of these rocks. Most popular is the idea that the devil, who in medieval times was nicknamed 'Old Harry', once slept on the chalk rocks.

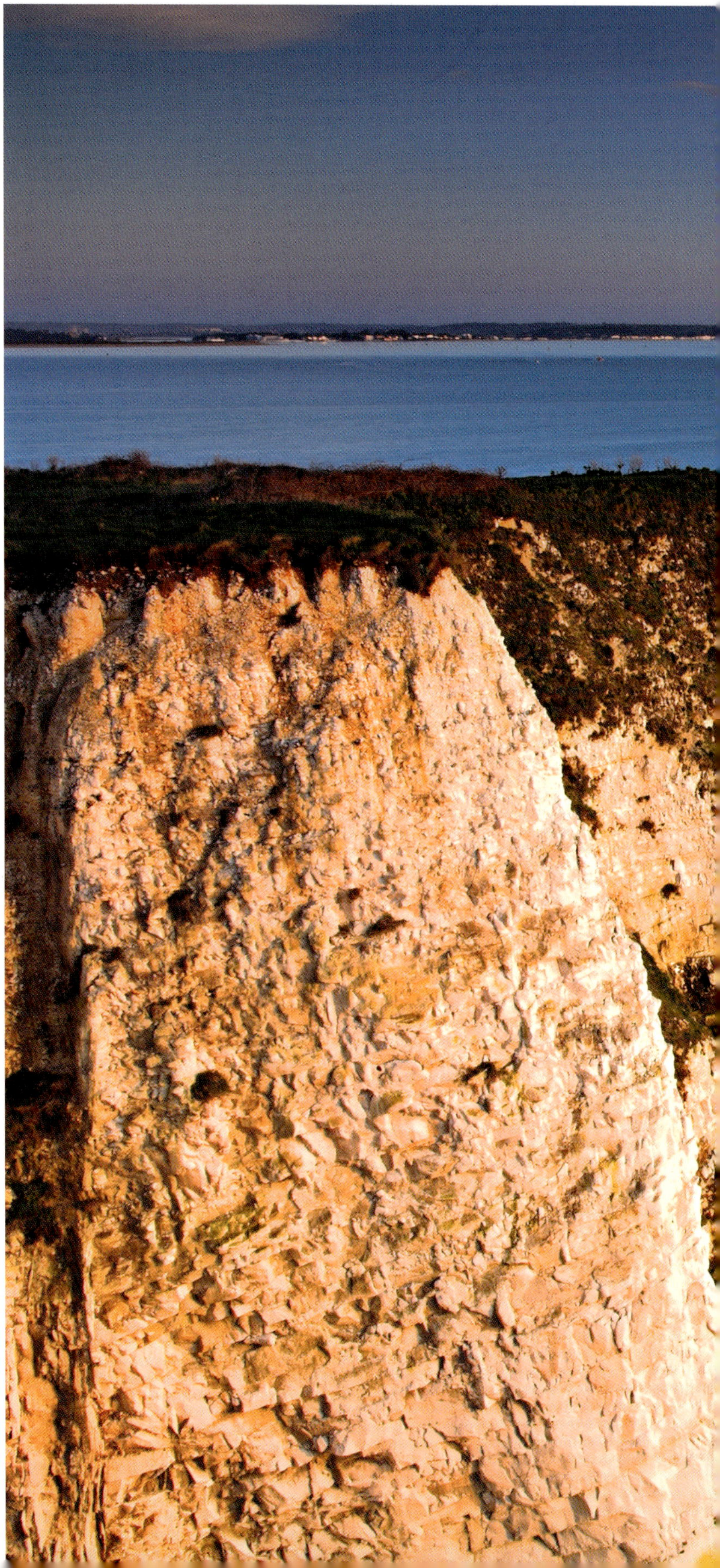

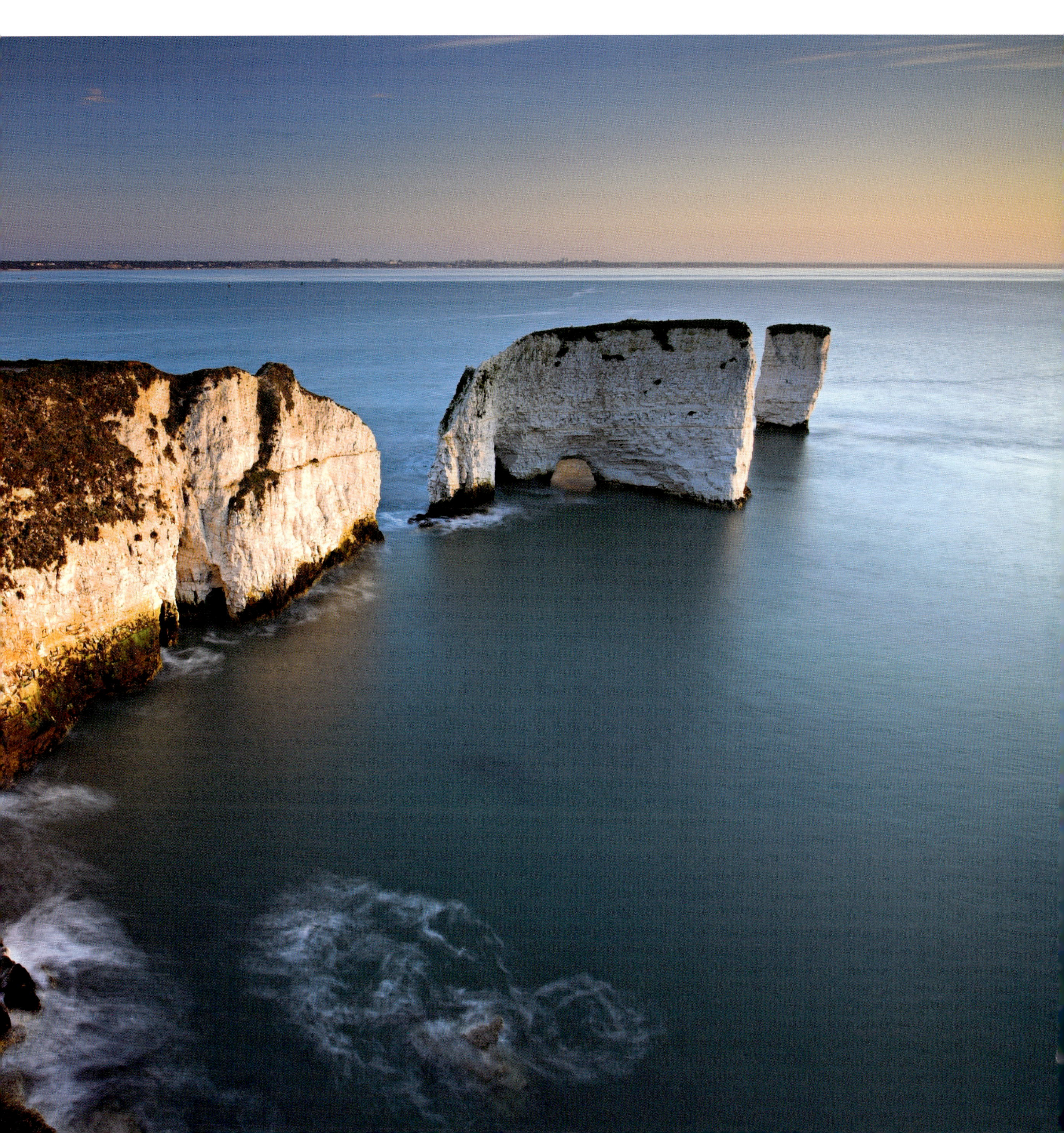

Handfast Point

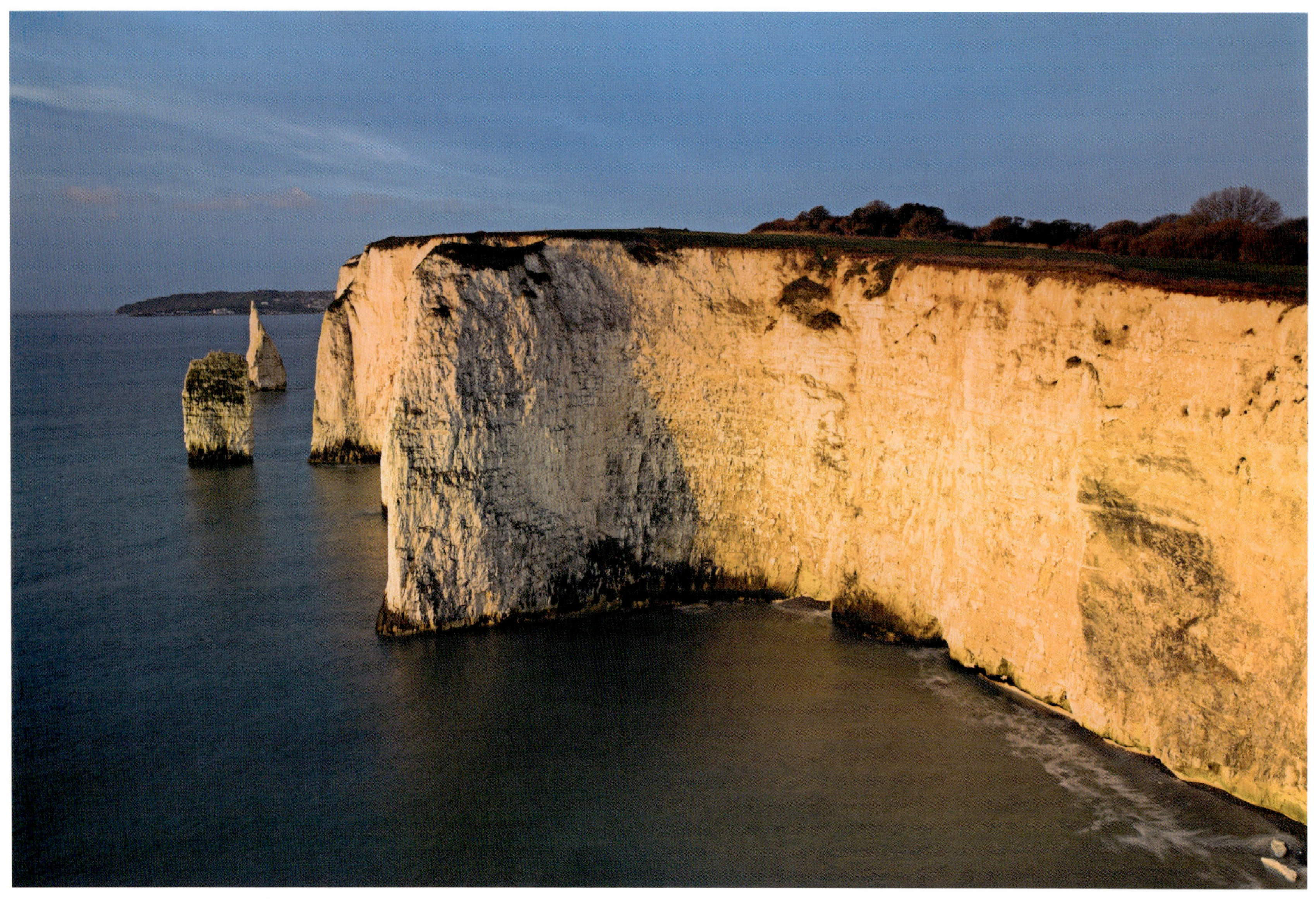

Early morning sunshine tints the
clifftops gold at Handfast Point.

Two chalk stacks called the
Pinnacles are present to the
southwest of Old Harry Rocks.
These can be viewed from the
clifftops of Ballard Down. This area
has wonderful wild chalk flora
which is complemented by many
species of butterfly, including the
Chalkhill Blue and Adonis Blue.

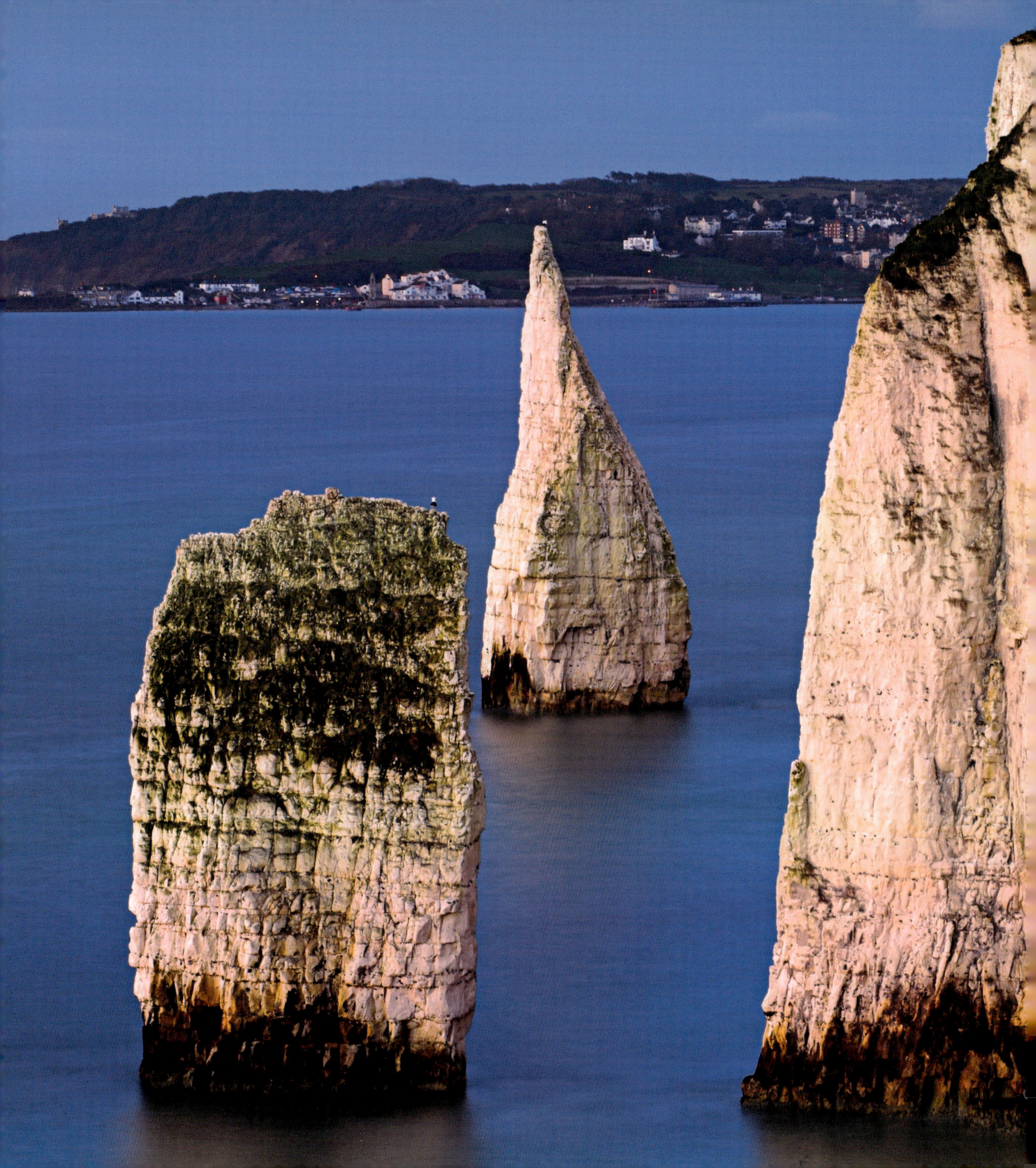

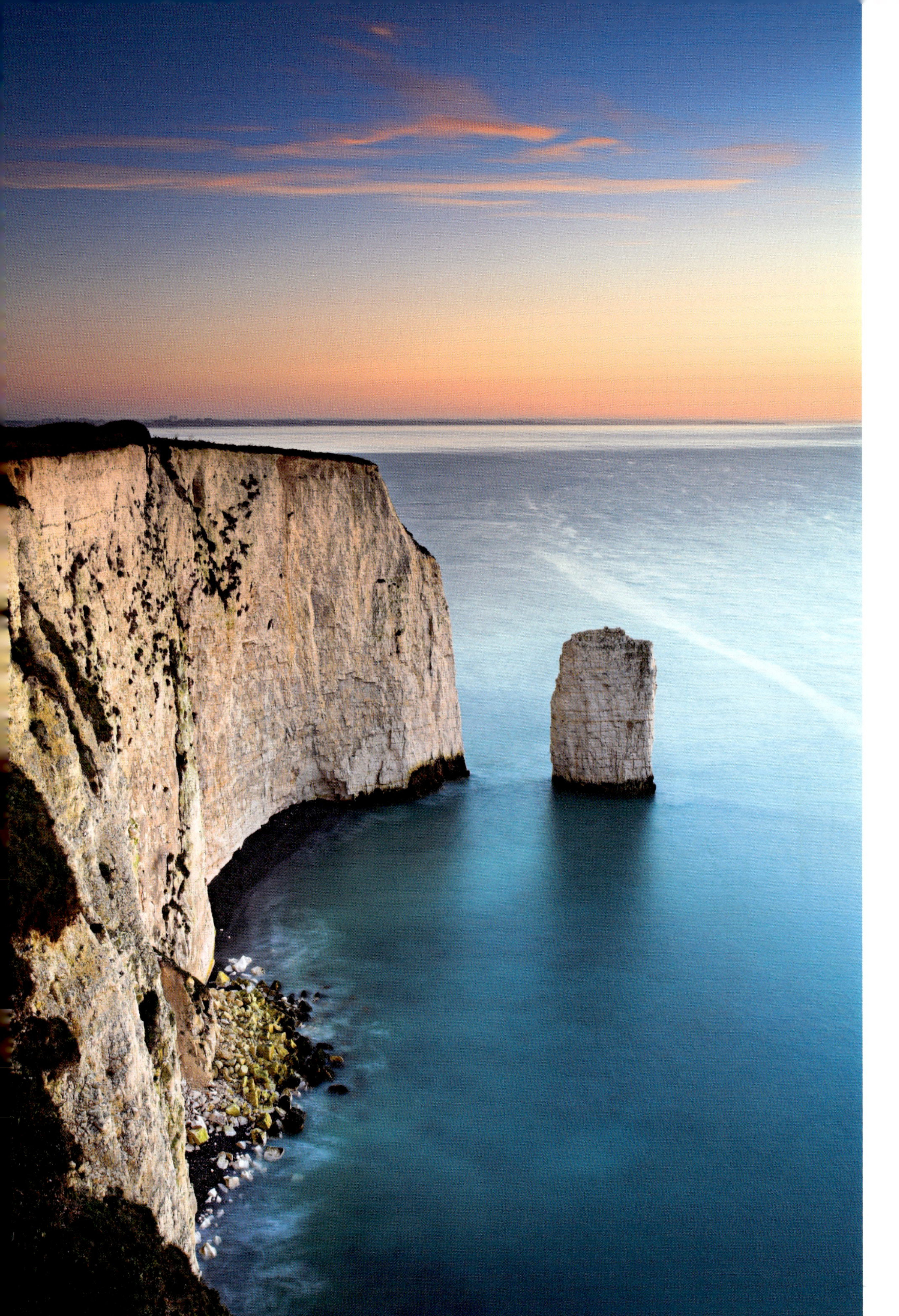

The dramatic white cliffs of Ballard Down are formed from thousands of tiny horizontal ledges of soft chalk. These fragile rocks are in a constant state of change, the headlands being eroded first into arches and then into solitary pillars of chalk. Soon, in geological terms, this rock stack will crumble to the sea and disappear from the landscape forever.

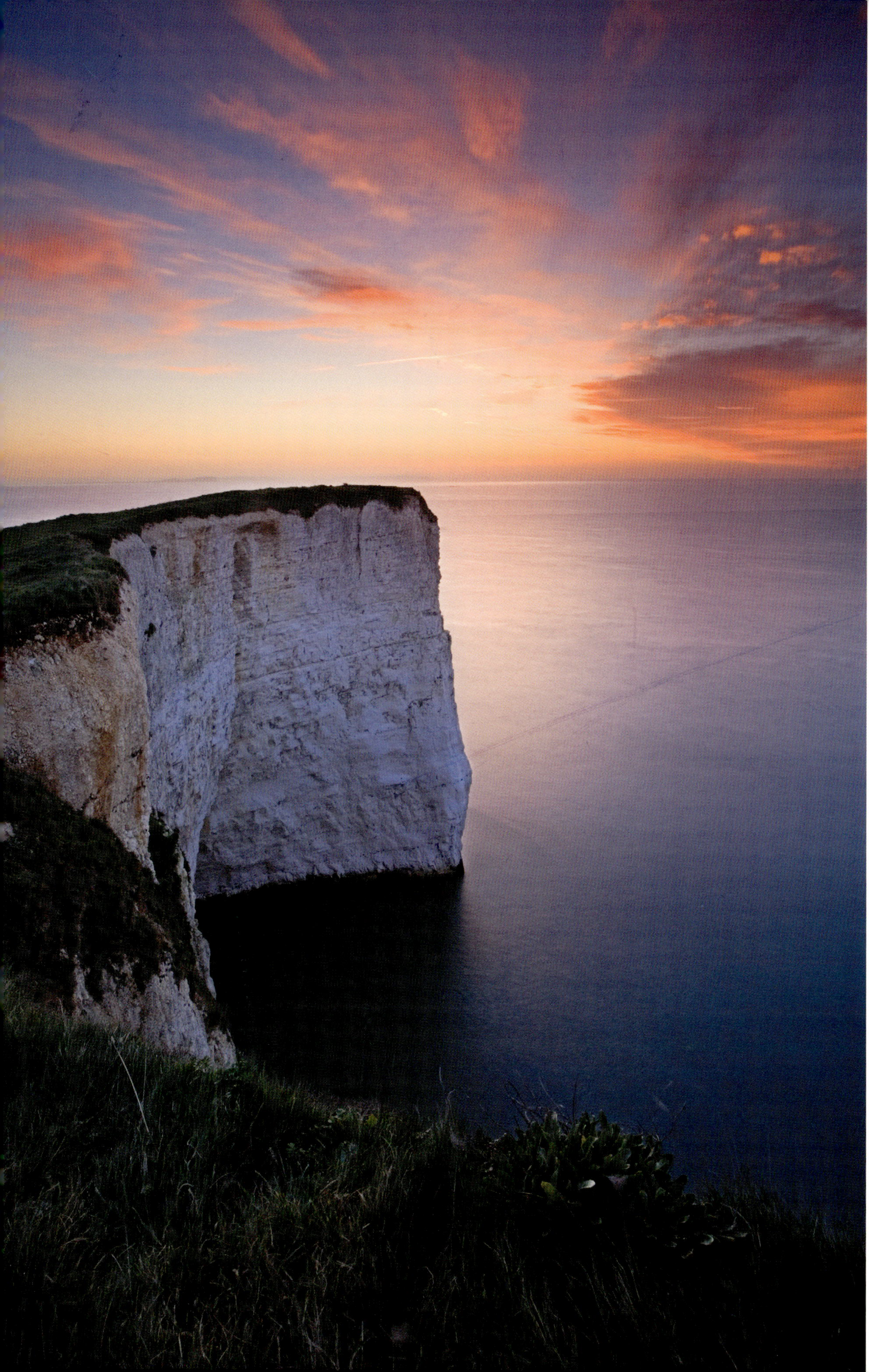

A beautiful sunrise is wonderful to experience, and the pink and red colours can sometimes remain for up to 30 minutes. For a photographer it is often the time before the sun has risen which is most spectacular.

Swanage

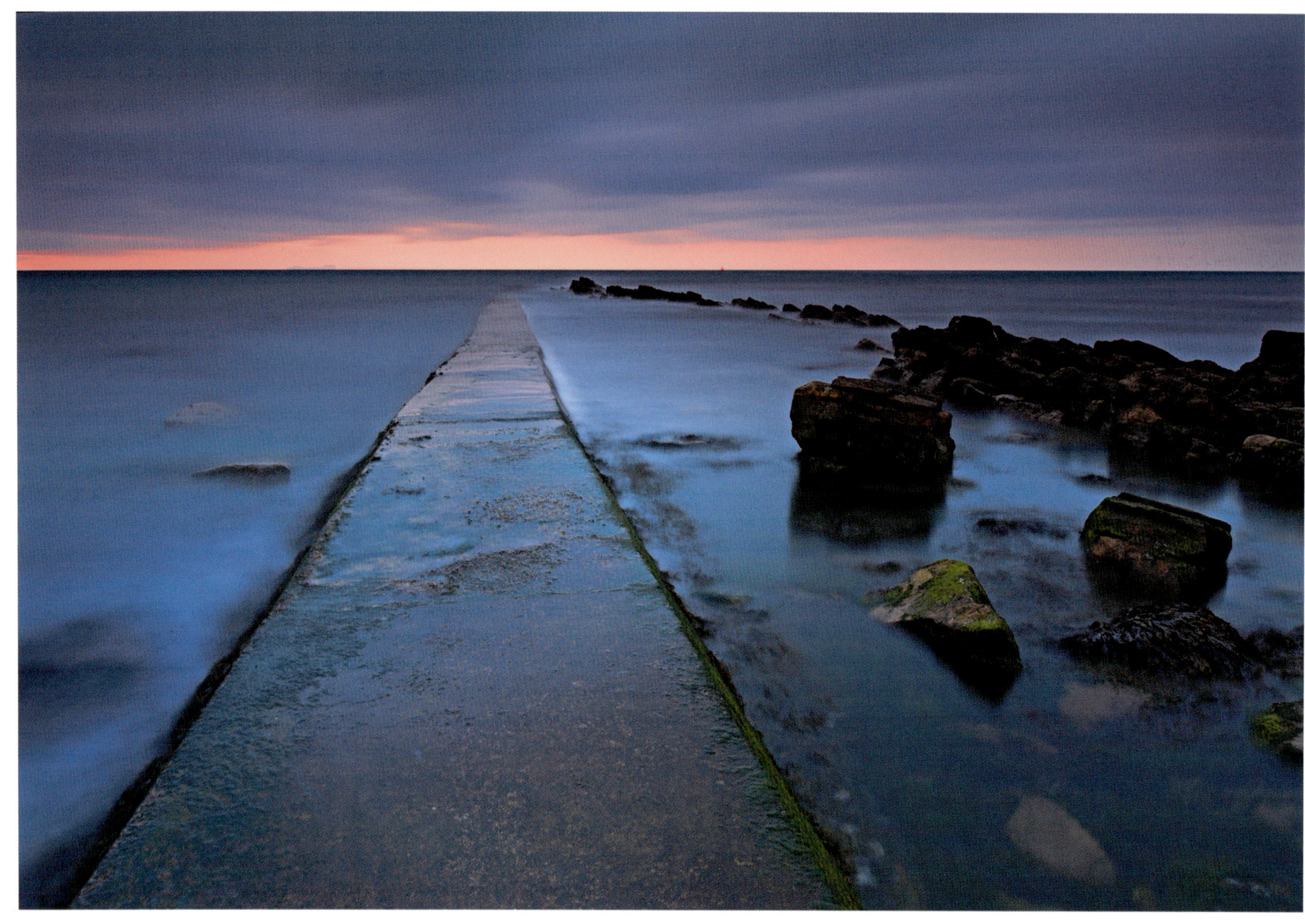

The pathway from Swanage ends at Peveril Point where it mysteriously disappears beneath the sea. It would not be difficult to imagine this was a mystical pathway to a long lost kingdom, a new Lyonesse or Atlantis. The truth is much more mundane; in reality this isn't a path at all, but a concrete casing surrounding an underground pipe.

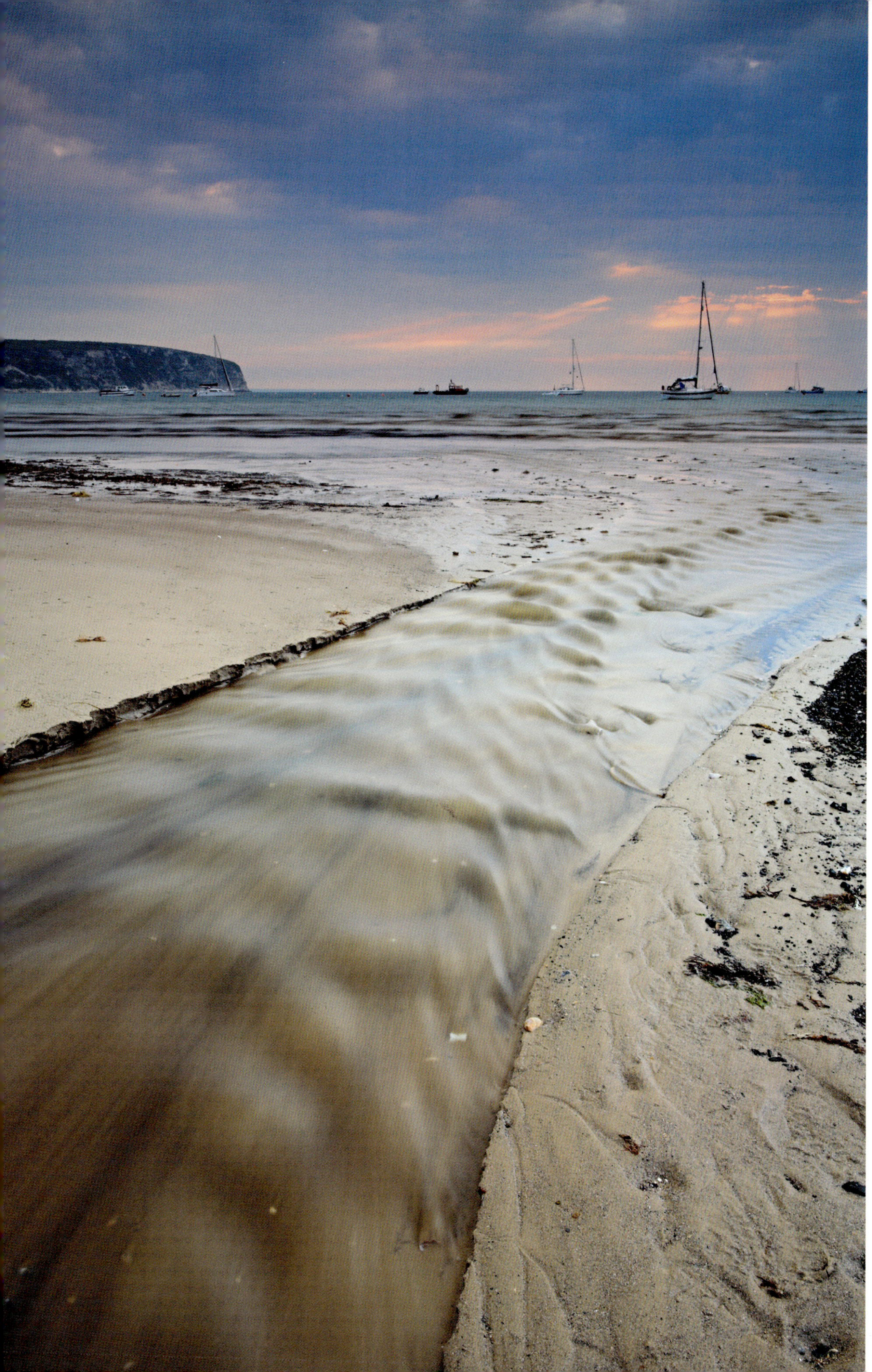

The idea of the Swanage sailing club began above a fruit and vegetable shop in 1935 and is still active. The traditional boats look very graceful while many people also enjoy the newer crafts such as the Wayfarers, Lasers, Toppers and Darts.

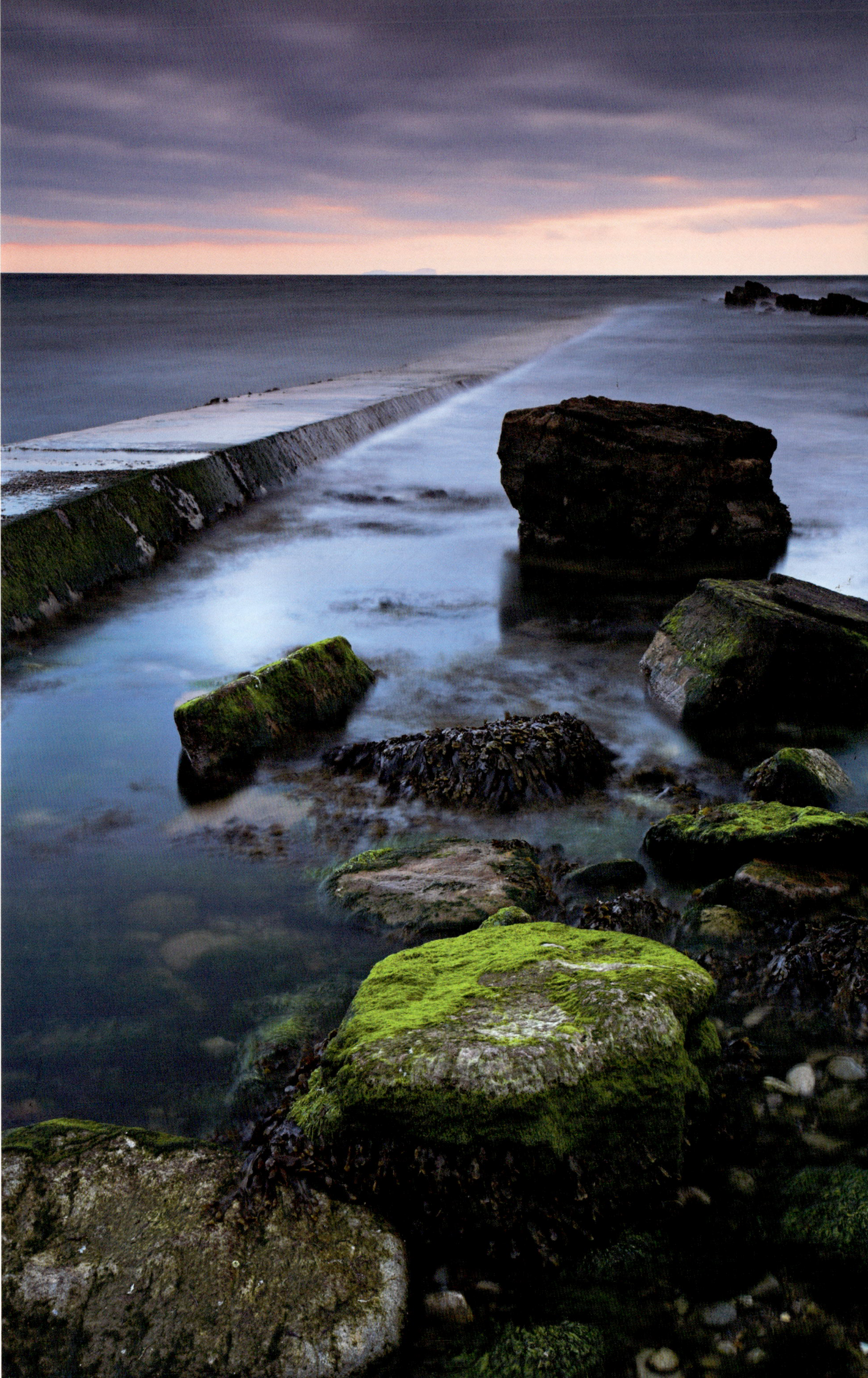

Algae-covered rocks are exposed at low tide at Peveril Point, their vibrant greens adding a splash of colour to an otherwise grey morning. Barely visible on the far horizon, it is just about possible to make out the cliffs of the Isle of Wight.

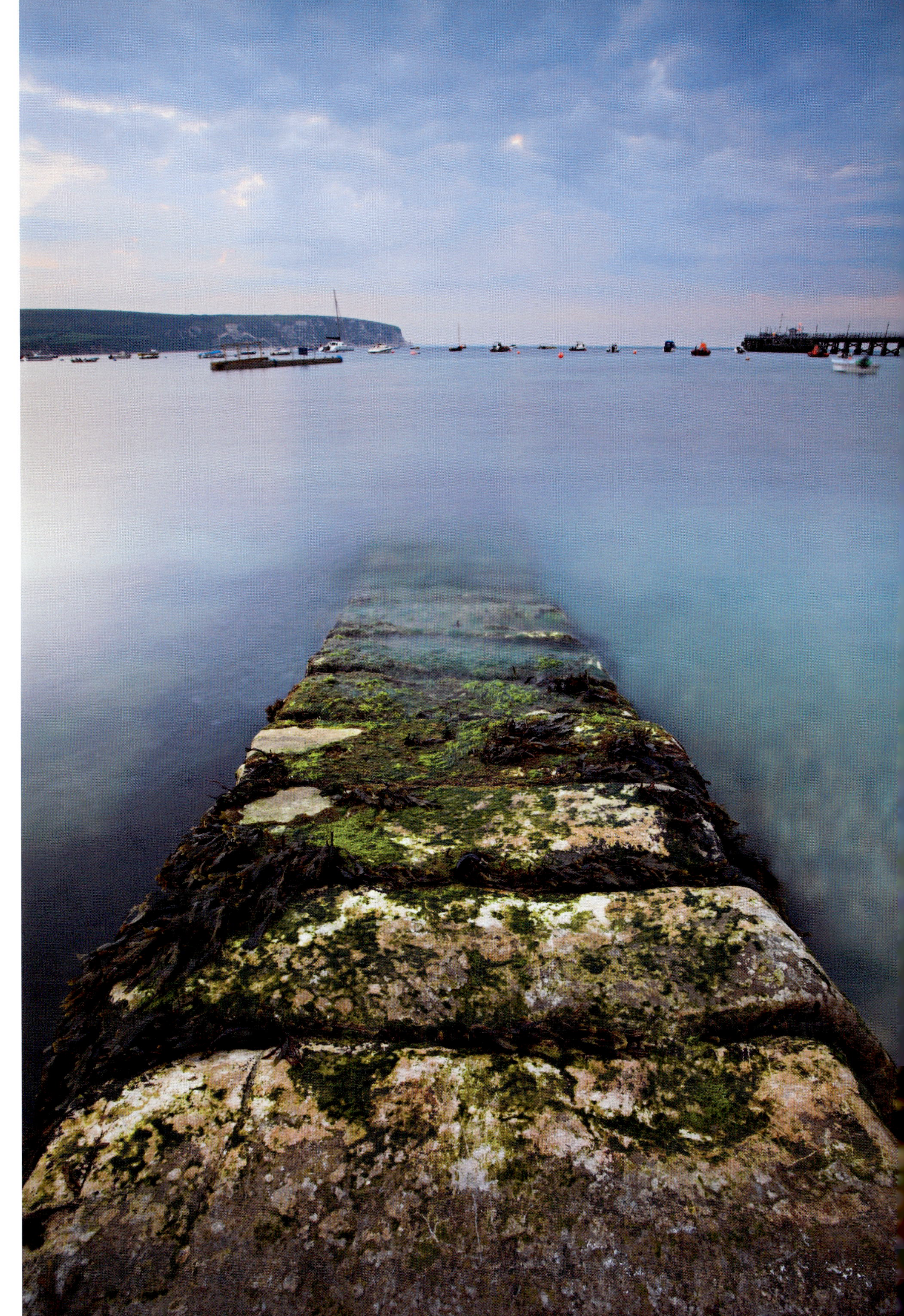

The sheltered conditions and clear water at Swanage Bay make it a popular location for scuba diving. Divers may encounter shoals of pollack, hundreds of spider and edible crabs, snails and hermit crabs amongst other sea creatures.

Despite once being both a busy fishing and quarry port, Swanage's main industry is now tourism. It has been a popular seaside resort since the Victorian period, complete with classic British pier and promenade.

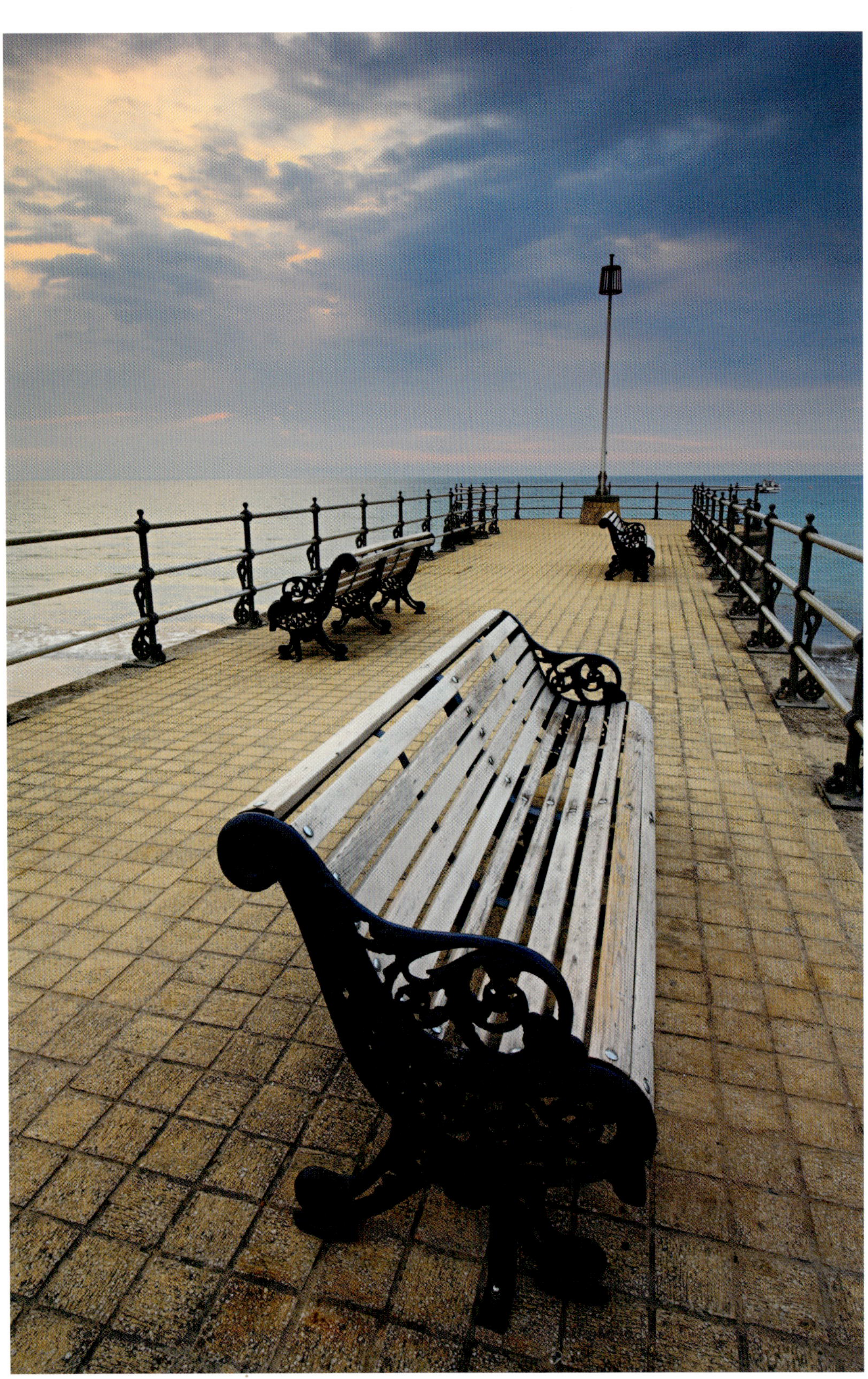

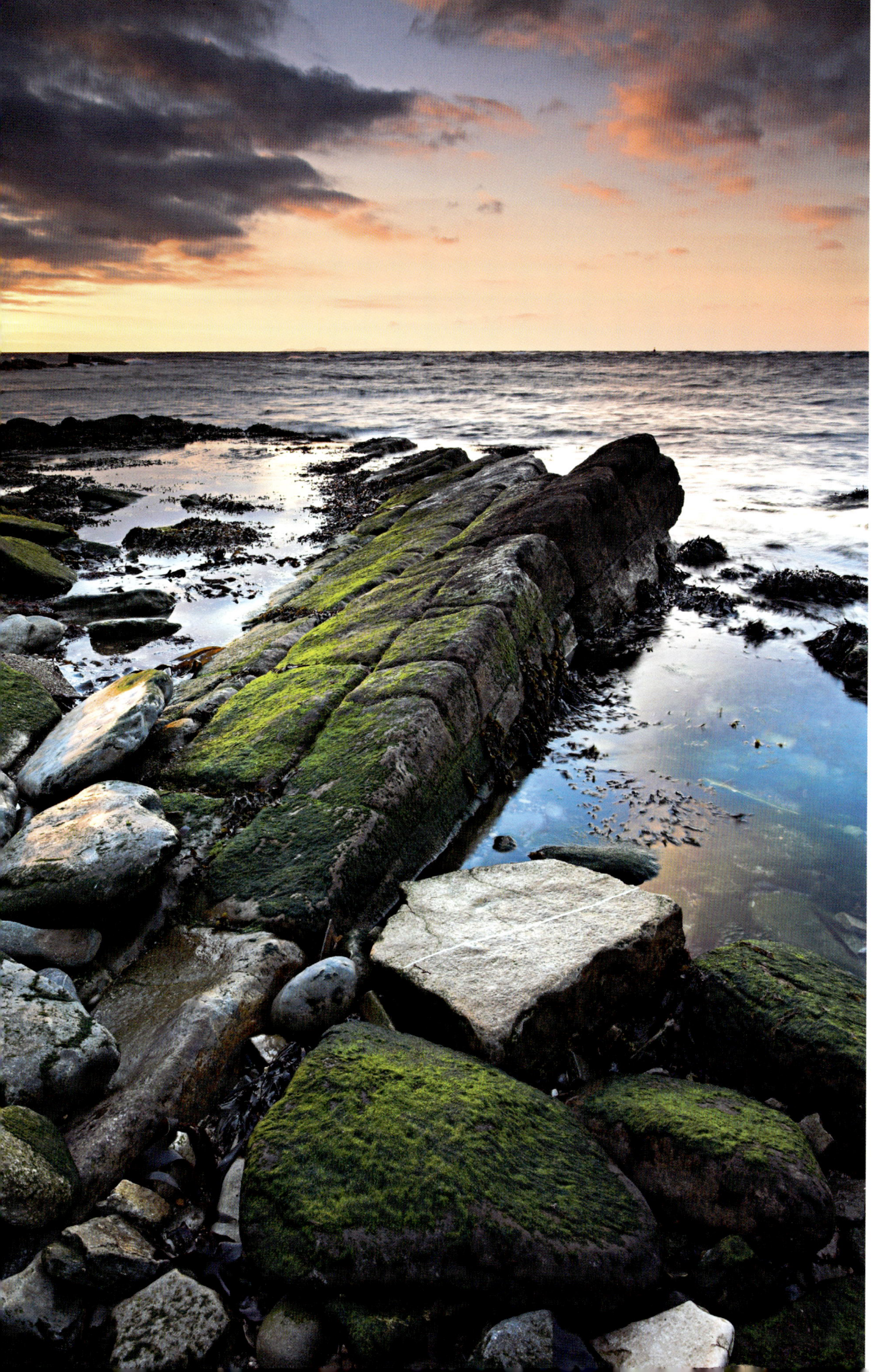

Peveril Point is one of the most treacherous locations for shipping on the Dorset coast. Strong tides and underwater rock ledges make dangerous hazards for passing boats. As a result, a National Coastwatch lookout station now stands on the Point, helping to keep passing boats safe.

Dancing Ledge

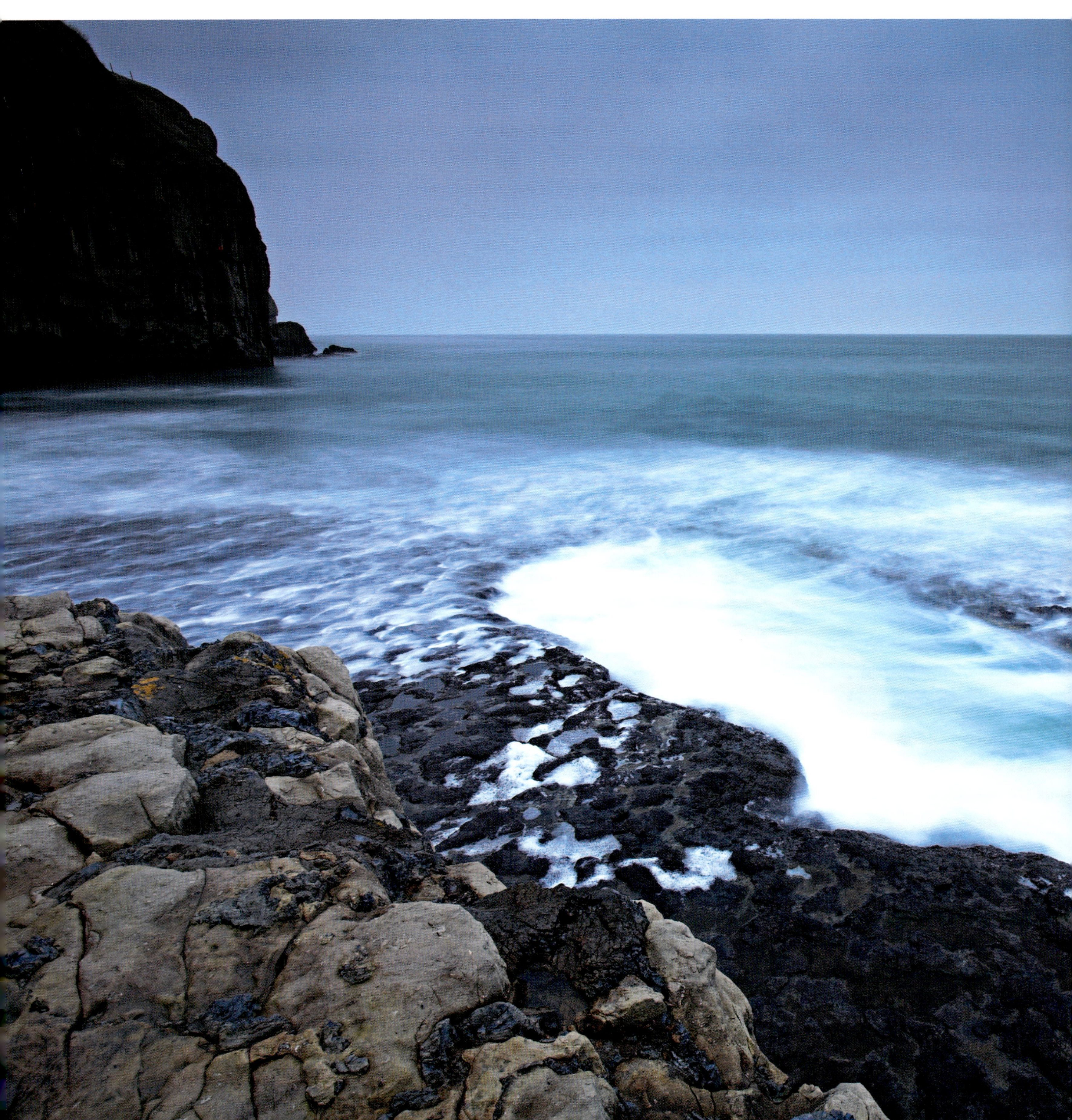

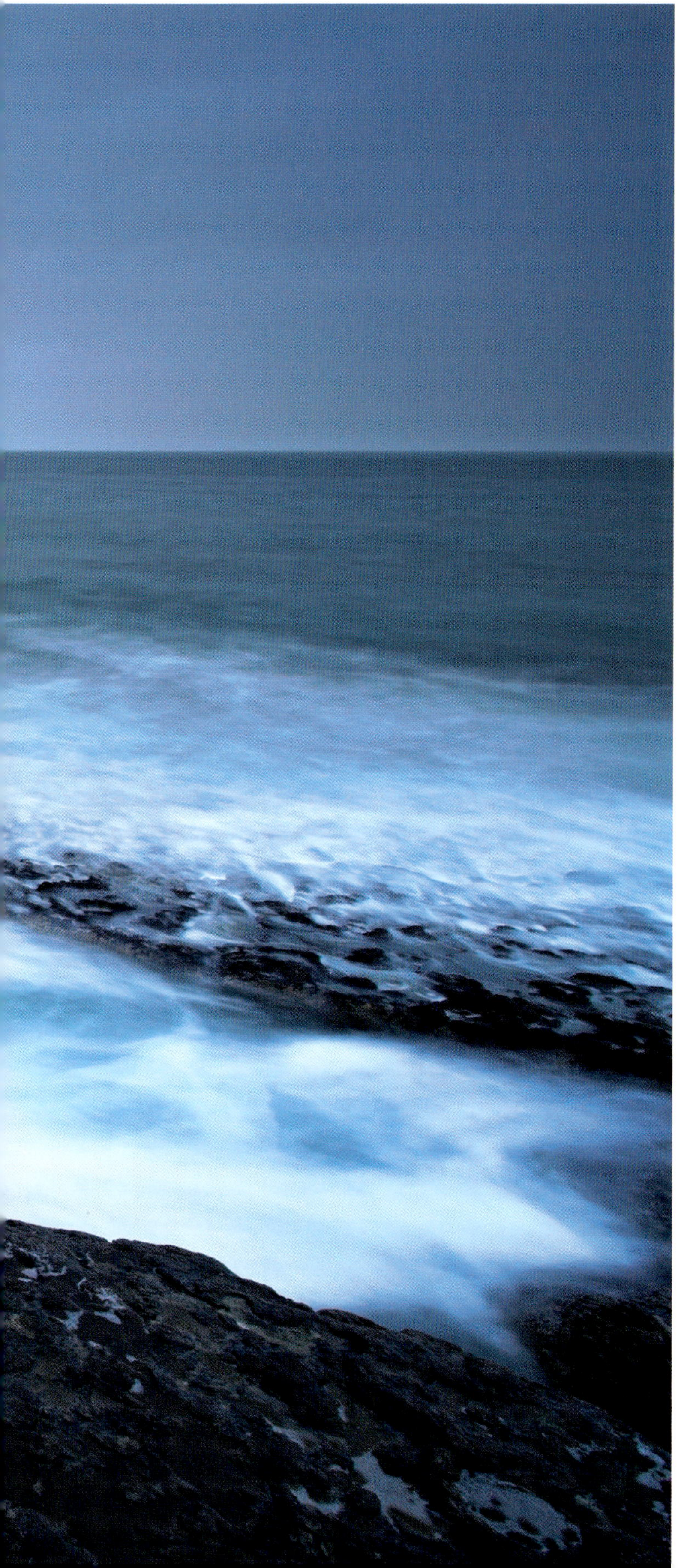

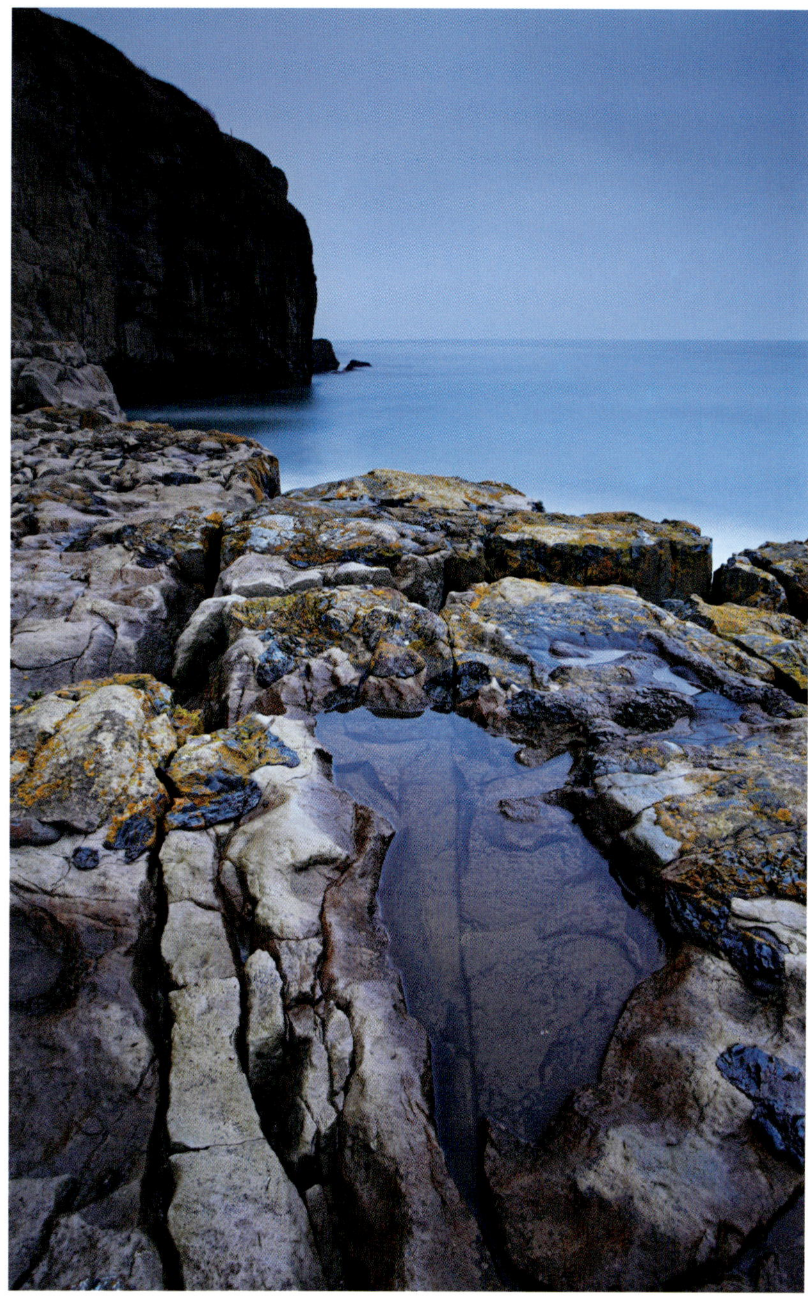

A cold blue winter's morning at Dancing Ledge. There are several rumours as to how the ledge was so named, one being that it resembles a ballroom floor.

The pool at Dancing Ledge was blasted from the ledge by quarrymen at the request of a local schoolmaster, who insisted that his pupils bathe in the sea every morning. Whenever the sea conditions proved too rough, rather than missing out on their exercise the boys could swim in the pool. Looking at the pool on such a bitter day, it's difficult to imagine anybody could be quite so foolhardy.

Seacombe

In a timeless struggle between the
soft water and hard rocks, the sea
will always end the victor, sculpting
this landscape in ever more unique
shapes.

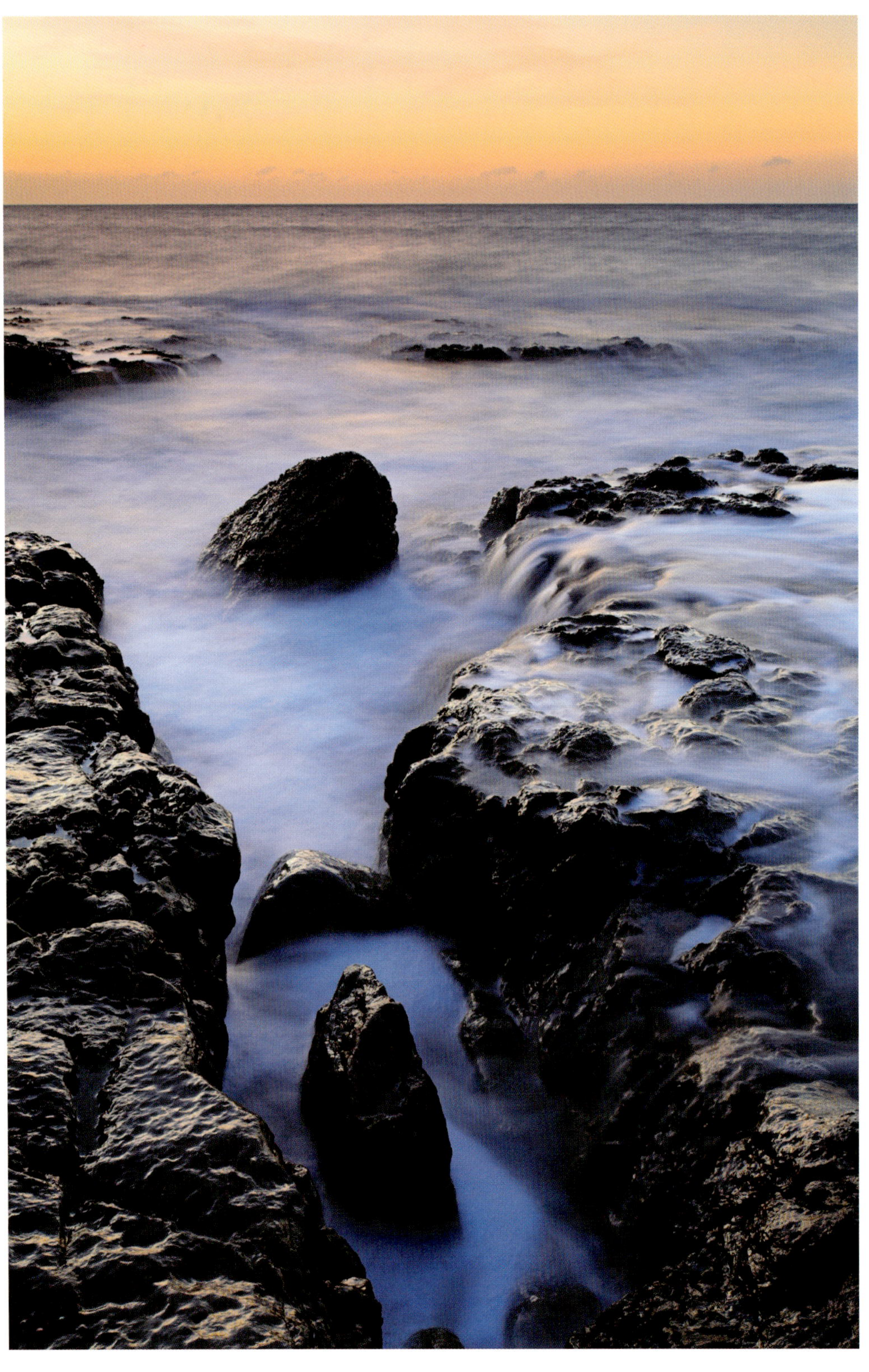

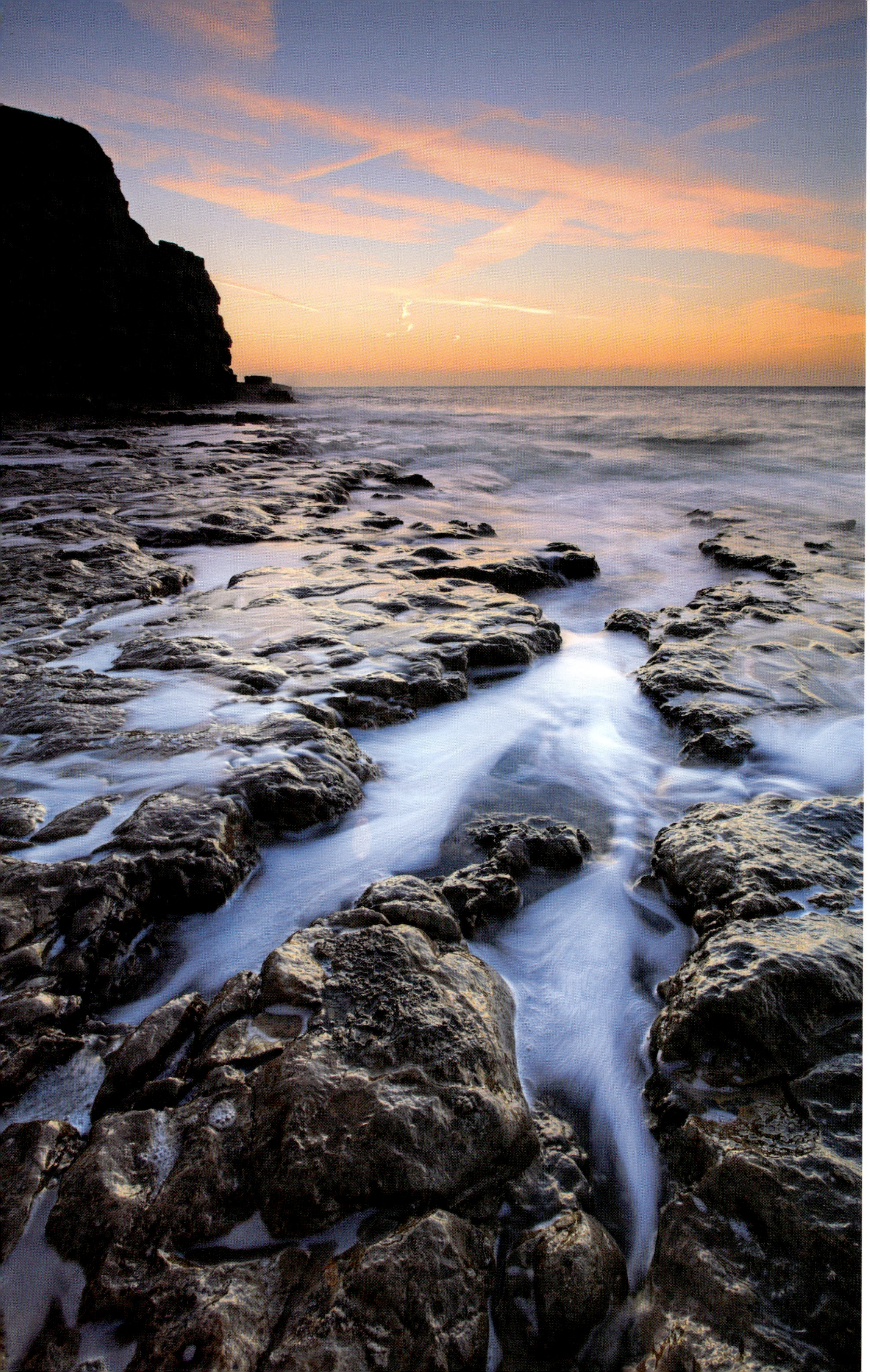

As a new day dawns over Seacombe, the ledges and rockpools are washed clean by an incoming tide.

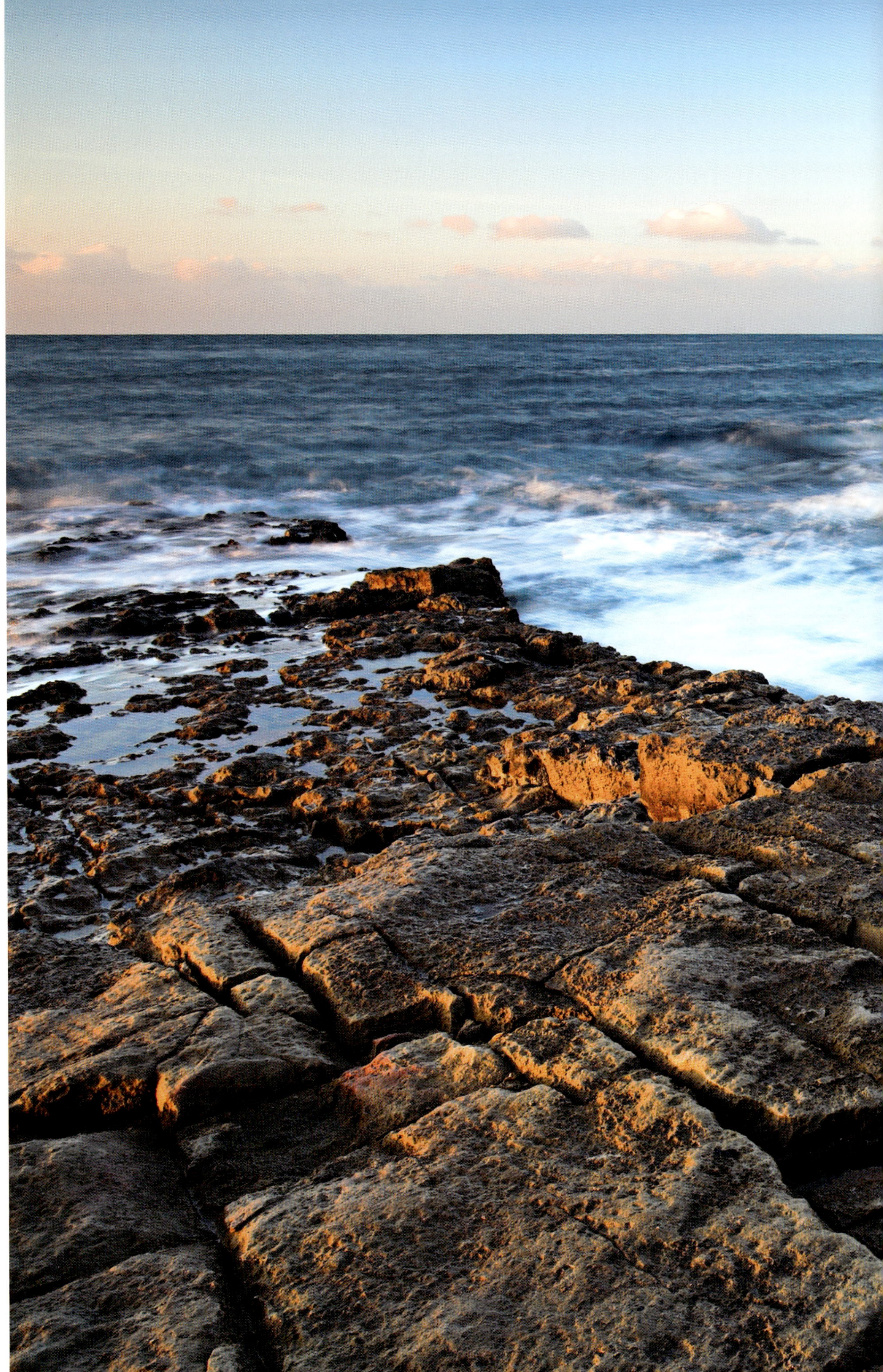

Early morning sunshine glows on
the ledges and cliffs at Seacombe.

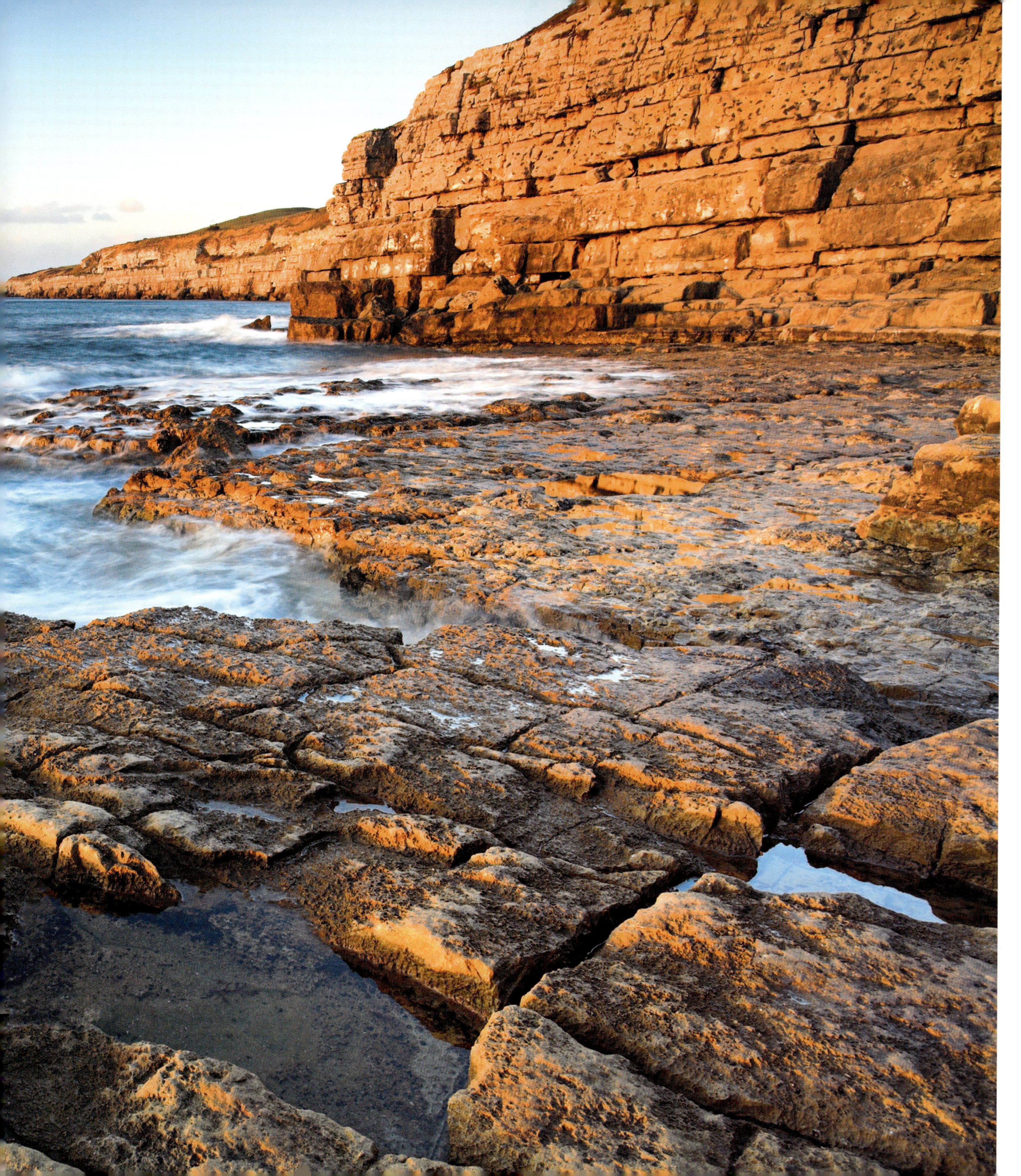

Winspit

A huge fossilised ammonite embedded in rock near the water's edge. As the cliffs which have long been its home crumble with erosion, this 140-million-year-old sea creature gradually makes its way back towards the ocean.

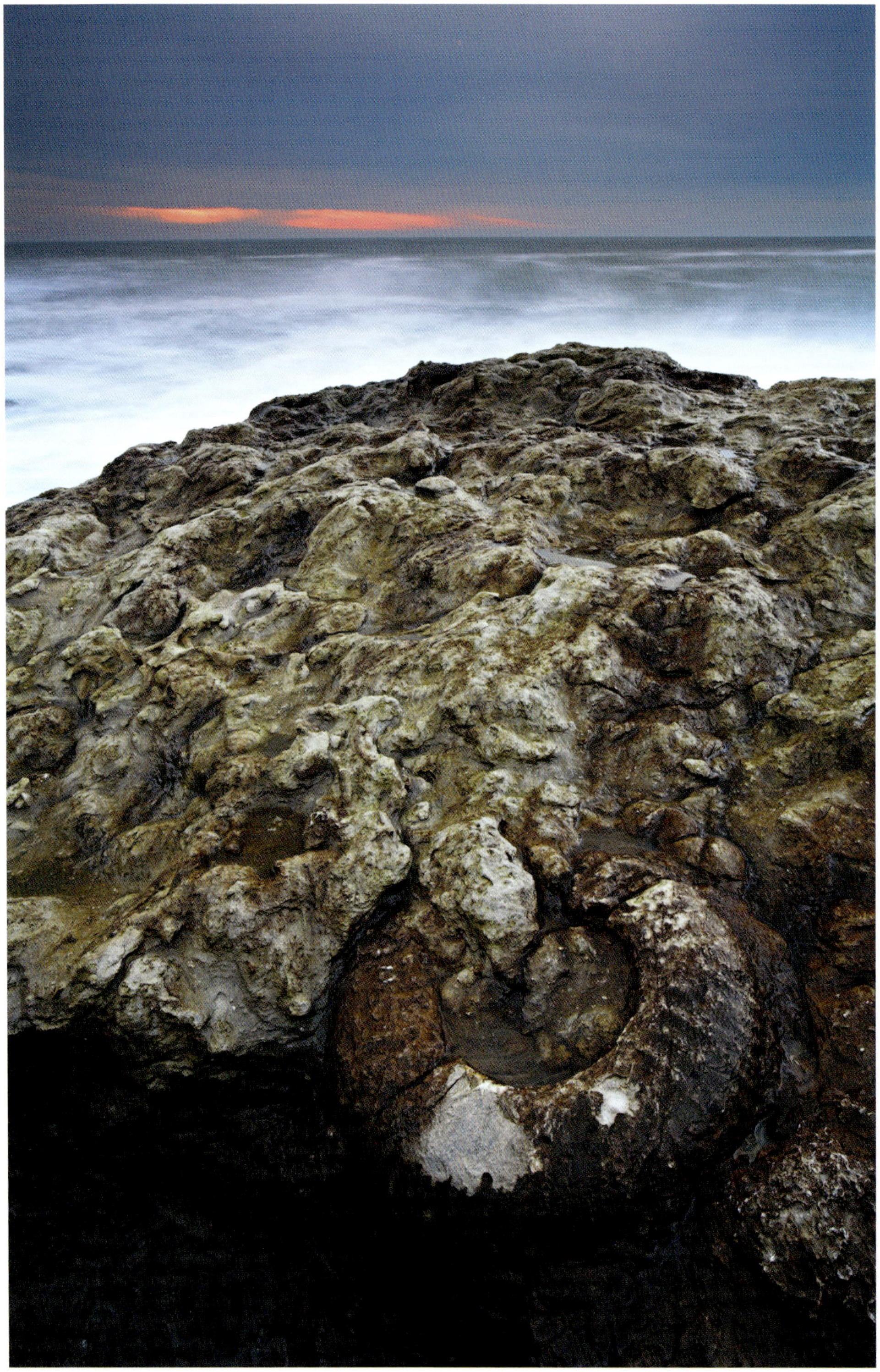

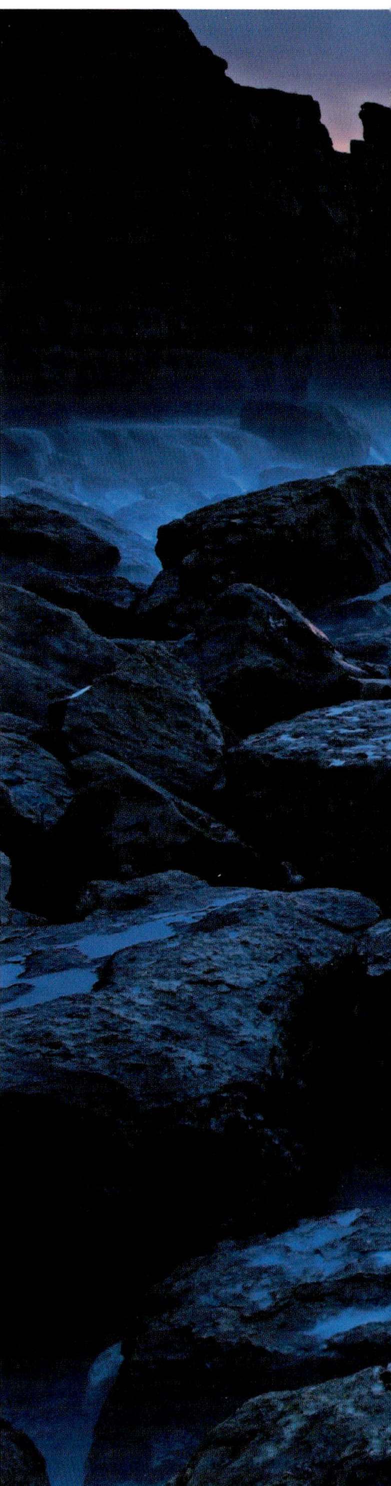

A small valley path winds down to
Winspit on the Purbeck coast. The
cove here, no more than a tiny
inlet, consists of a jumble of broken
limestone boulders facing an
everlasting assault by the sea.

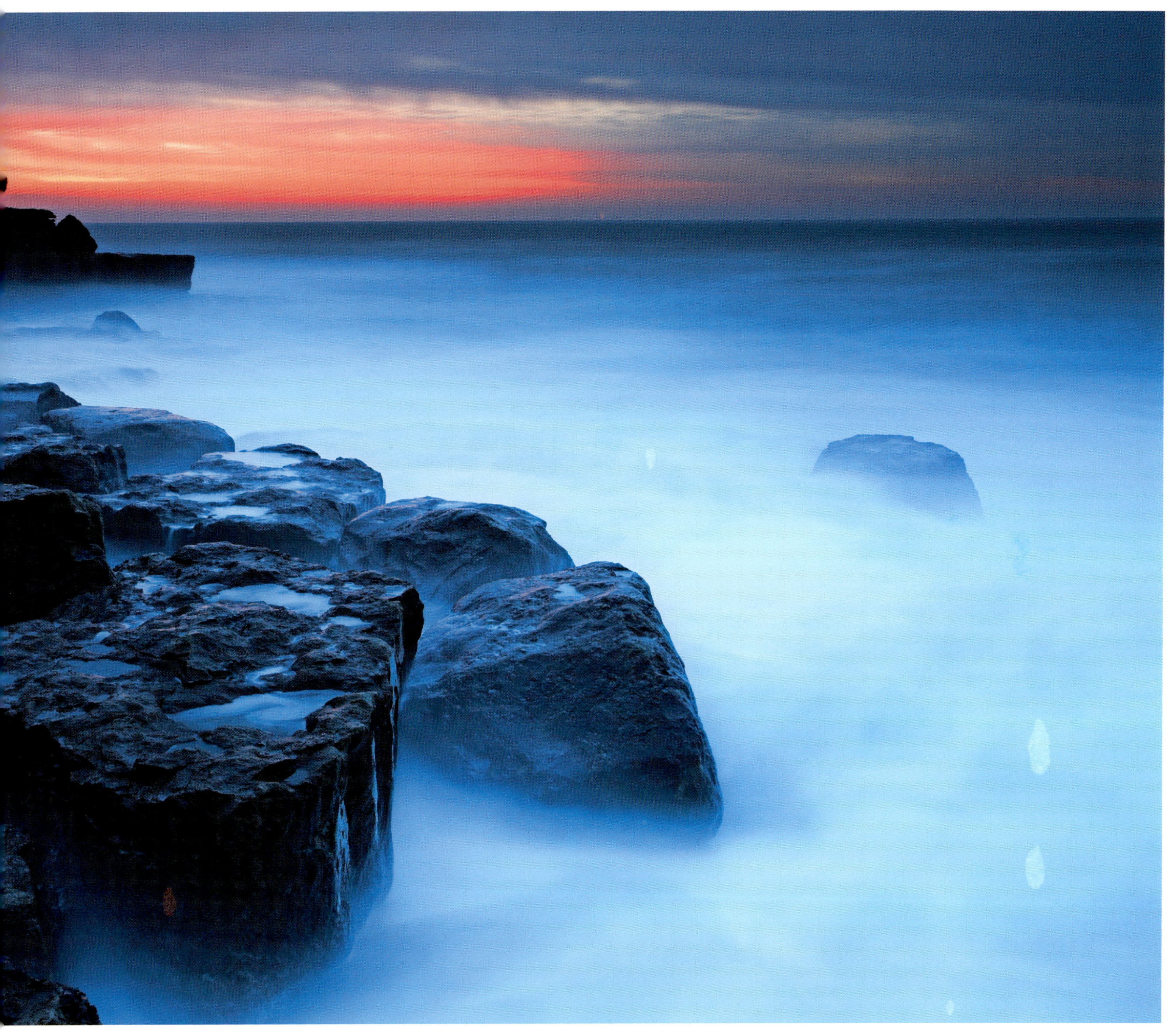

St Aldhelm's Head

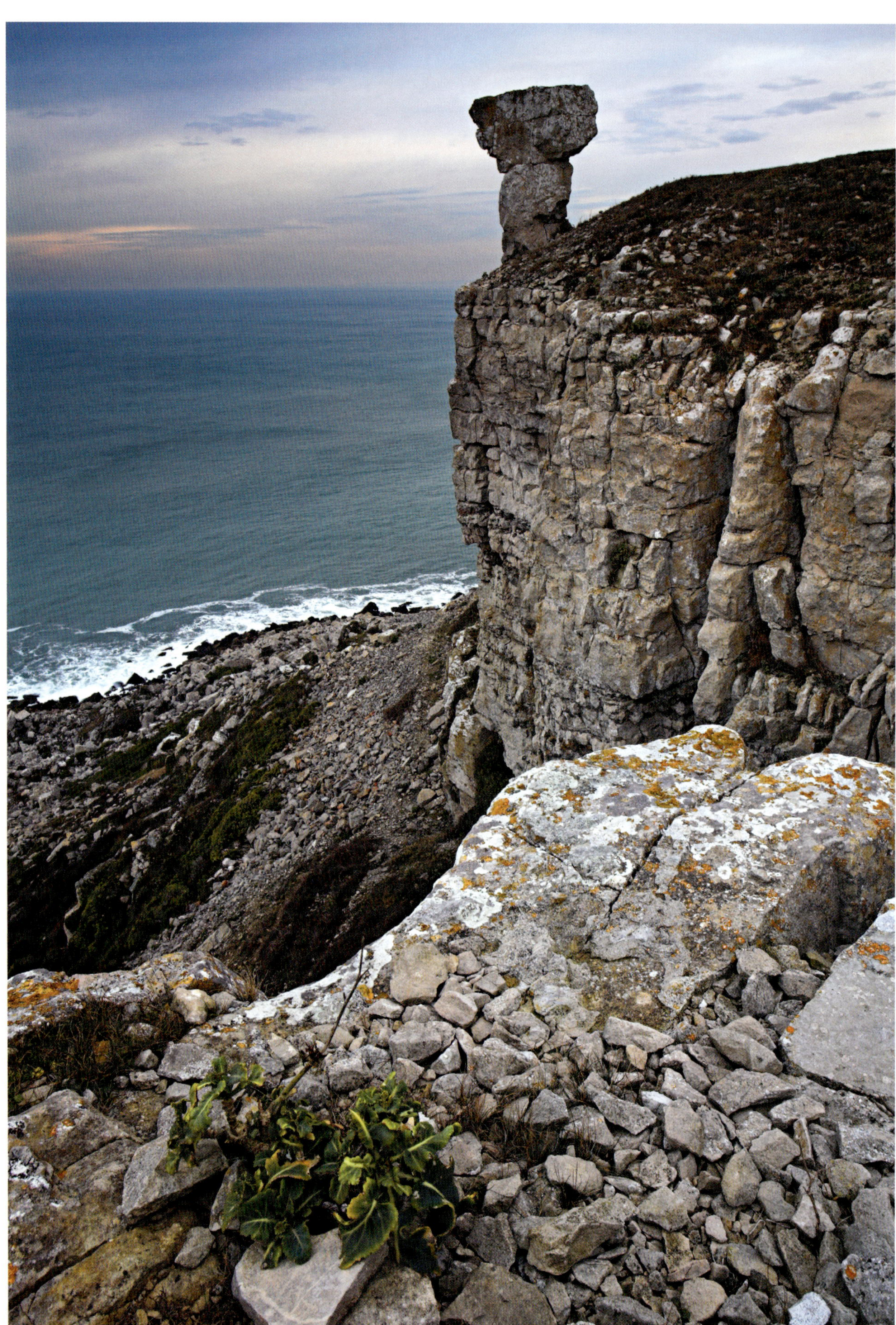

Balancing precariously on the cliff edge, the stone pillar at St Aldhelm's Head was left by quarrymen in the nineteenth century. This head, also known as St Alban's, marks the southernmost tip of the Isle of Purbeck.

Kimmeridge

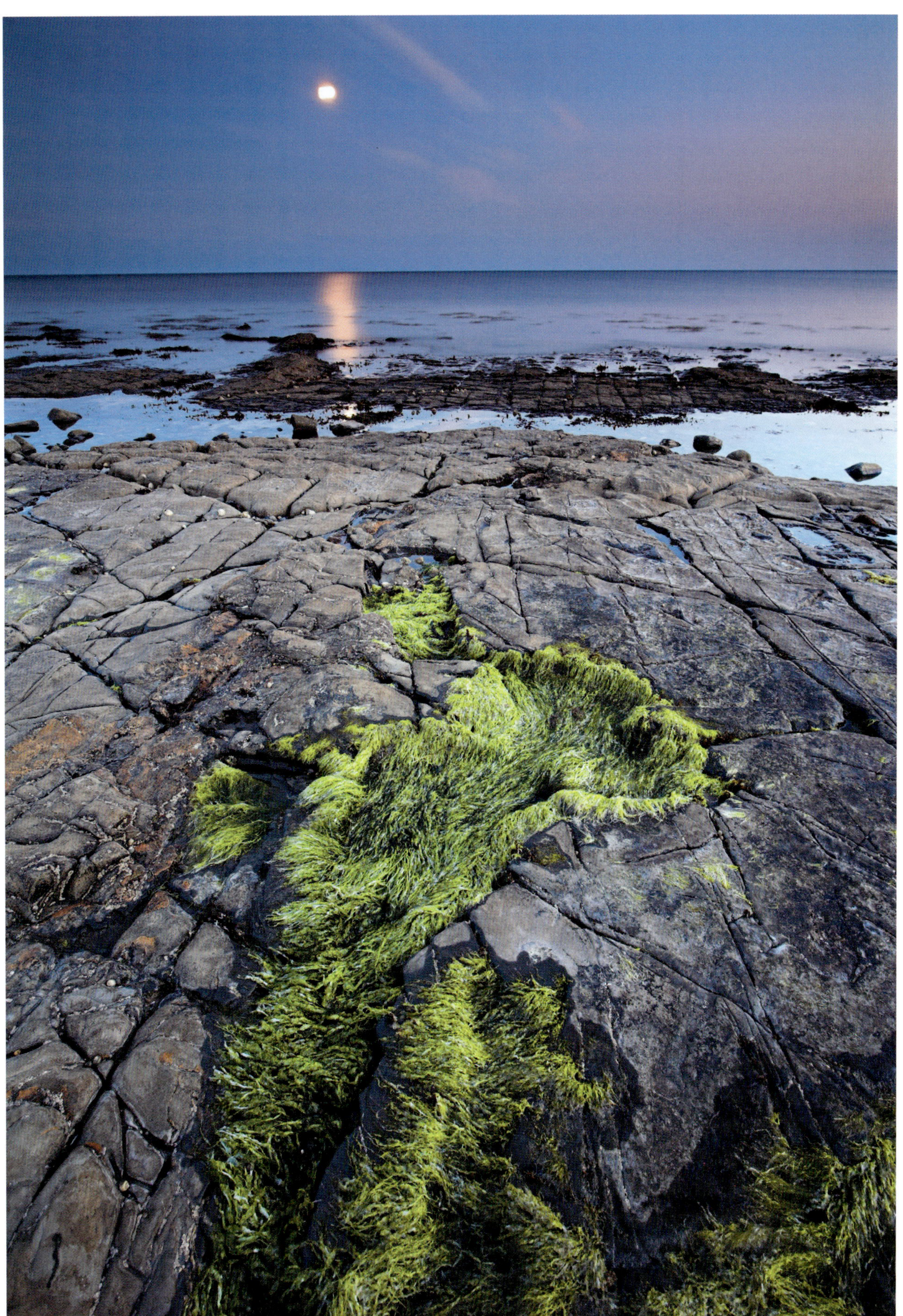

Seaweed and algae thrive in this constantly changing environment and add a splash of vibrant green to the silvery moonlit Charnel Bay.

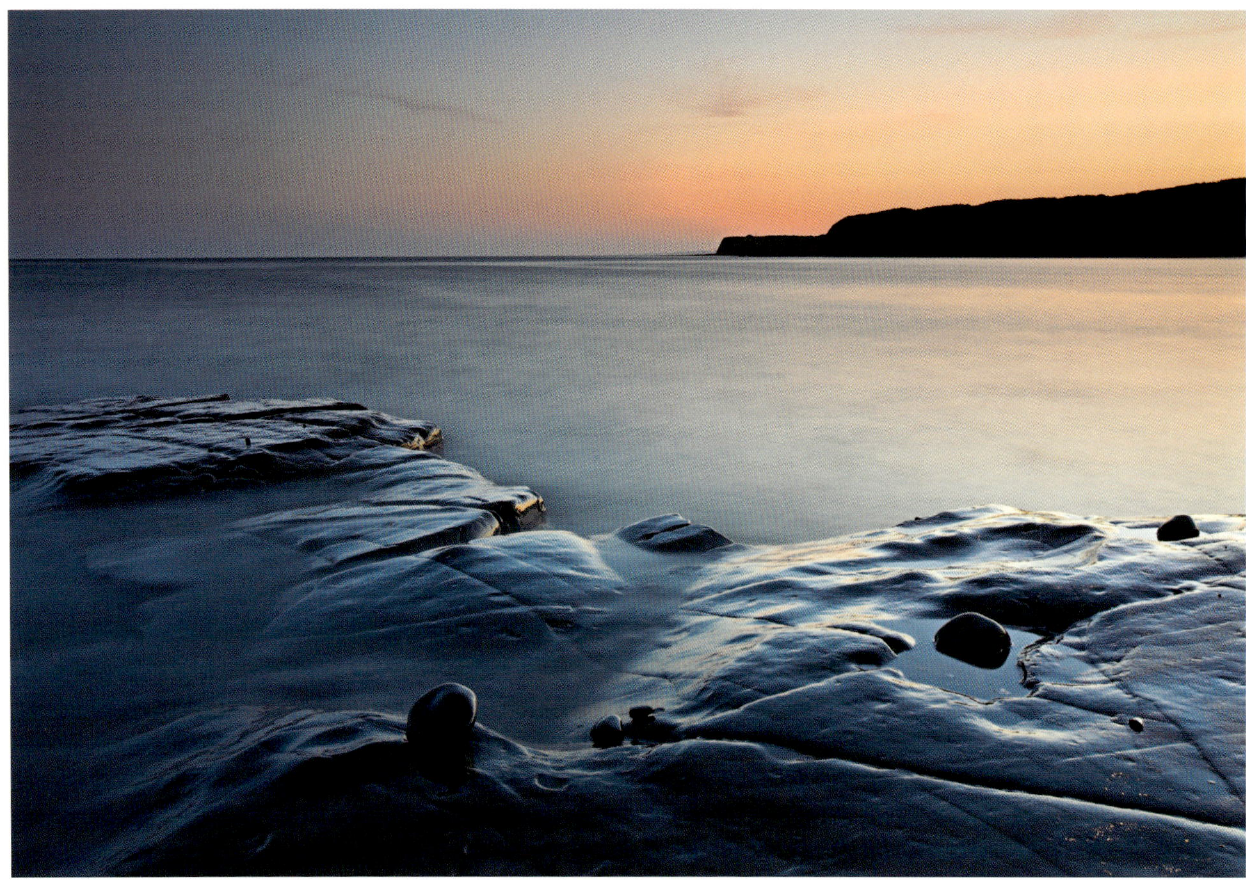

The long camera exposure captures a deceptively calm image of the Kimmeridge shoreline, which is dominated by long smooth rock ledges.

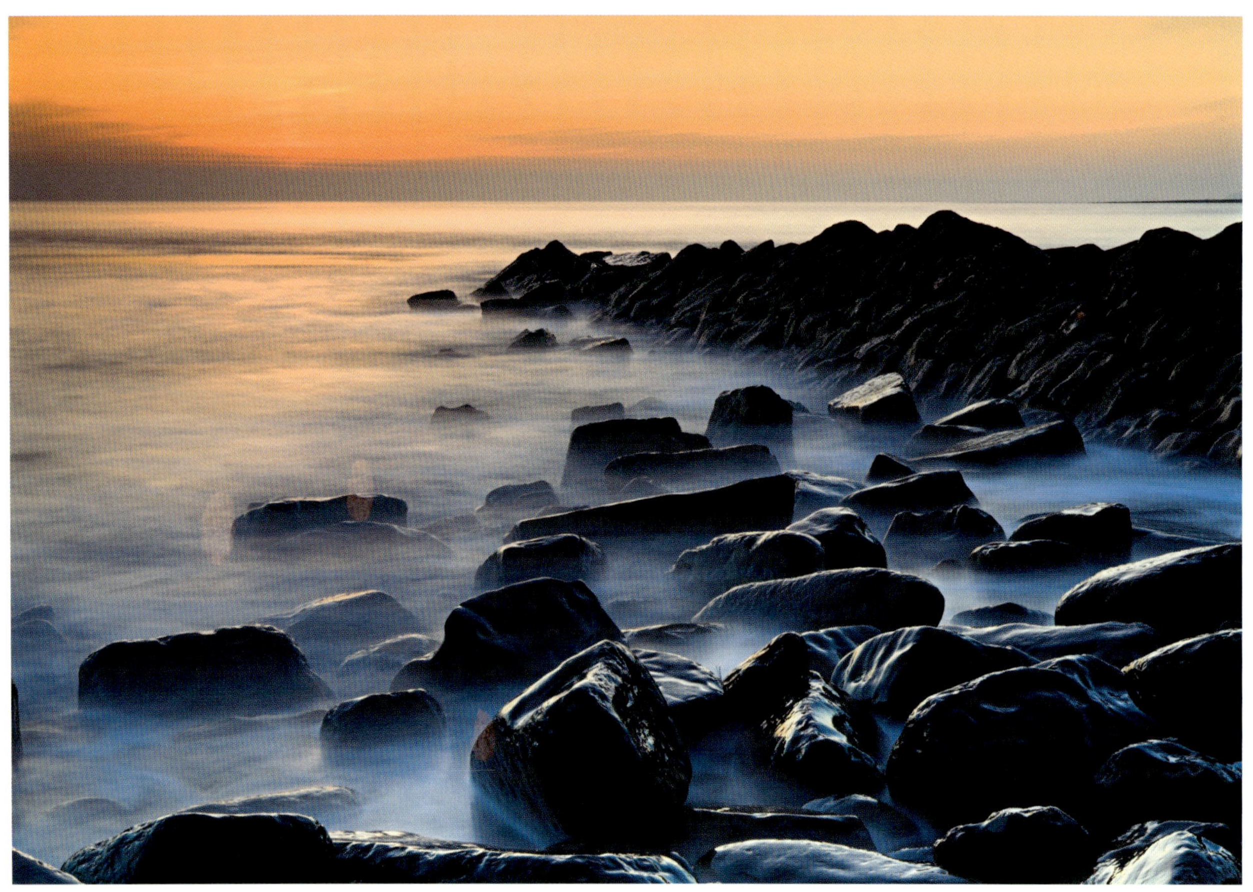

As the sun sets on another summer's day, the sky over Kimmeridge Bay assumes an orange glow. The broken chunks of Purbeck limestone shine with inky blackness as they are splashed by the waves.

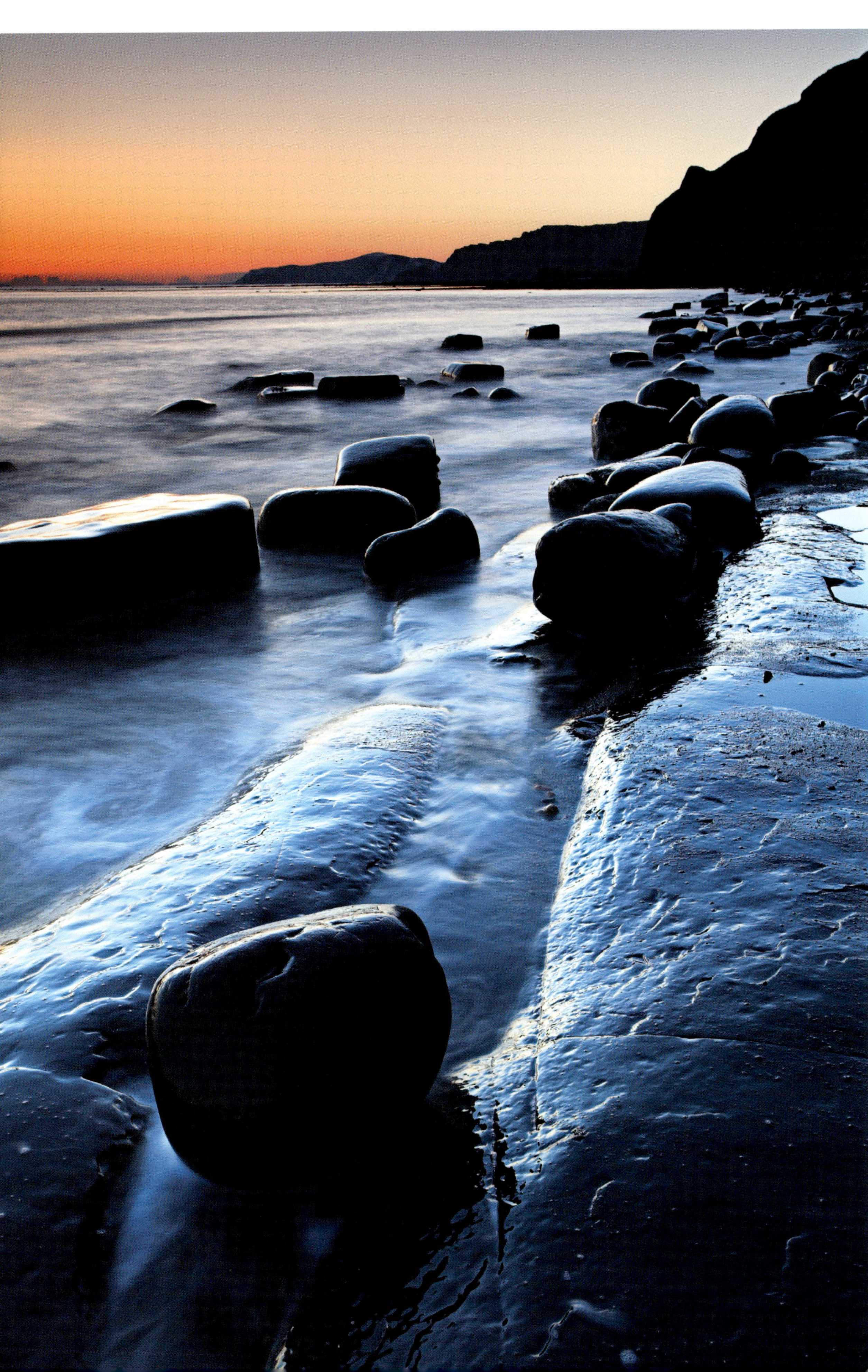

The endless cycle of the tide gently sculpts this coastal landscape, smoothing both the flat ledges and rounding the boulders and pebbles which are found here in abundance.

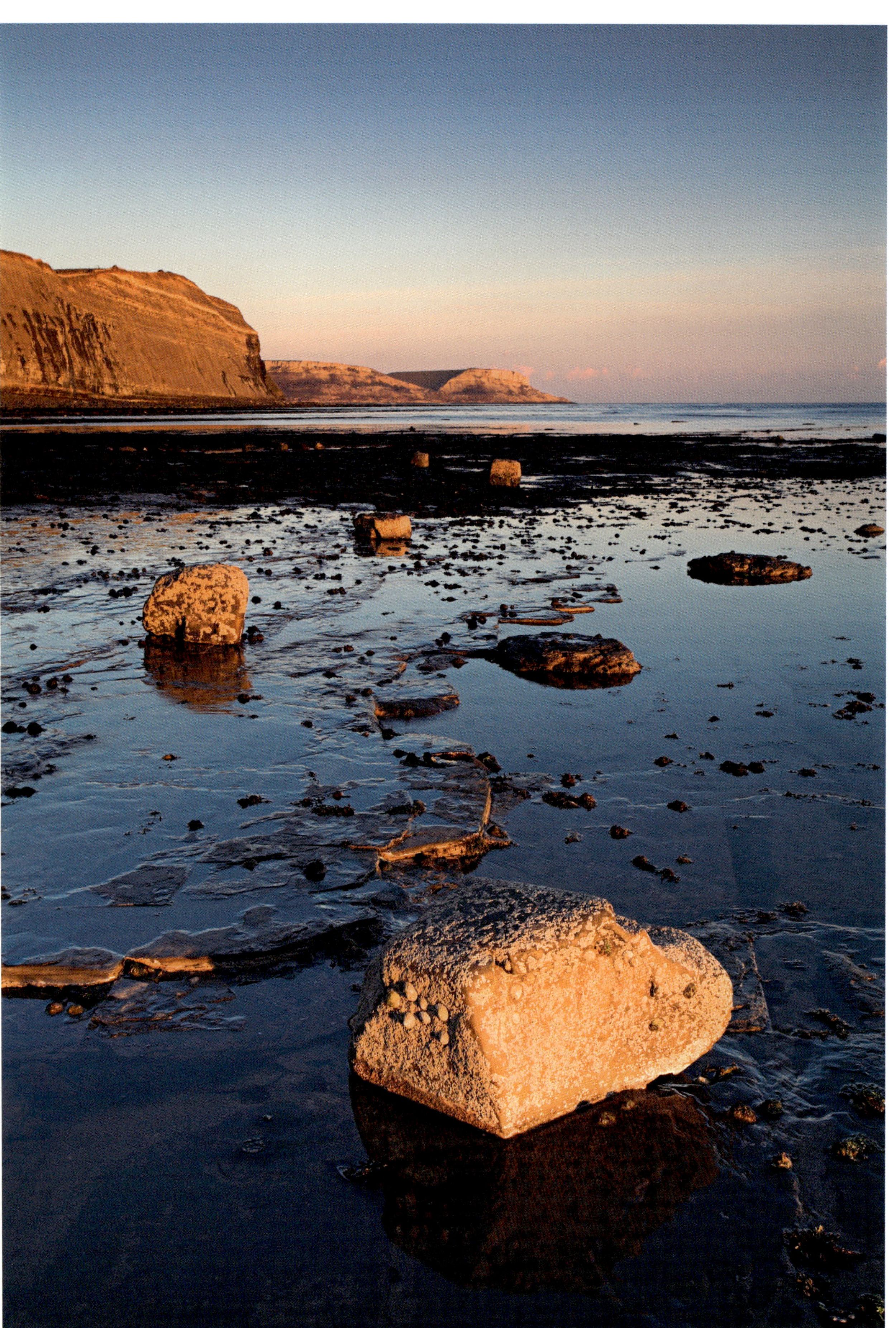

The ledges at Kimmeridge stretch far out into the sea; at low tide they present a rare opportunity to walk a long way out and gain an unusual view along the impressive coastline.

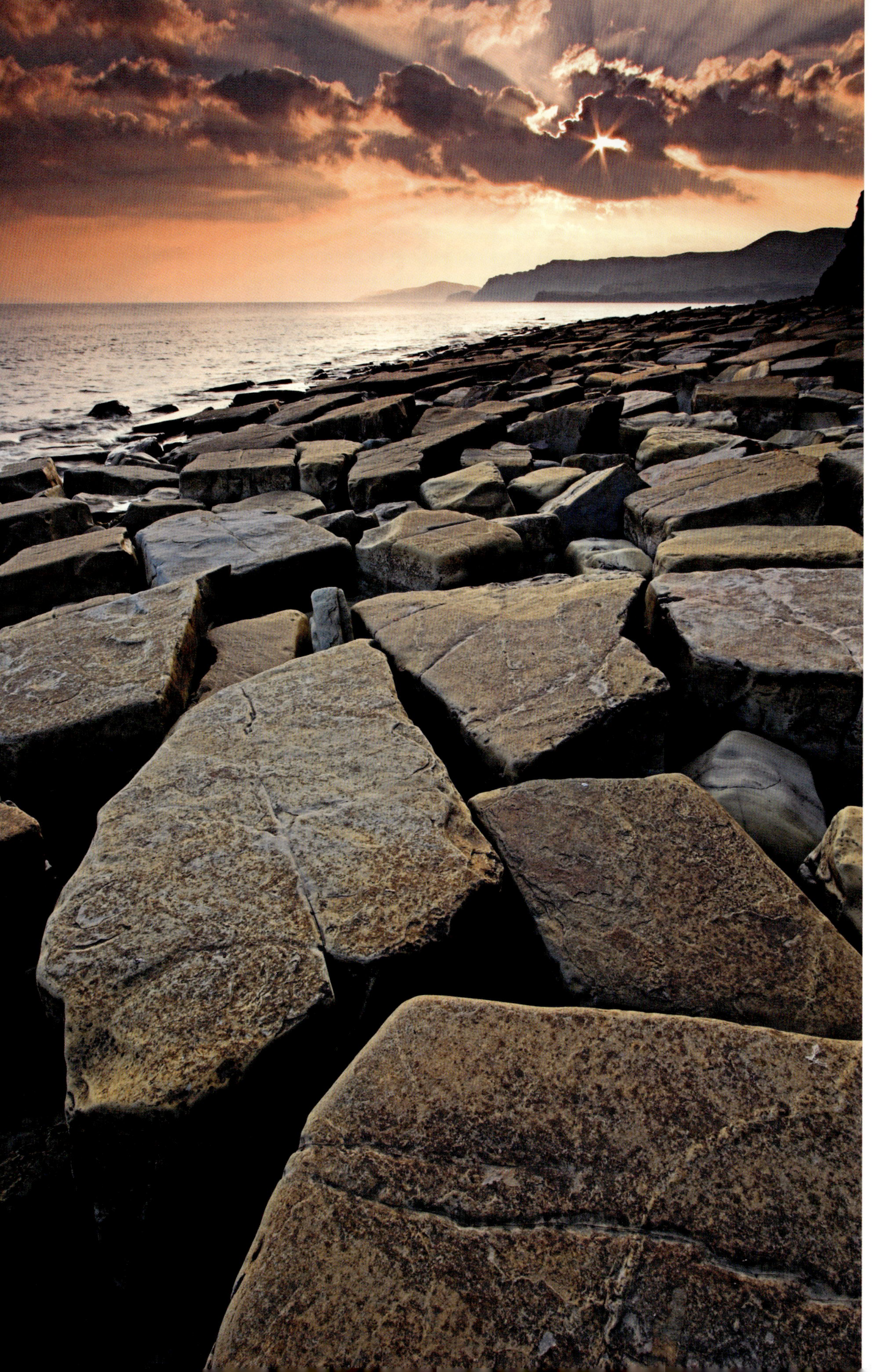

The Purbeck limestone lies within the thick Kimmeridge Clay sequence which is home to many important fossils from the Jurassic period. These rocks were the floor of a deep tropical sea rich in prehistoric life 155 million years ago. Today many holidaymakers walk over the rocks unaware that humans were not yet in existence when the rocks formed.

Hobarrow Bay

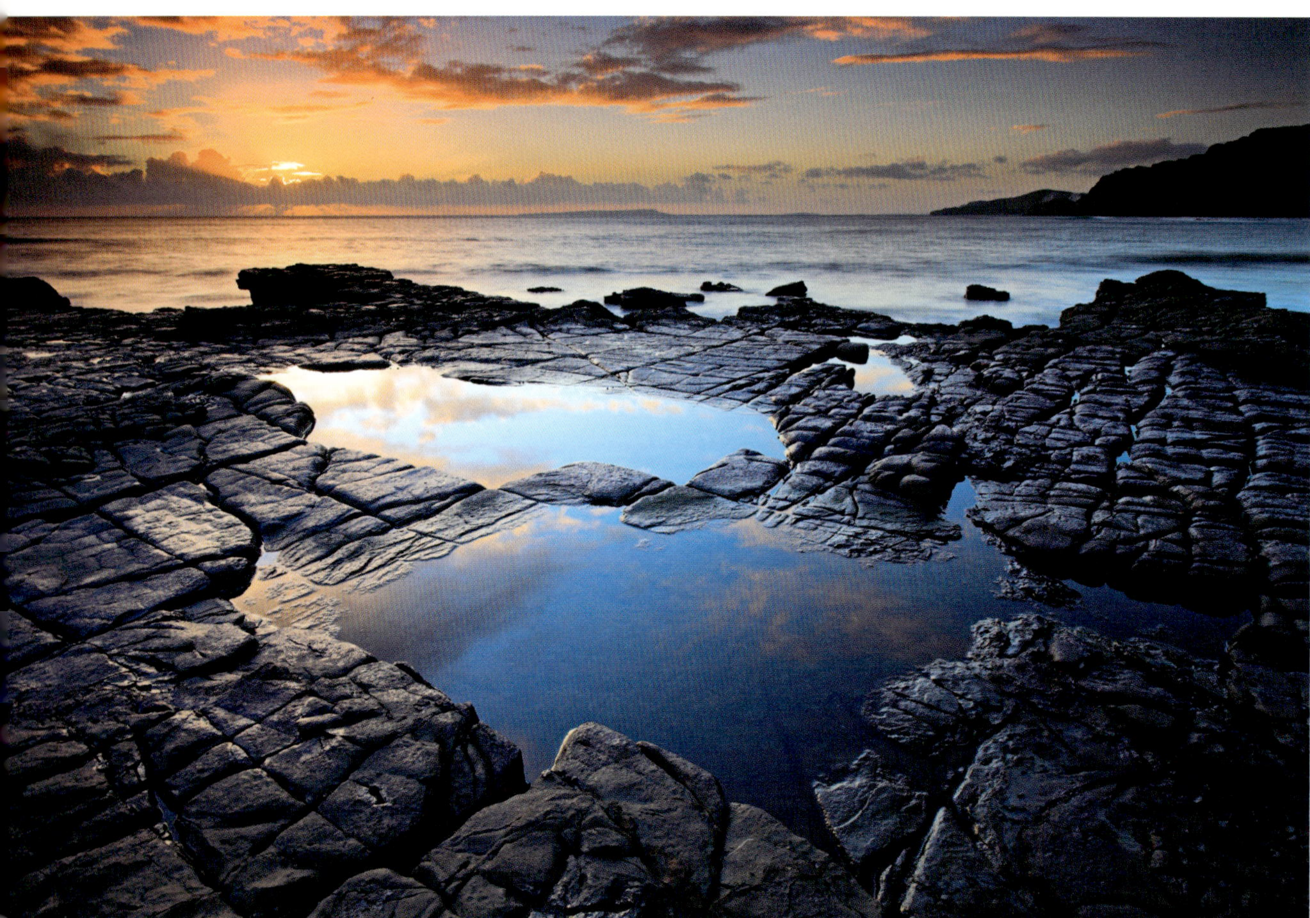

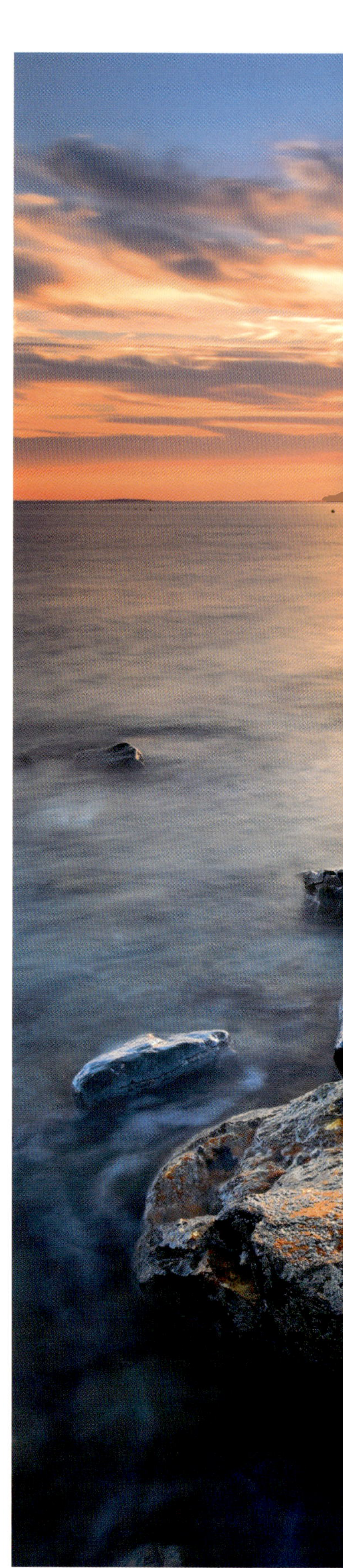

Looking towards Hobarrow Bay from Broad Bench, this stretch of coast is owned by the MOD and has restricted access to the public. But on the occasions that access is permitted it is well worth the trip. The sea-level views of the huge Gad Cliff are remarkable, and in such a highly visited part of England the explorer to this bay will rarely see another soul.

far right

Dominating the horizon is the imposing Gad Cliff. A herd of wild goats live on the lower slopes of the cliff, completely isolated from human contact. It is believed that the goats either escaped from a farm or were survivors from a shipwreck long ago.

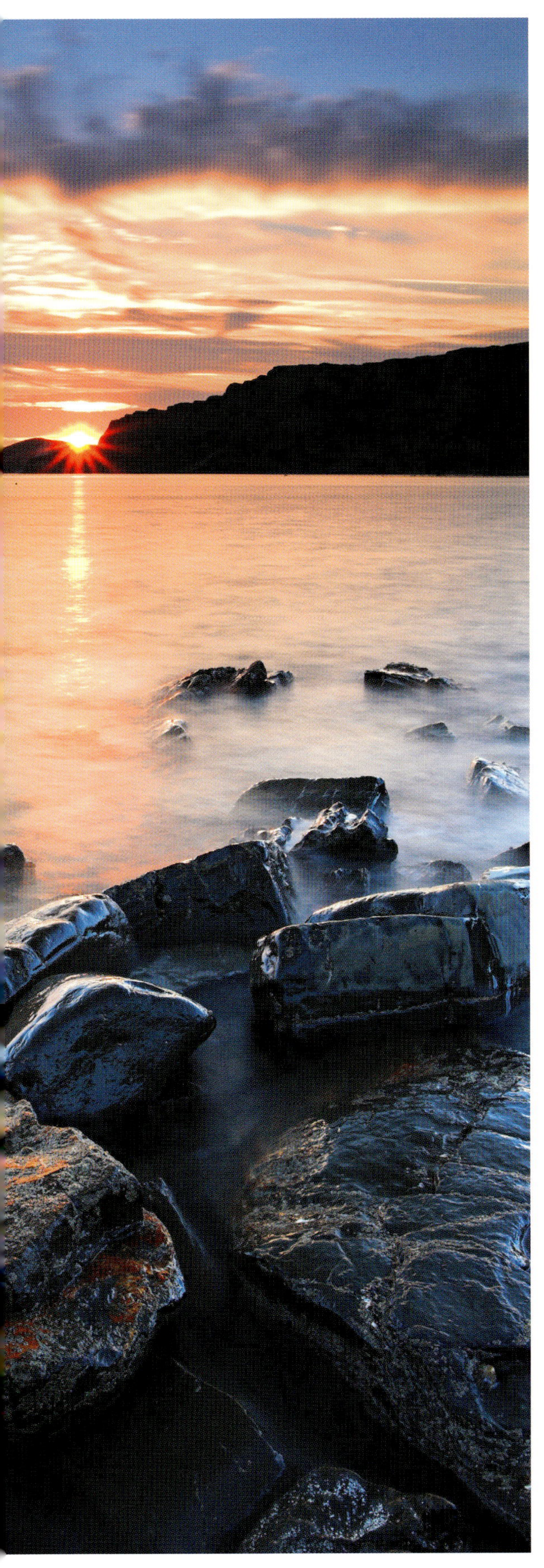

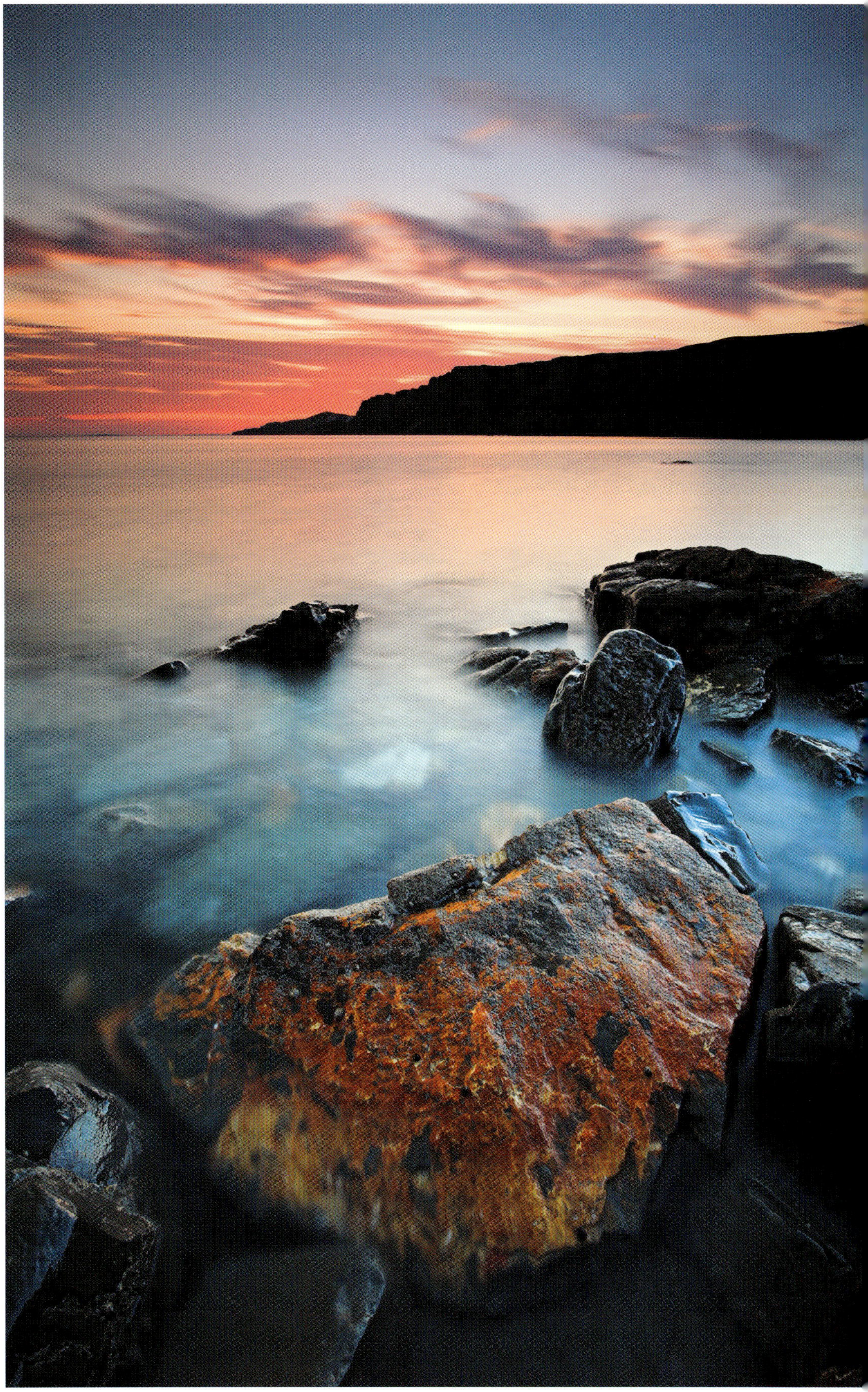

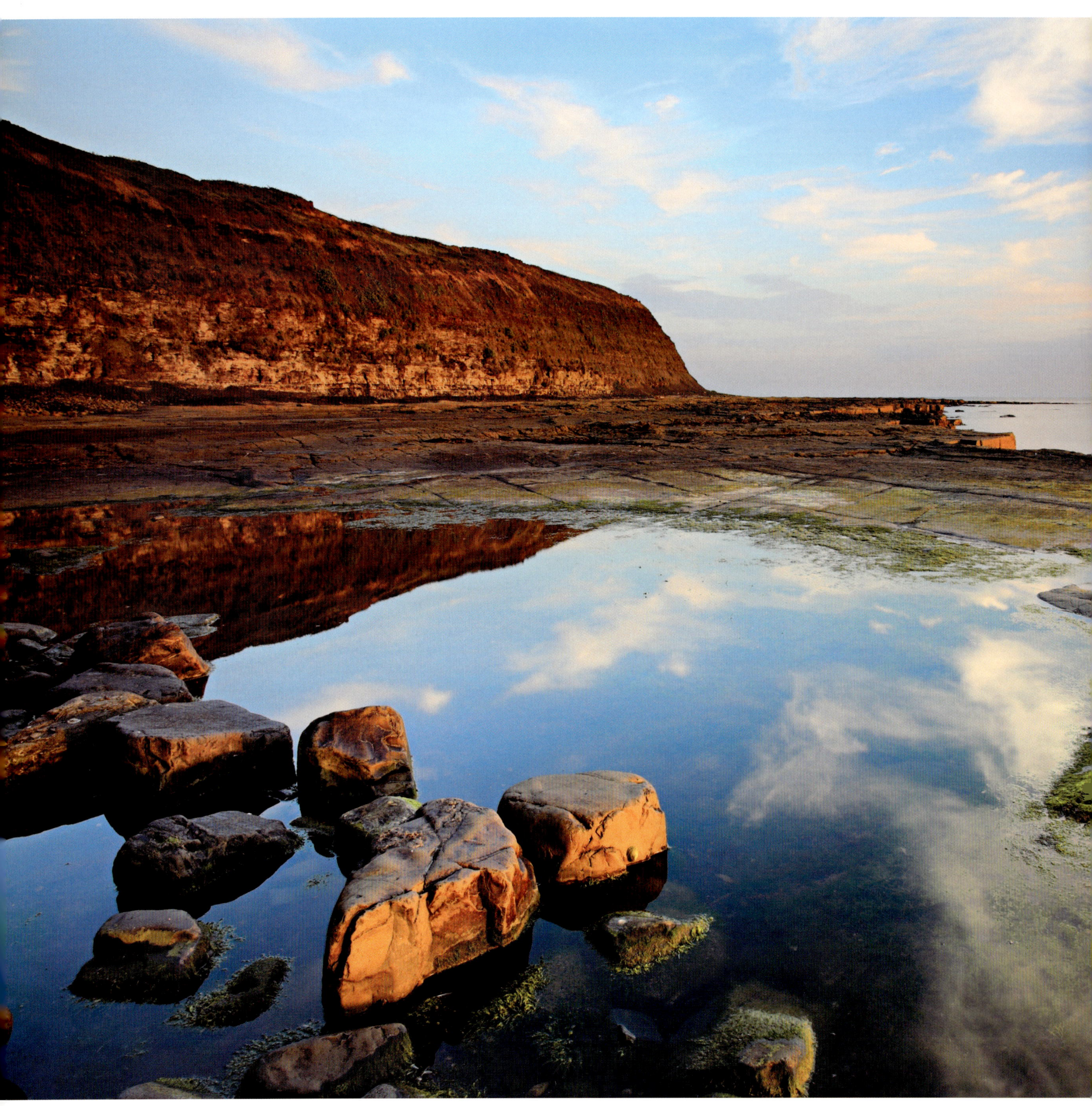

A reflective shot such as this is only possible to capture when the wind is very low, which is a rare occurrence at the coast but well worth the wait!

These beautiful layers of cyclical shales show the passing of time many thousands of years ago.

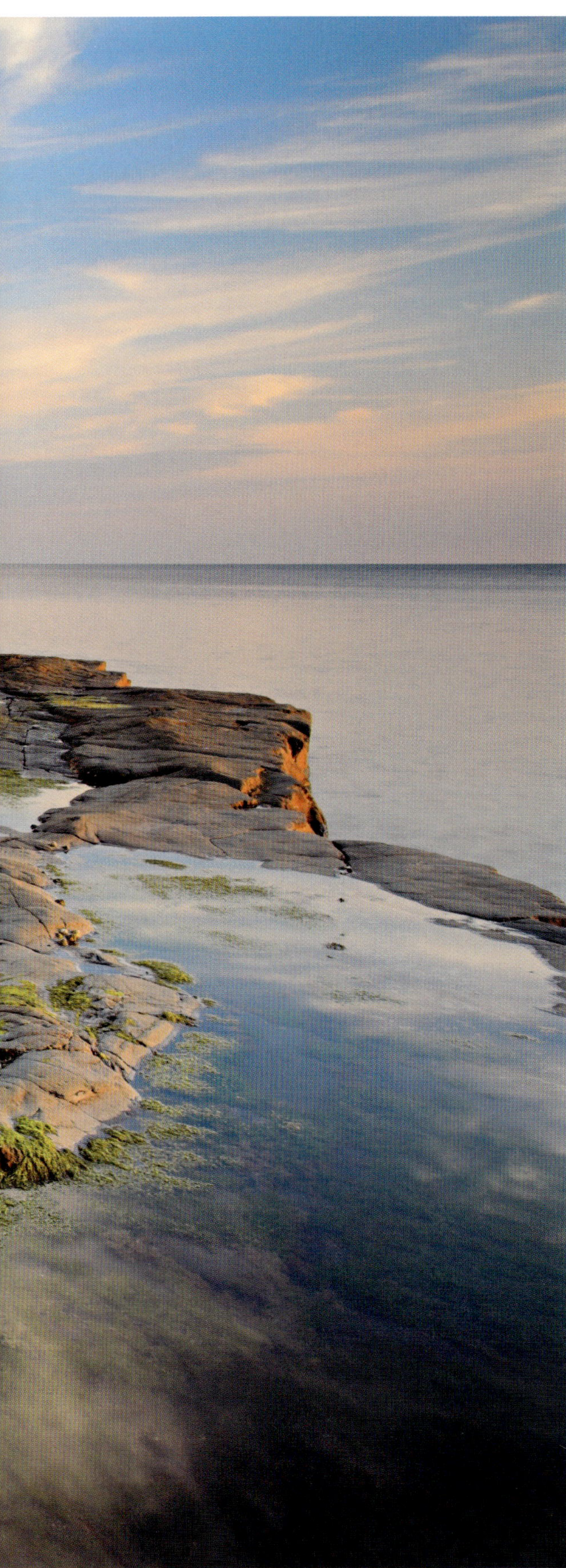

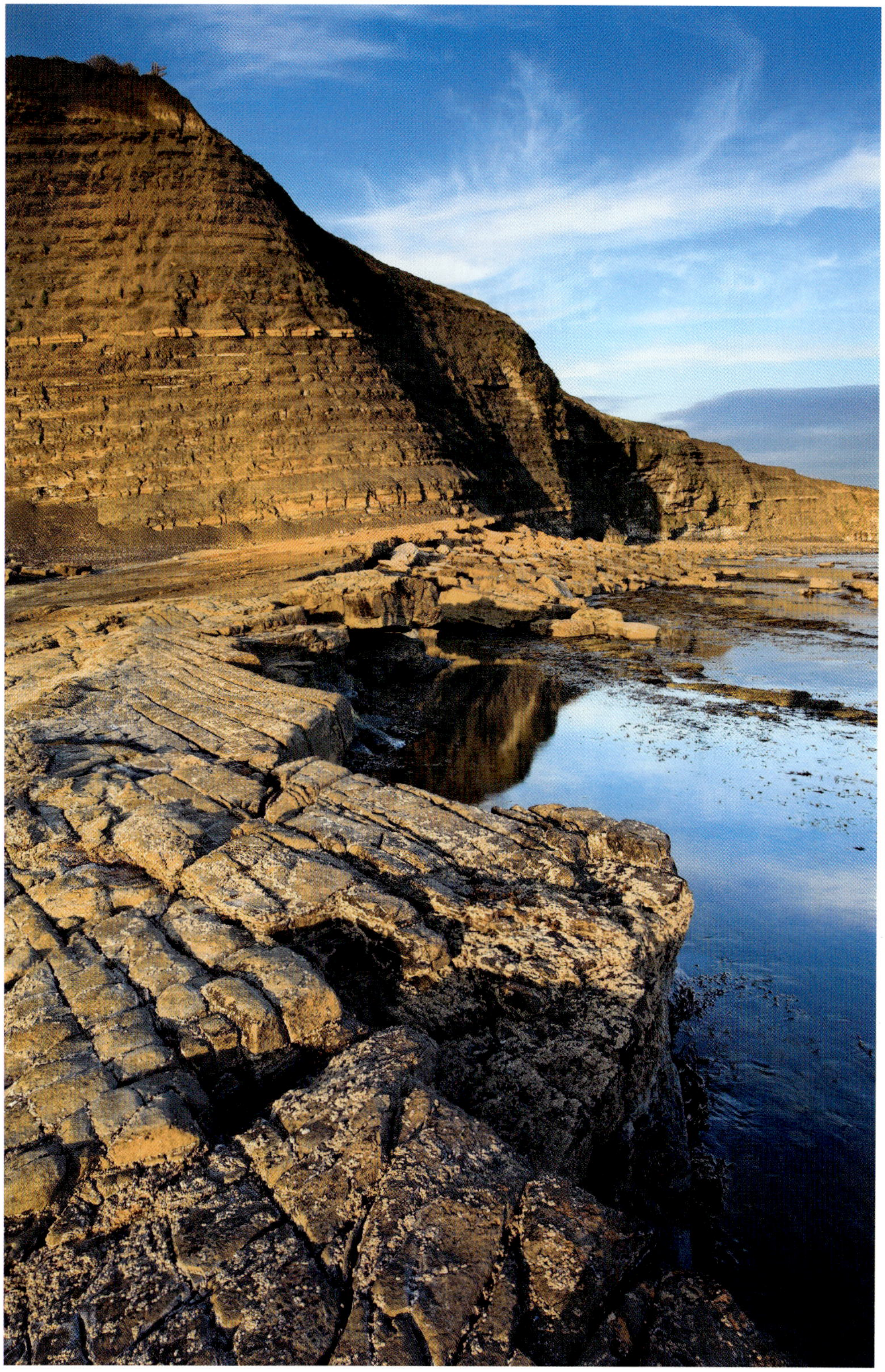

Pondfield Cove

Dinosaurs once roamed the landscape that is now Pondfield Cove, their footprints discovered here in recent years. On a day such as this the surroundings here can ignite your imagination and almost enable you to peer into this time long ago.

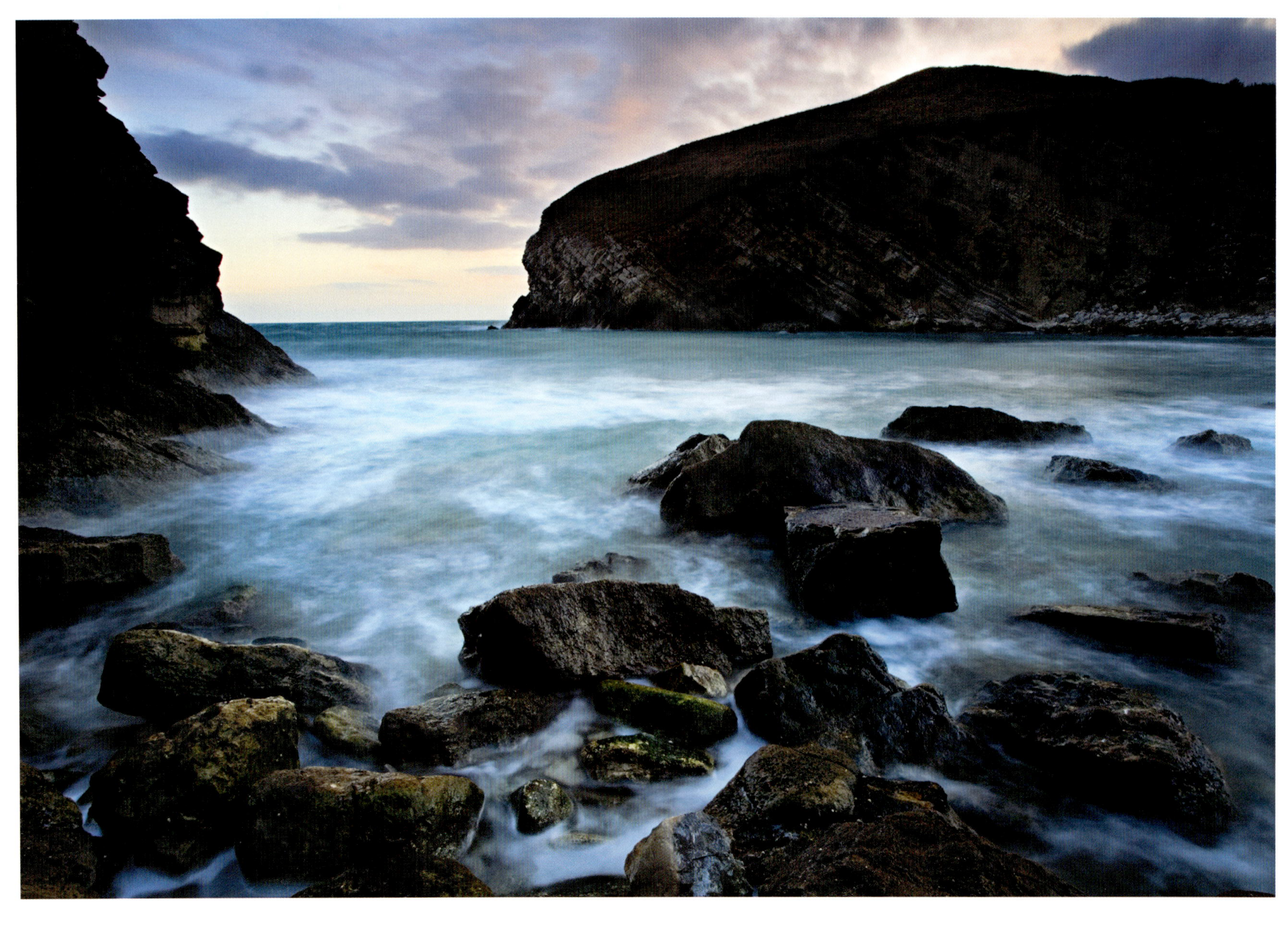

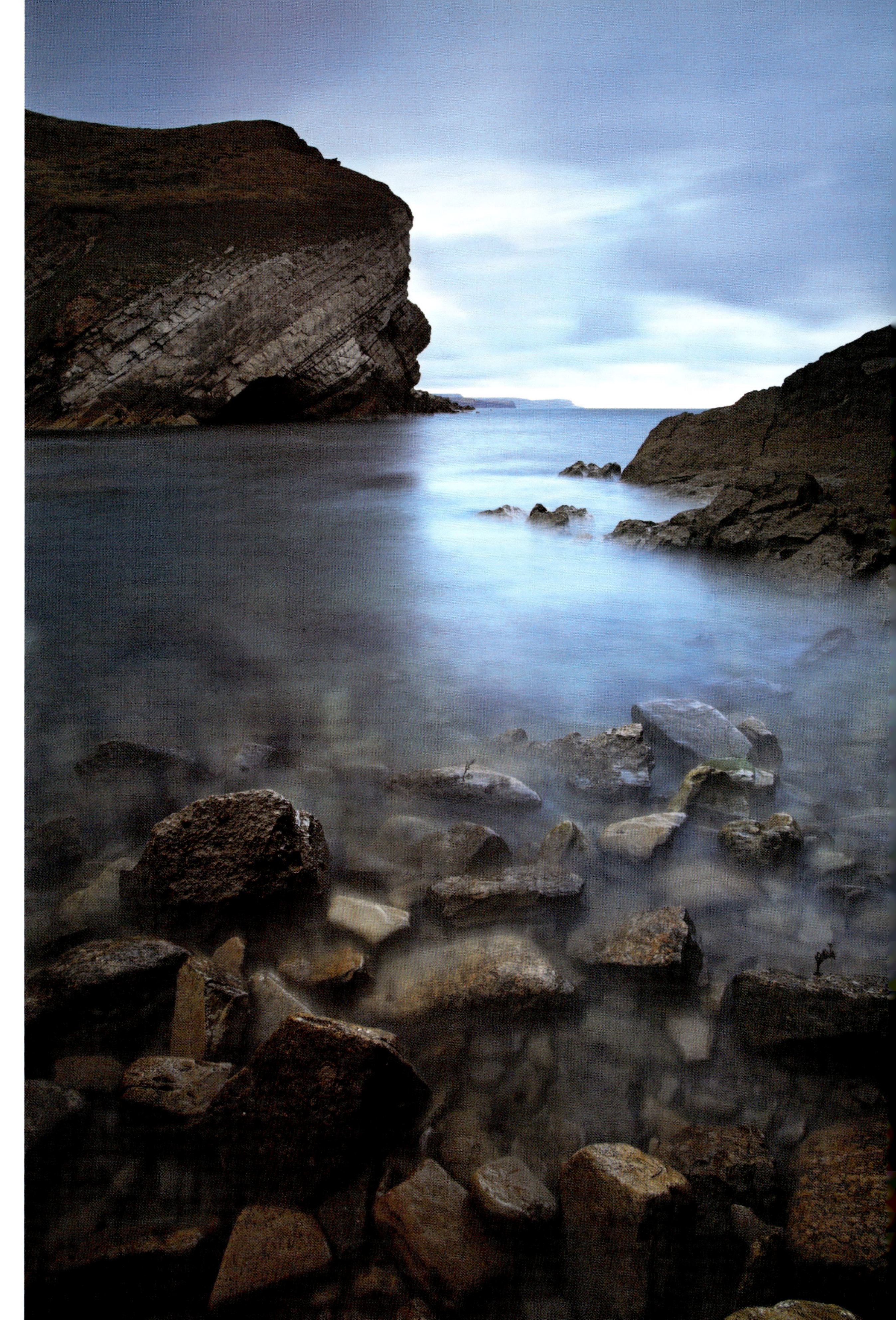

Snorkelers and walkers alike enjoy the dramatic scenery at Pondfield Cove with its small caves hidden under the layered rock types of the Purbeck formation.

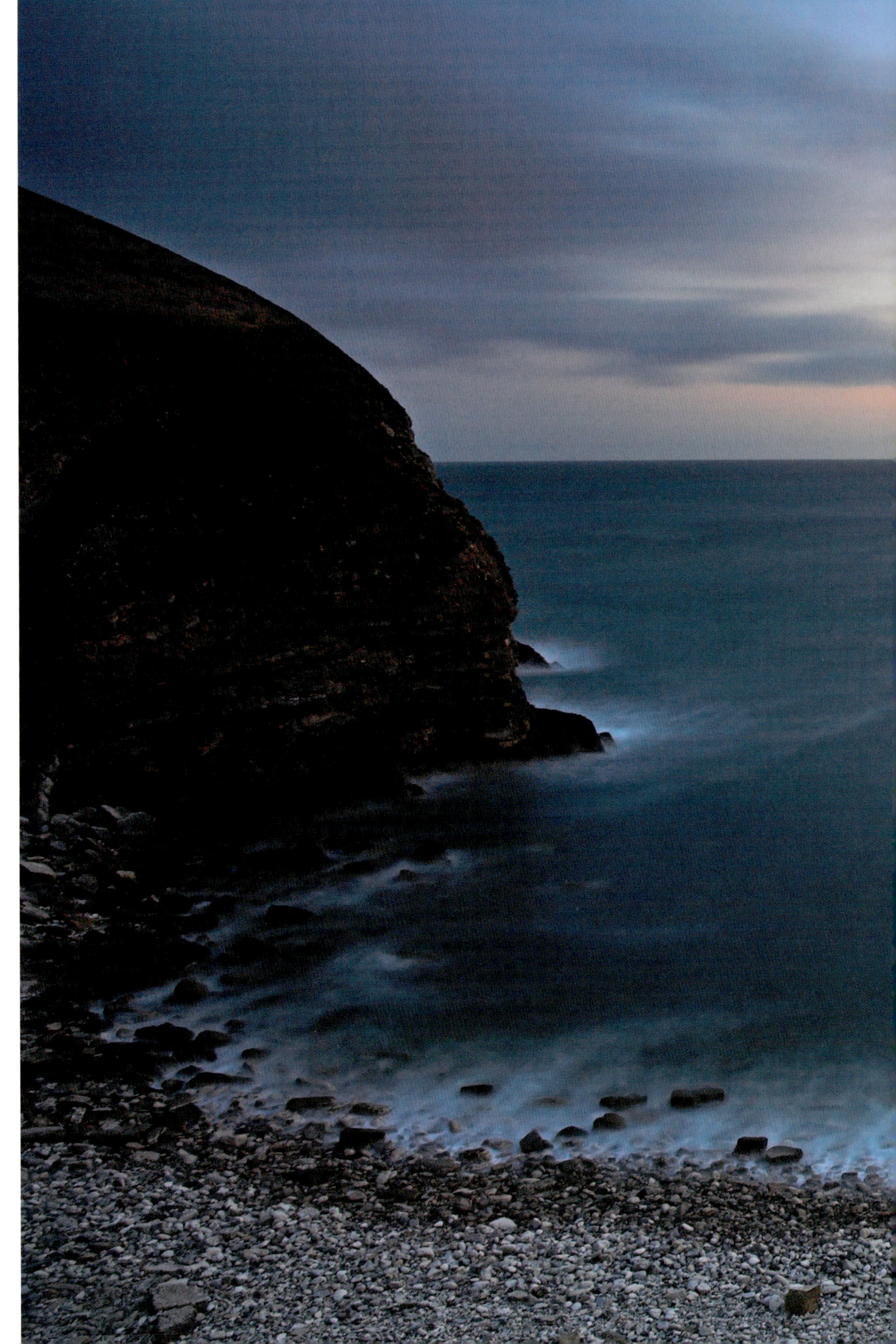

The full circular view of Pondfield Cove is best appreciated from the clifftop and resembles a smaller version of the better known Lulworth Cove. The peaceful and constant clatter of pebbles can be heard as waves surge in and out of the bay.

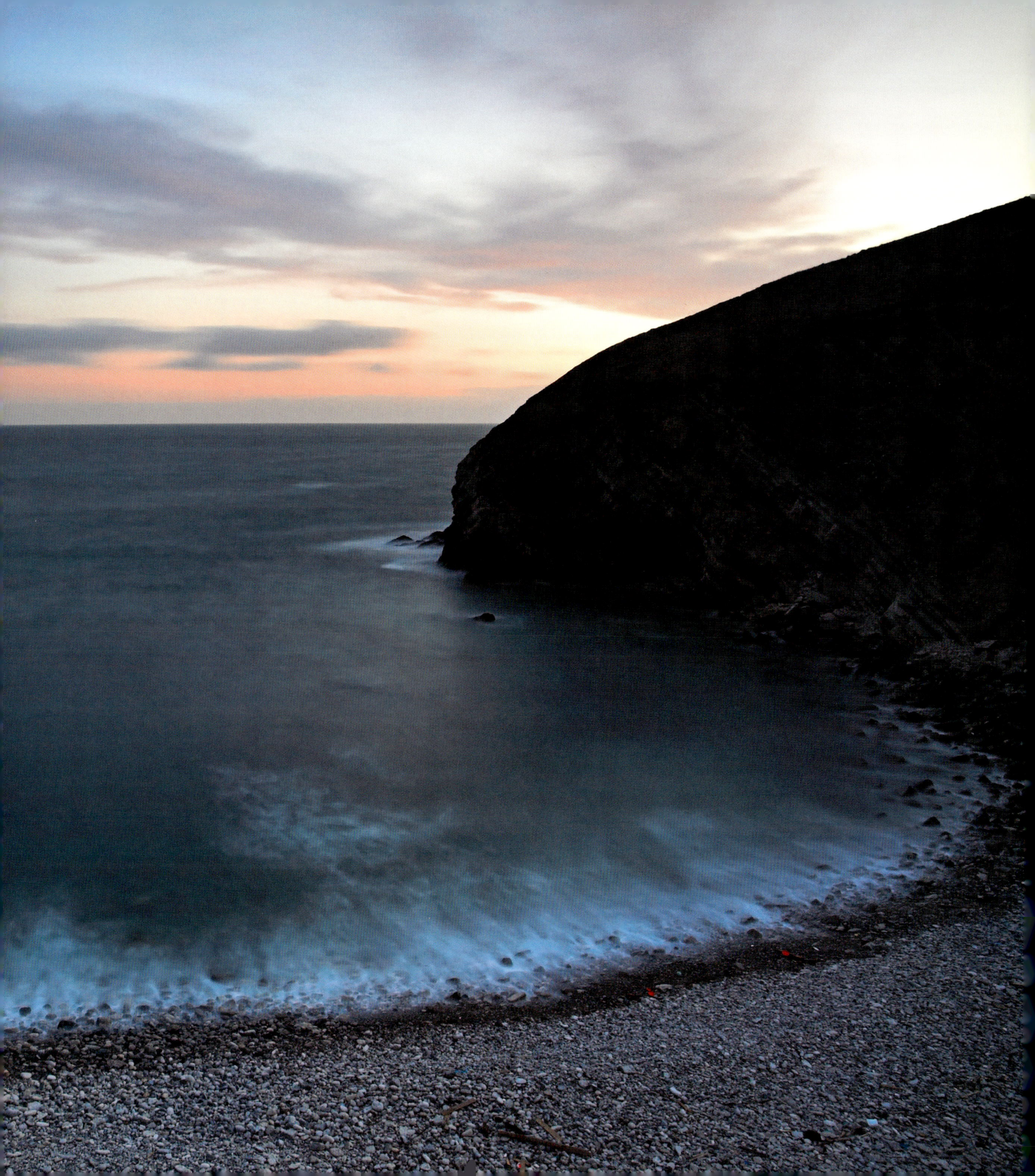

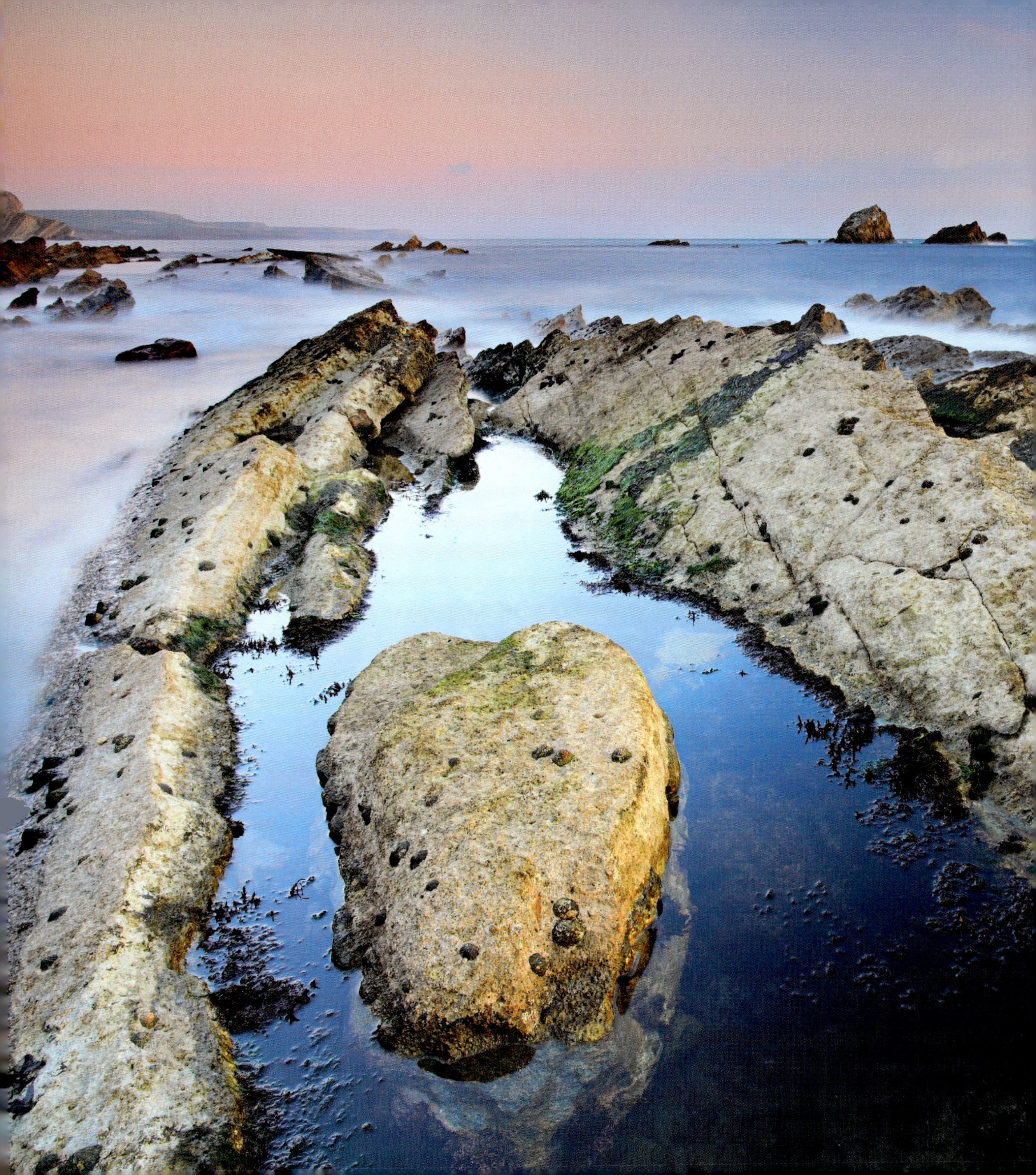

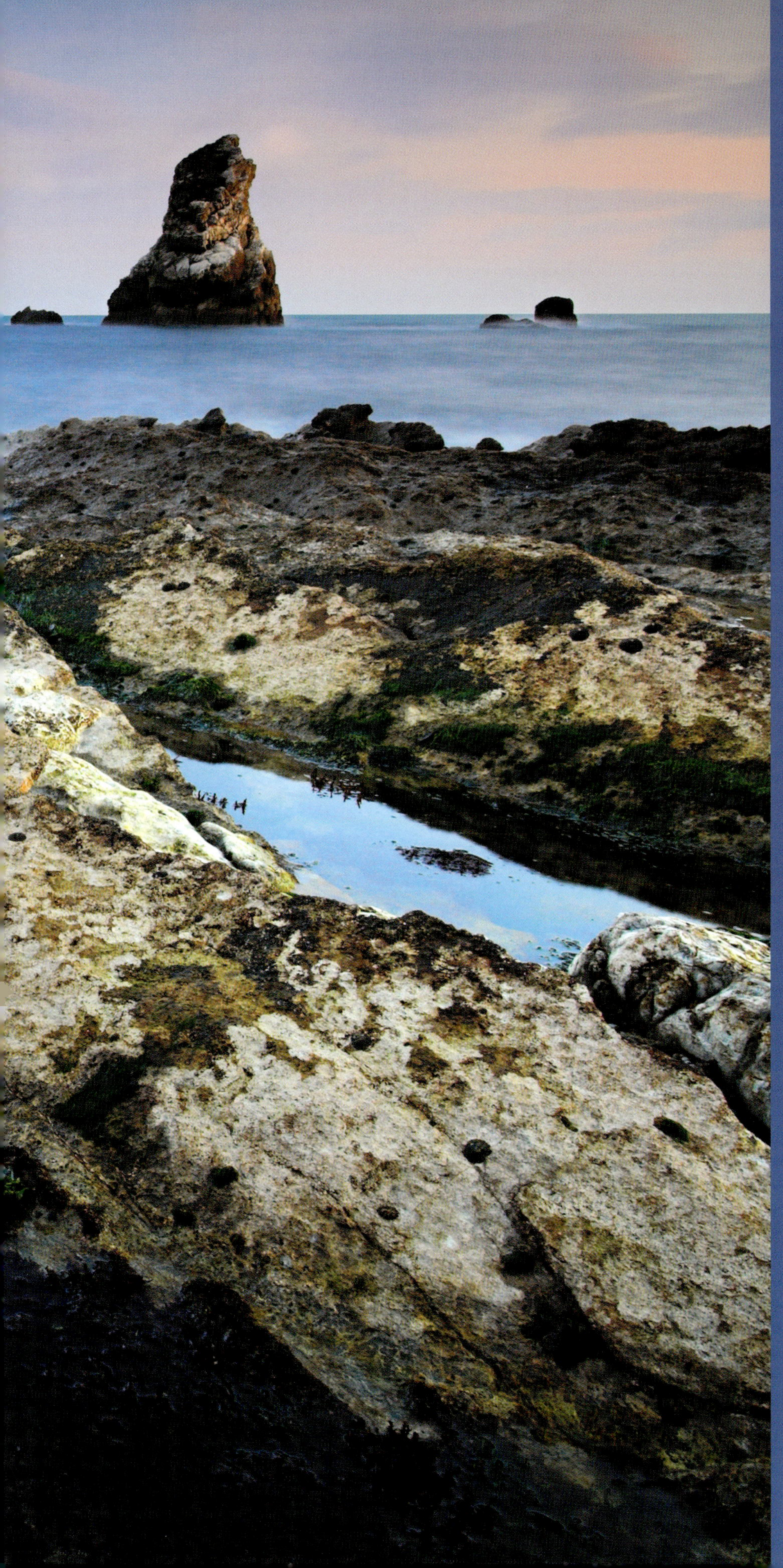

Worbarrow Bay to Osmington Mills

Mupe Bay is one of the hidden gems encountered along the South West Coast Path, which runs for 630 miles from Studland Bay to Minehead in Somerset. Throughout this long journey, the trail passes by some of the most spectacular coastal scenery to be found anywhere in the world.

Worbarrow Bay

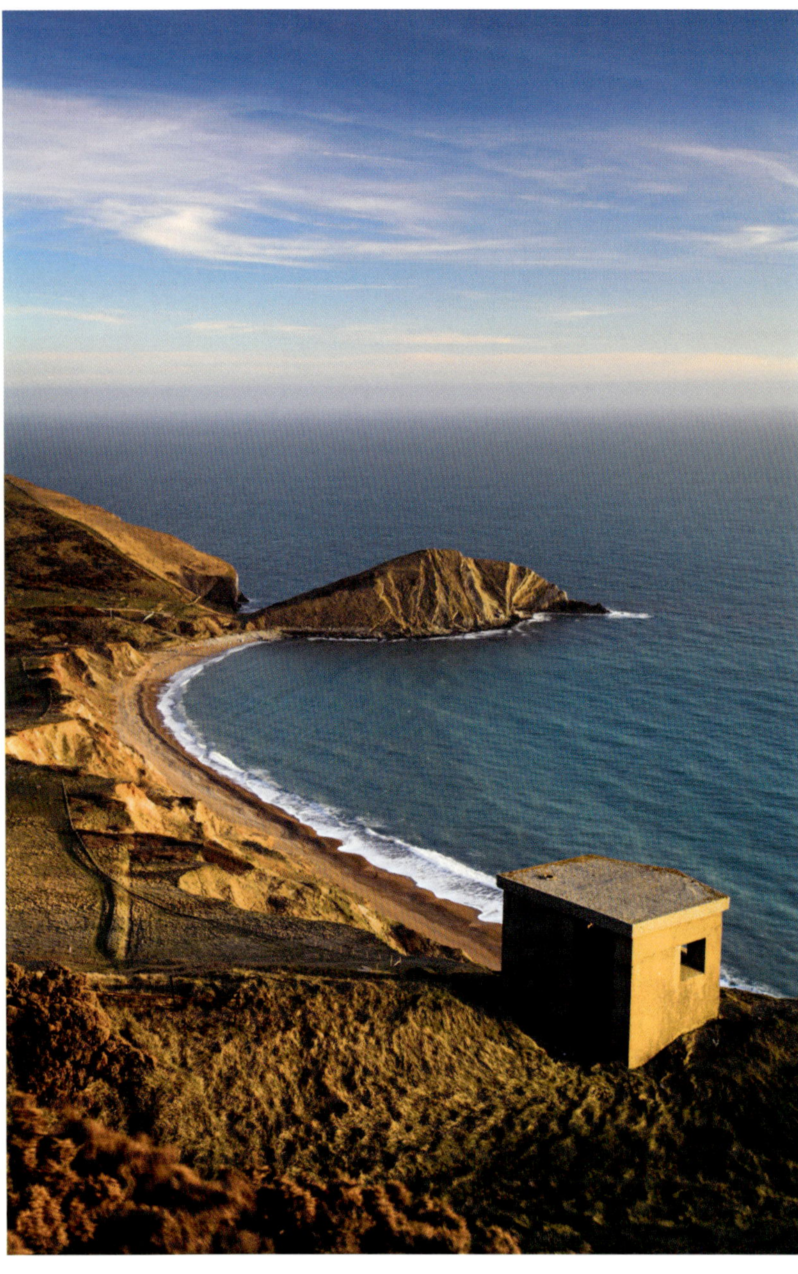

The path to Worbarrow Bay runs over restricted access MOD-owned land used as a firing range. As a direct result of this restriction, the bay can only be accessed via a walking track and remains completely undeveloped, which has helped to preserve the delicate beauty of this area.

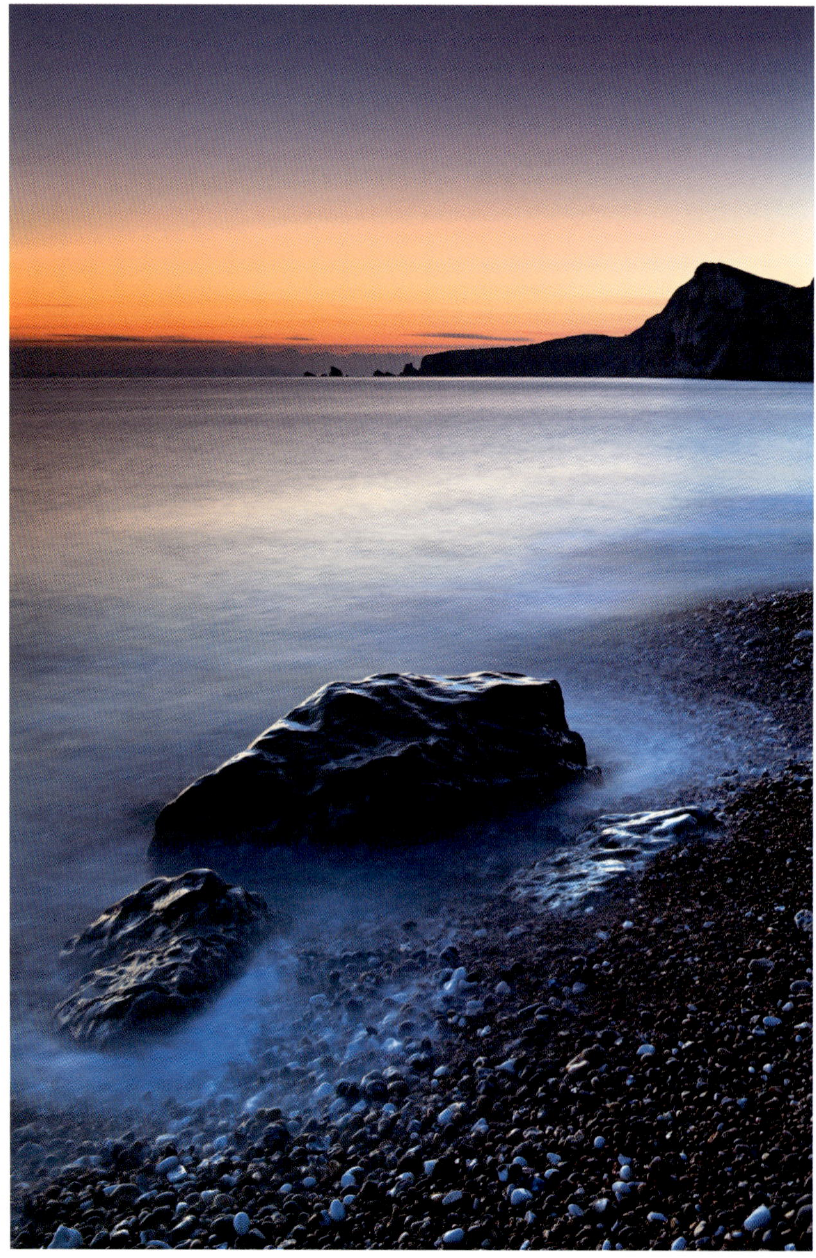

High above Worbarrow Bay this Second World War pillbox has been built upon a much earlier defensive aid, an Iron Age rampart. Now perilously close to a crumbling cliff edge, each of these historical treasures faces a turbulent future.

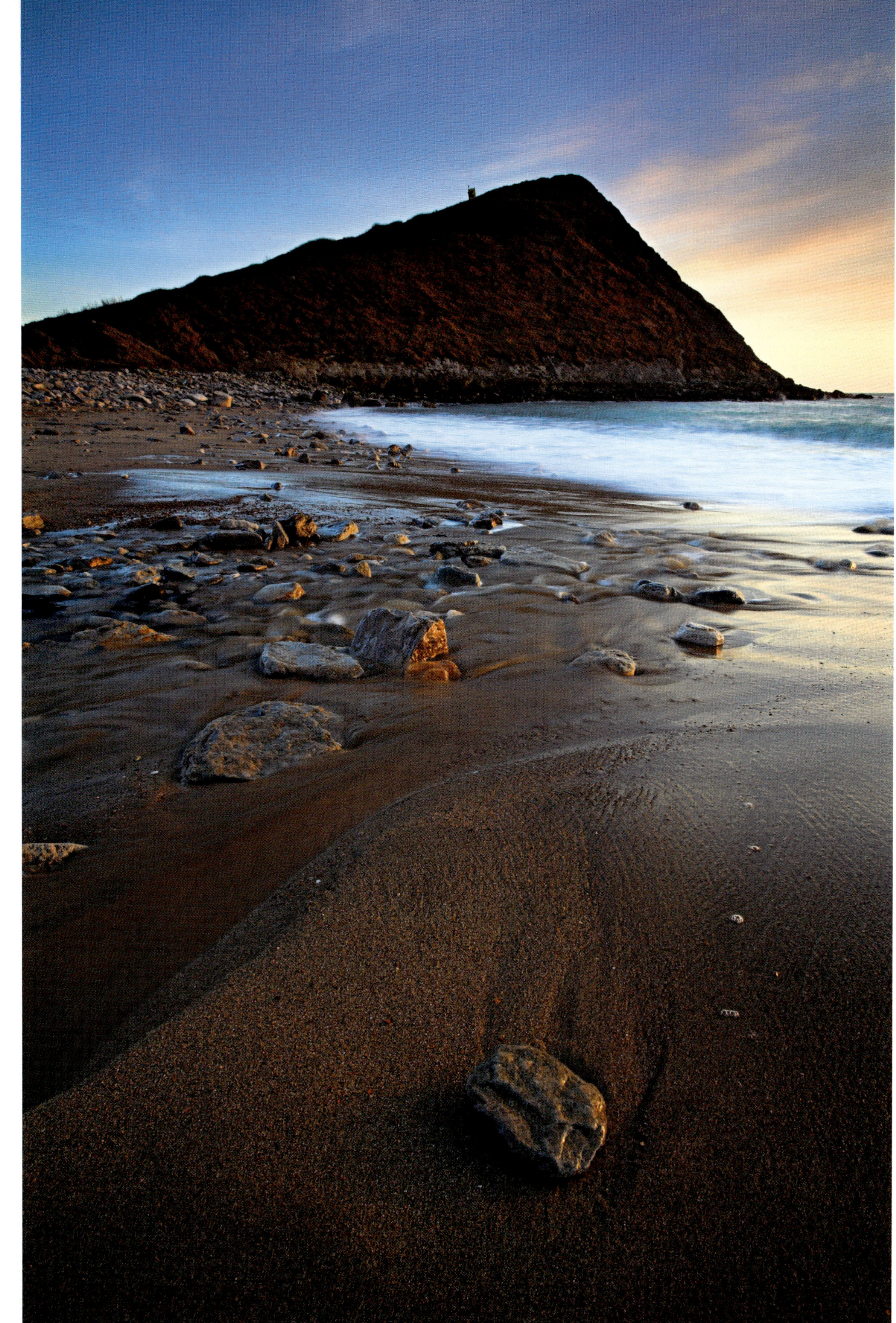

The triangular shaped headland found at the eastern end of Worbarrow Bay is called Worbarrow Tout. The steep cliffs that form the tout separate two very different bays: the sweeping Worbarrow Bay on the western side and the tiny rocky Pondfield Cove on the eastern.

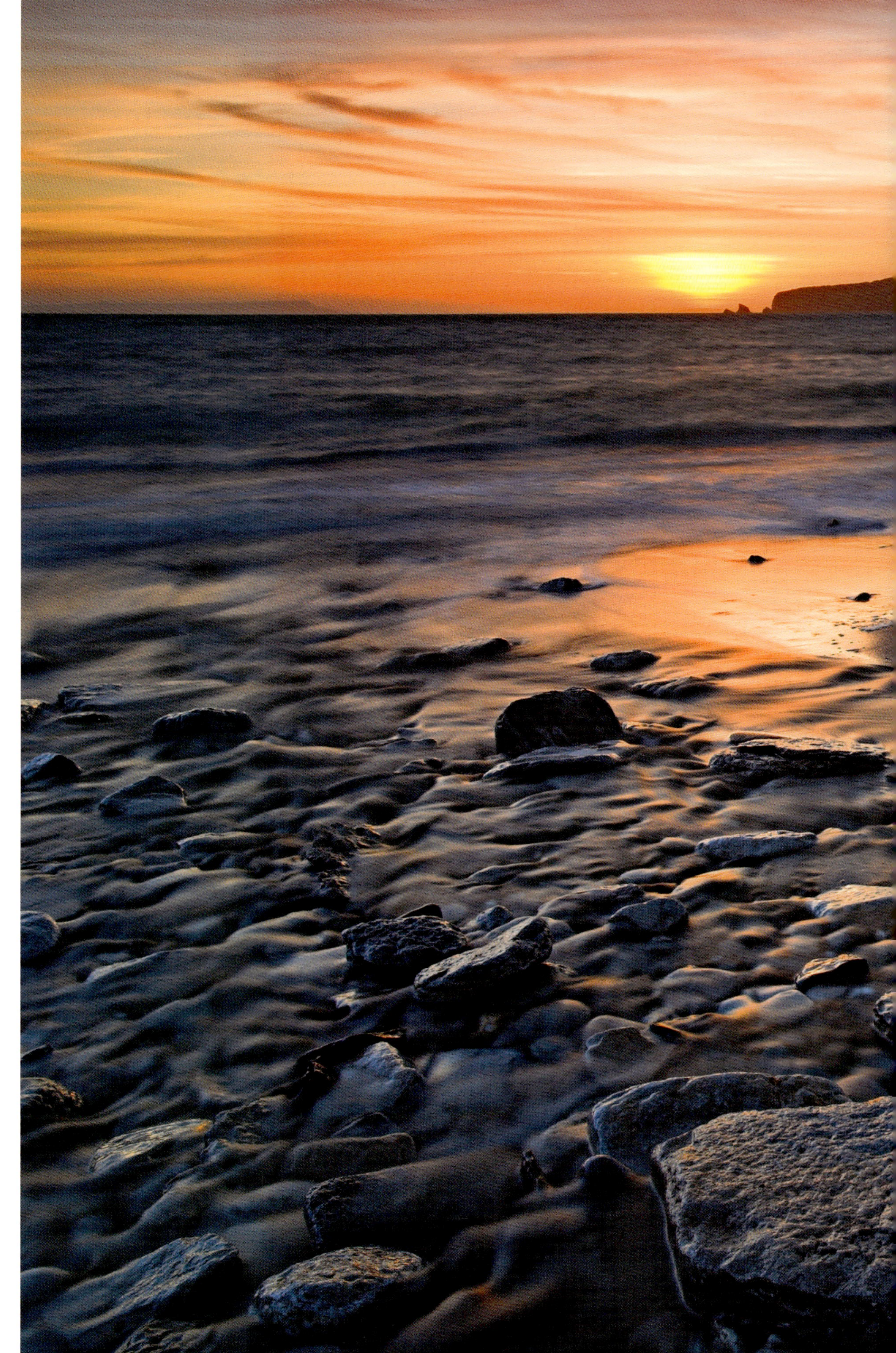

While it remains relatively unknown compared to its illustrious neighbours Lulworth Cove and Durdle Door, Worbarrow Bay is no less breathtaking to behold. The bay sweeps around in a wide arc backed by towering cliffs over a pebbly beach. The sea stacks of Mupe Rocks are just visible on the distant horizon.

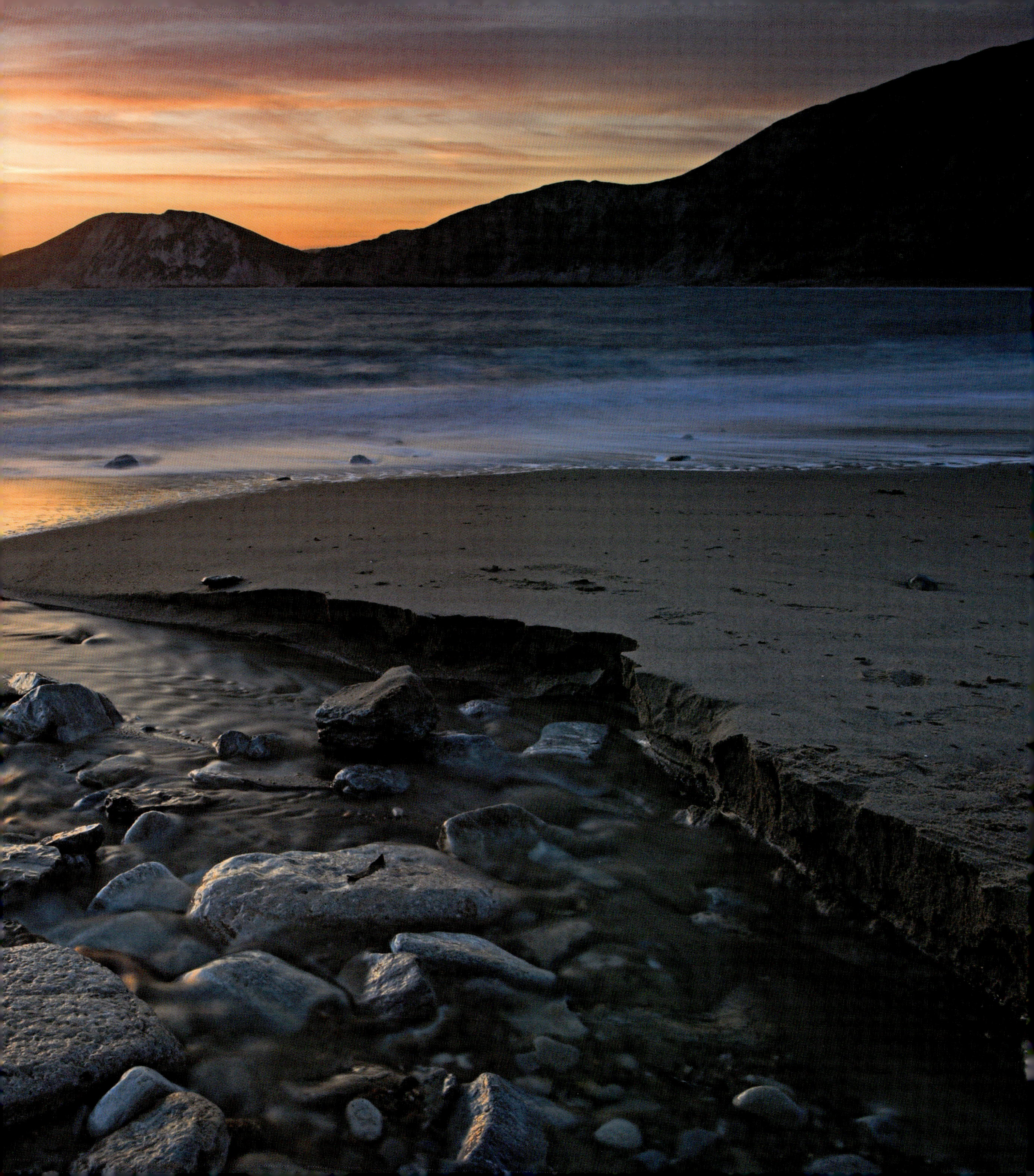

Mupe Bay

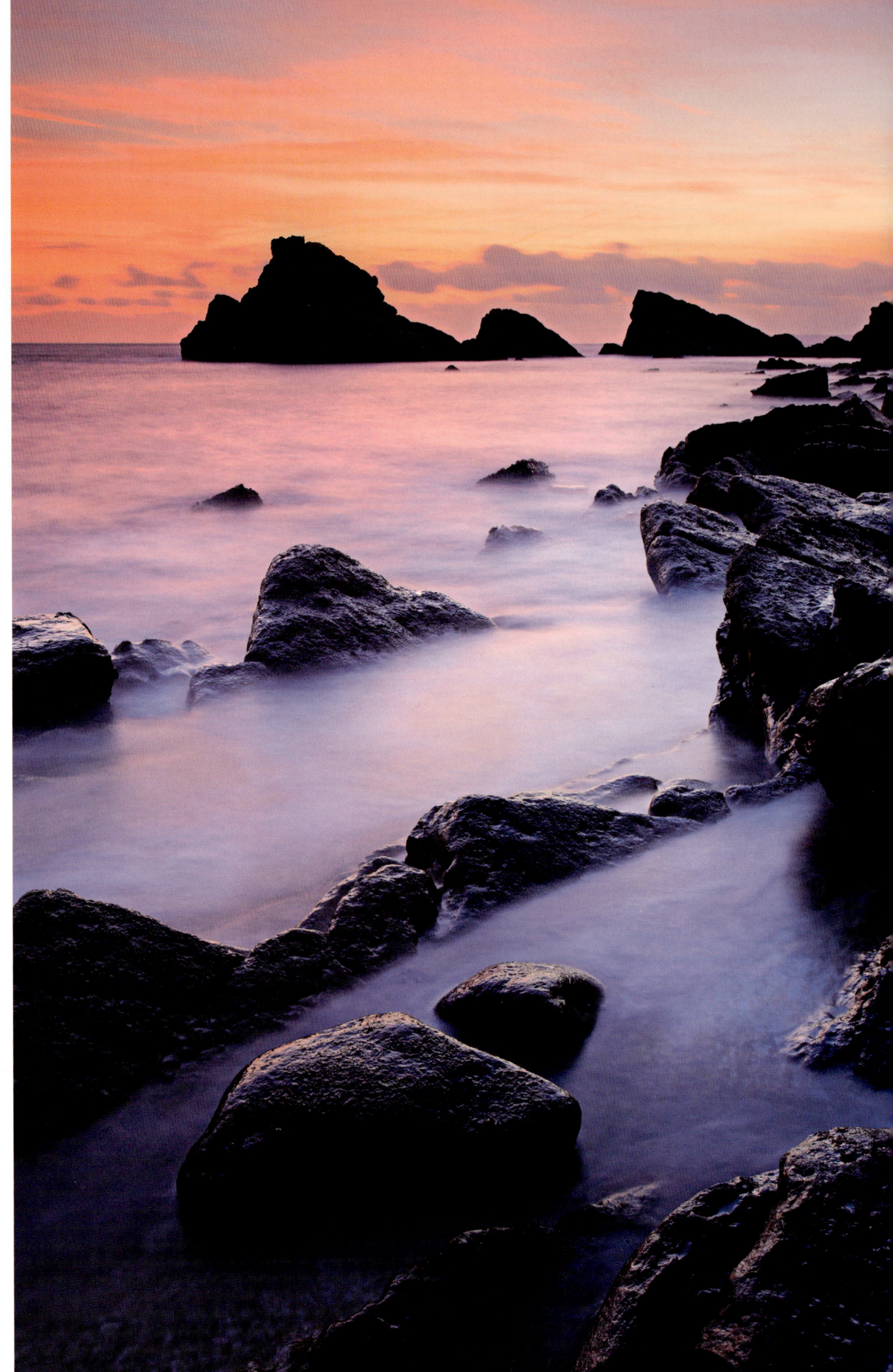

A glorious sunset presides over the
ruggedly beautiful and isolated
Mupe Rocks.

Mupe is not exactly your typical beach destination, but can offer tremendous variety to the adventurous. Being part of the Lulworth Ranges MOD land, access is restricted mostly to weekends. Even then you can only reach the coast via a strenuous walk eastwards over Bindon Hill or much longer walk westwards passing Flower's Barrow. On arriving at Mupe you are rewarded with not only a sandy bay, but also jagged limestone ledges, rocky islands and even an authentic smugglers' cave.

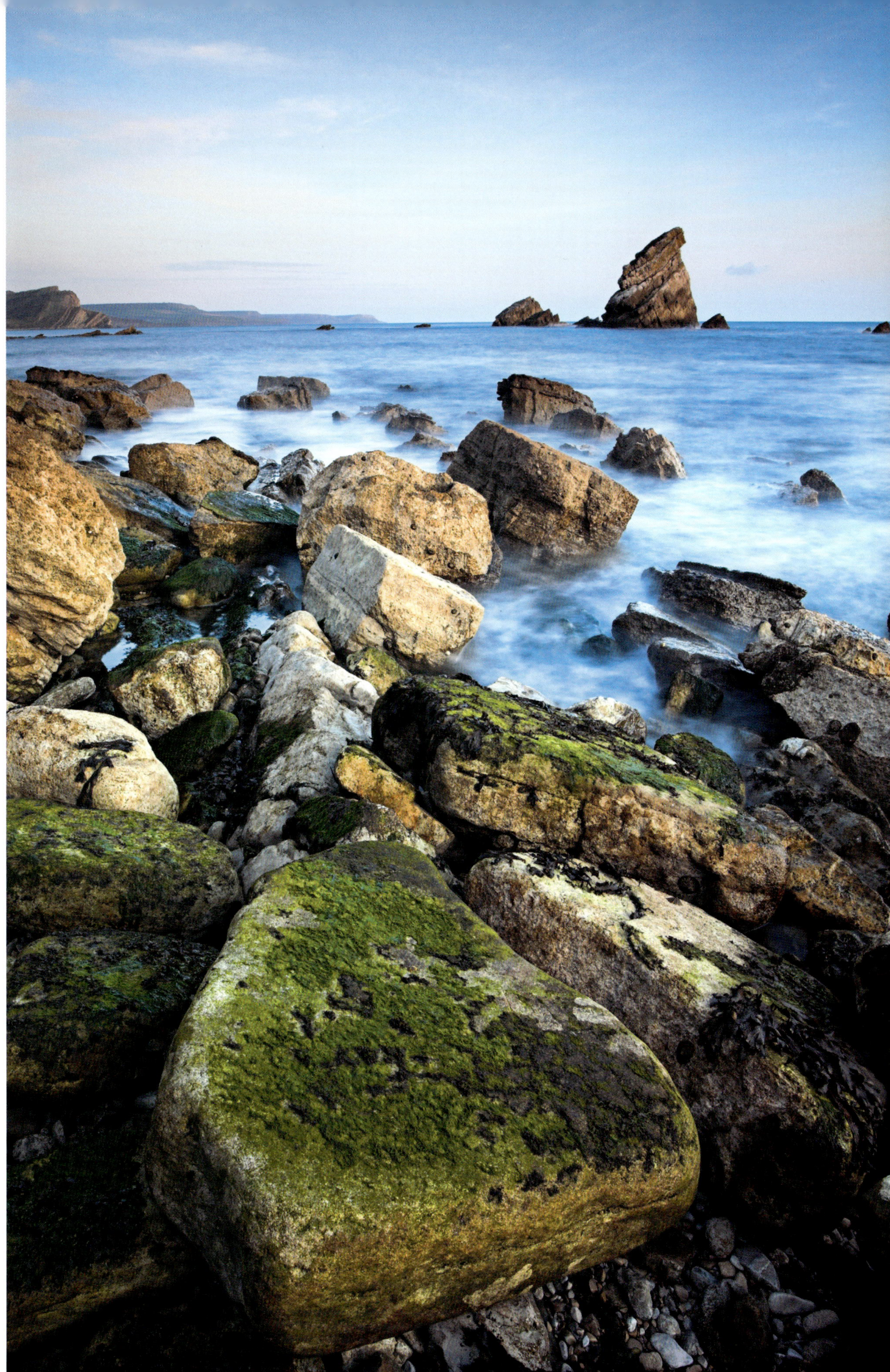

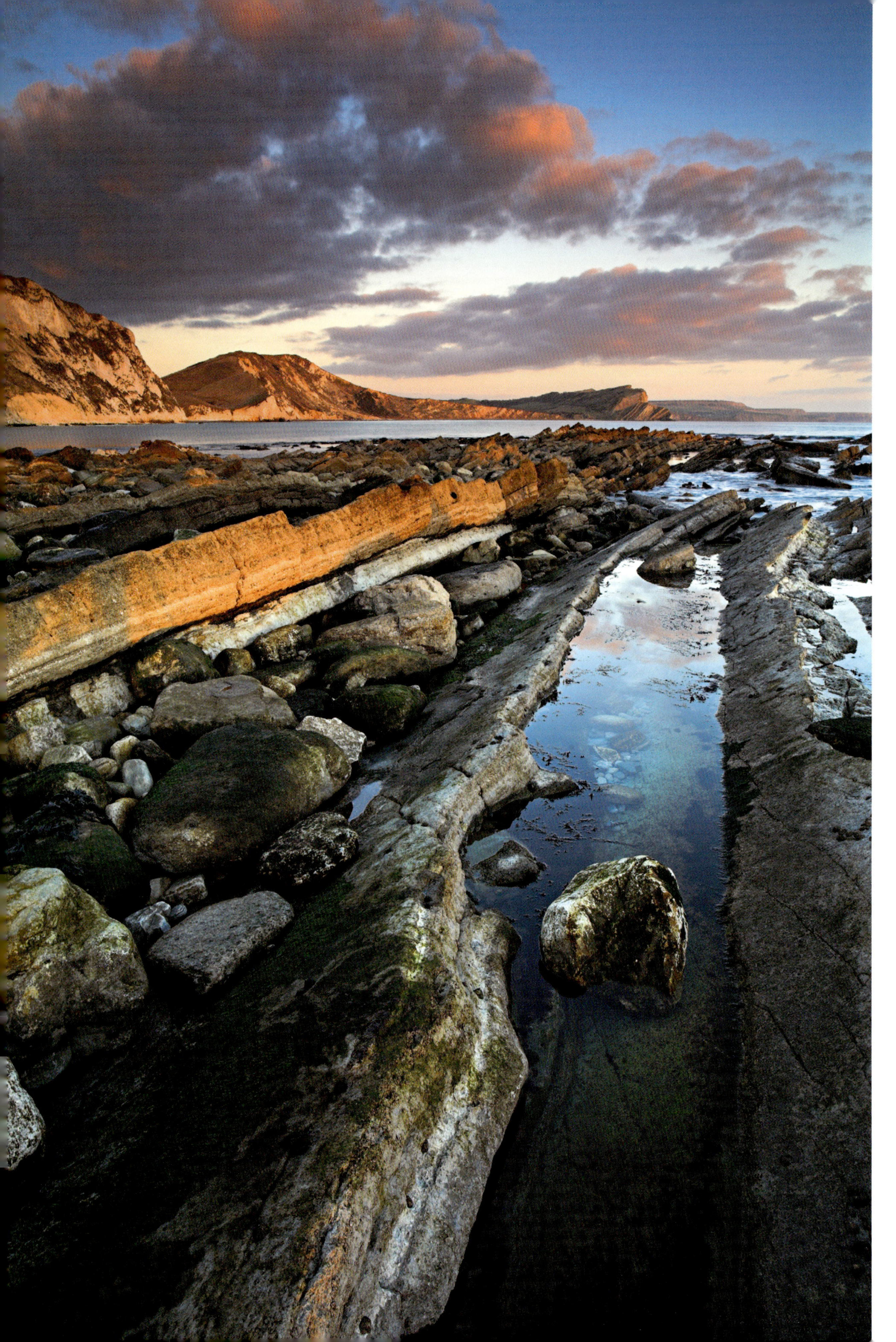

Golden winter sunshine lights up the ledges and white cliffs of Mupe and Worbarrow Bays.

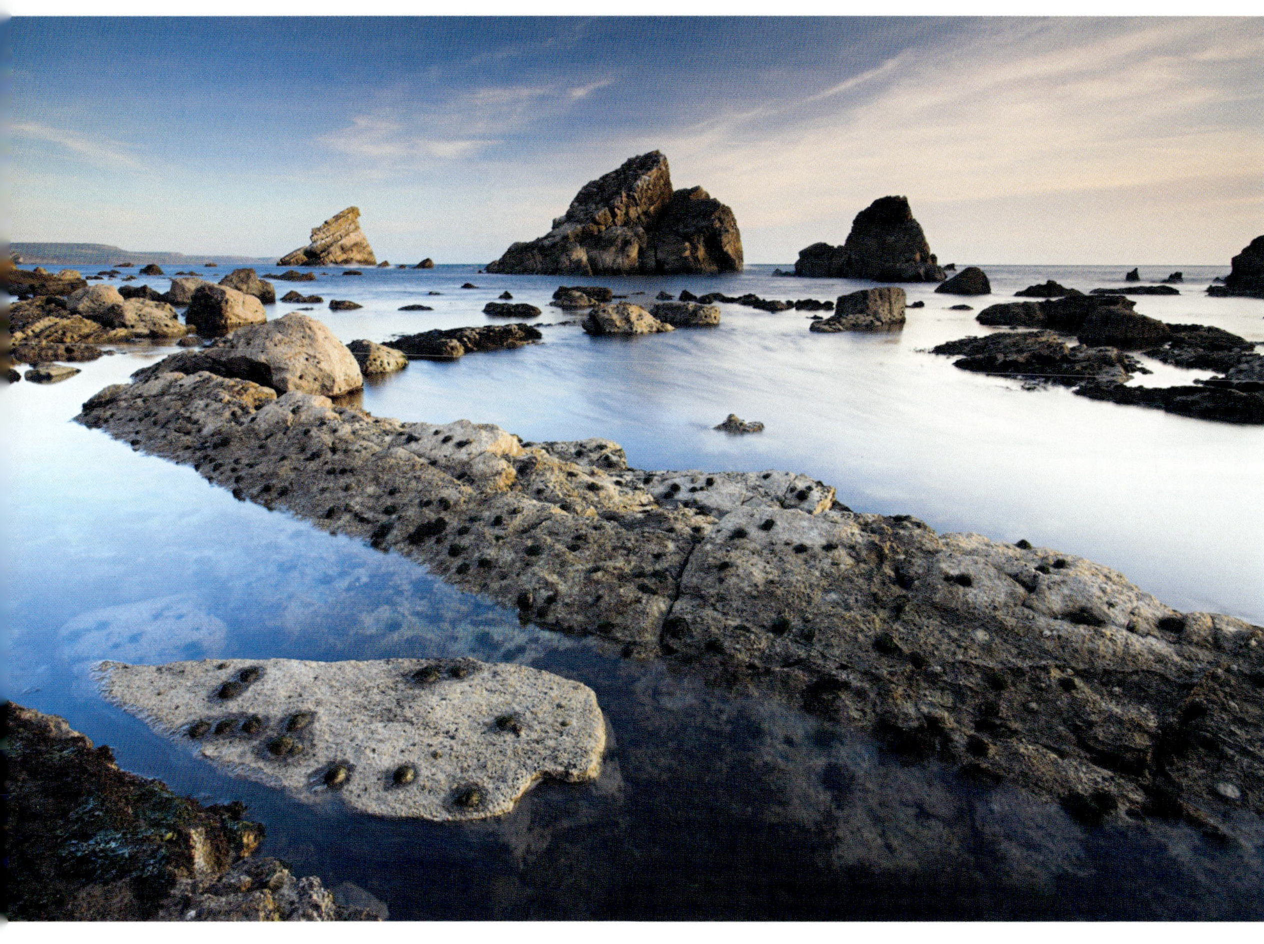

The rocky Purbeck stone outcrops at Mupe provide a spectacular vista to all who visit them. There are more sea stacks in this location than any other single place on the Dorset coast.

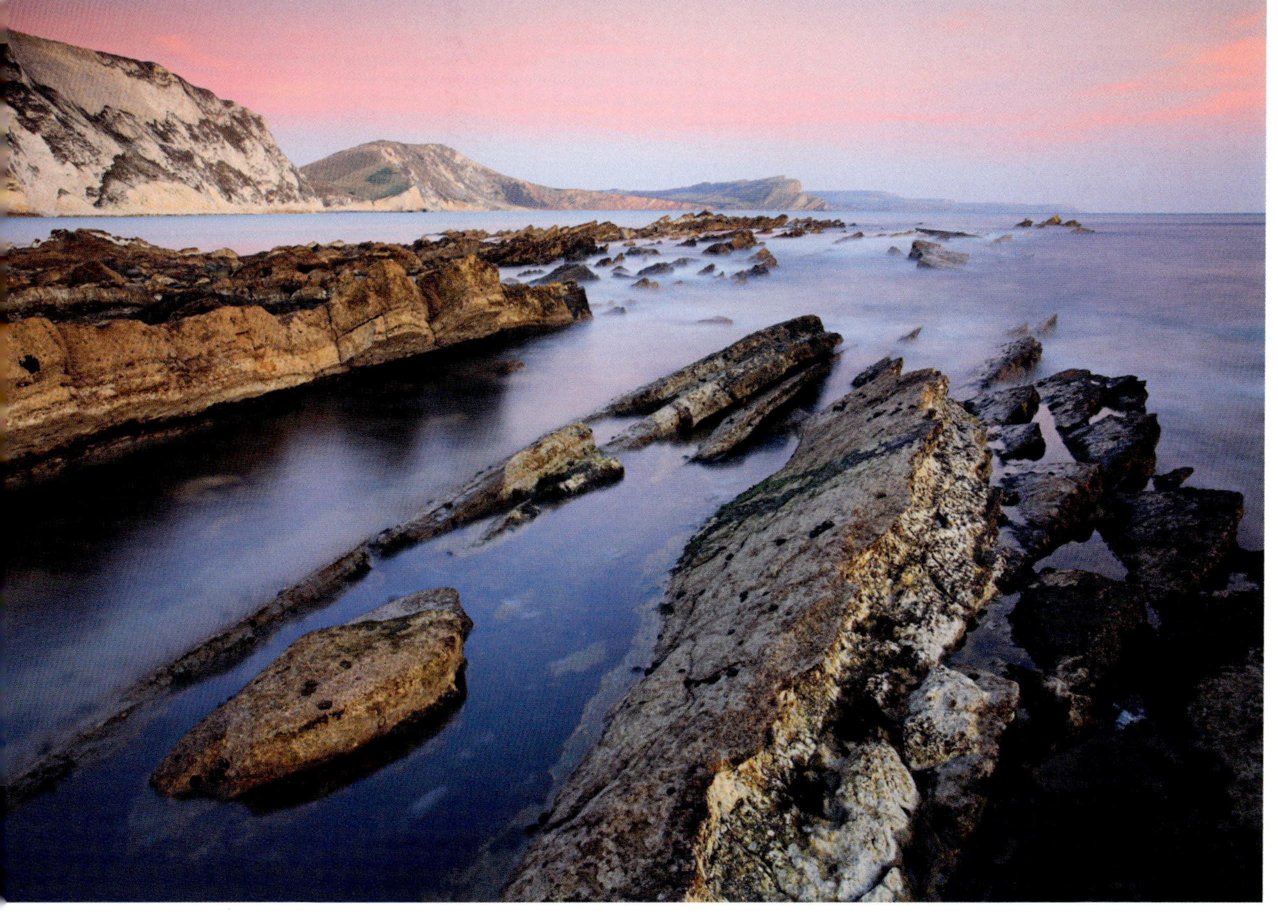

The jagged ledges stretch out past Mupe Bay before disappearing beneath the water's surface under Worbarrow Bay. On an evening blessed with special light, the view is truly memorable.

Lulworth Cove

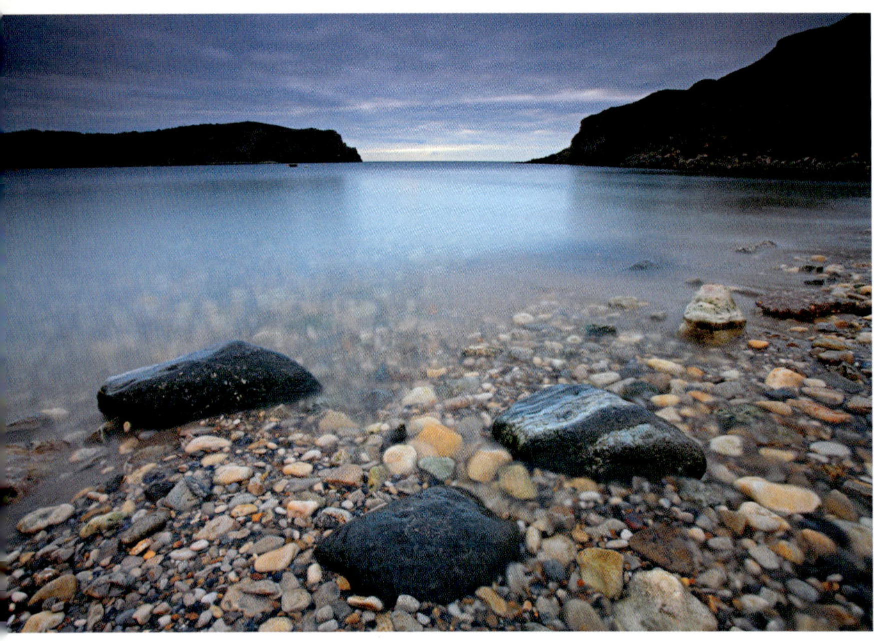

The bay at Lulworth was formed through coastal erosion initially to the outer Portland limestone cliffs. Once a weakness was found in this hard rock, the water surged in to begin the erosion of the much softer clay beds behind.

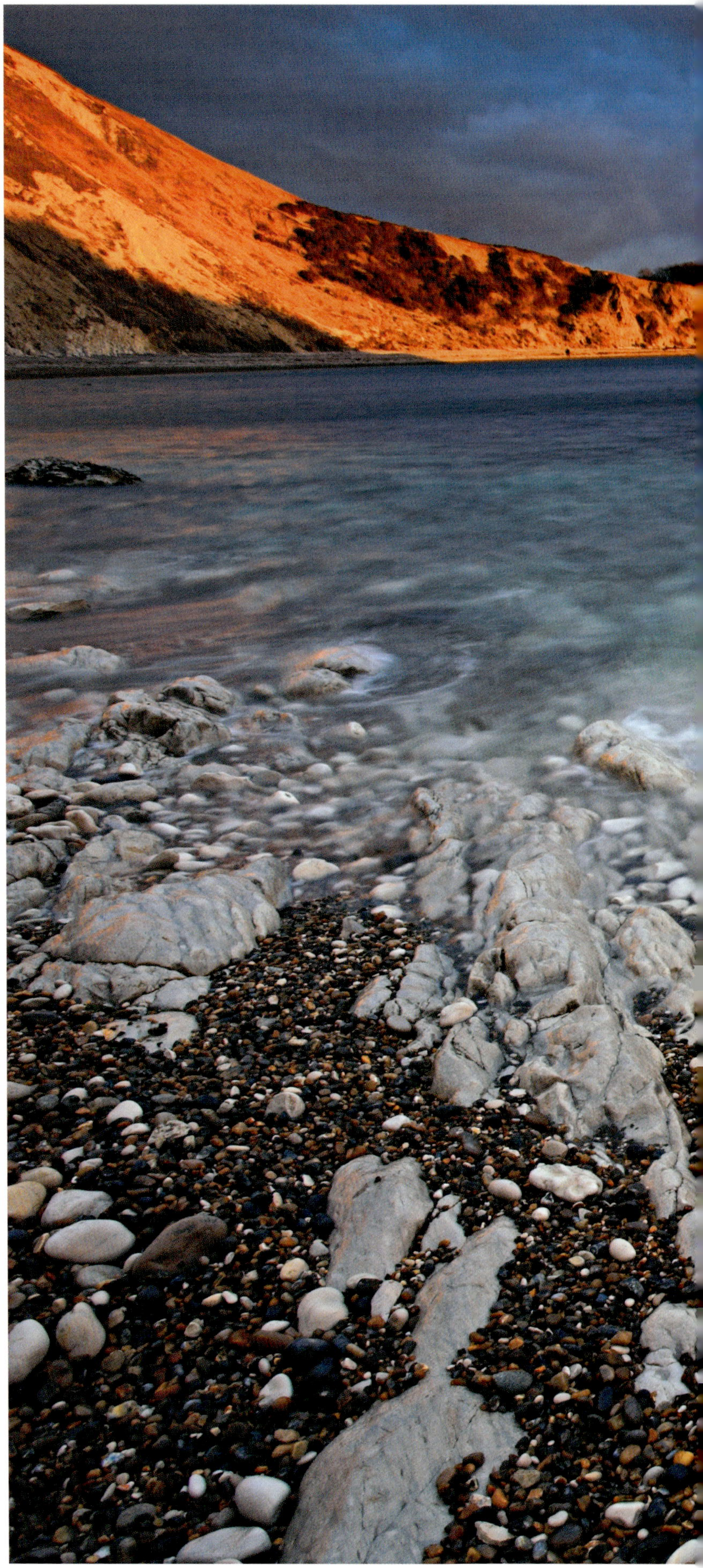

Chalk ledges running beneath the water at Lulworth Cove can change the appearance of the sea, charming the viewer with scenes reminiscent of a Mediterranean bay. The golden light on the cliffs compliments this picture, appearing to portray warm summer evenings beside inviting water. The reality, however, is all too different. This image was taken only two days after Christmas on a bitterly cold evening!

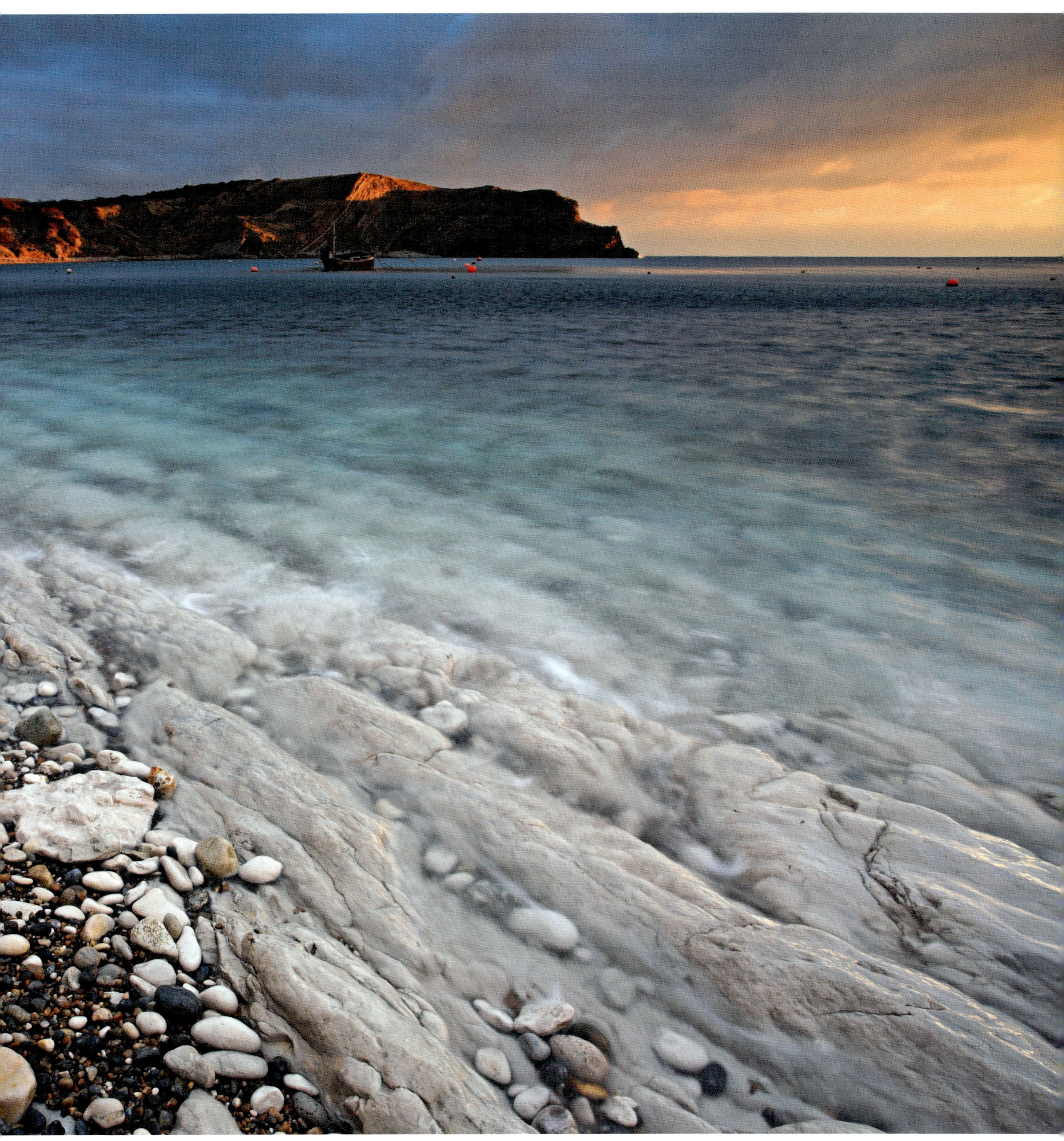

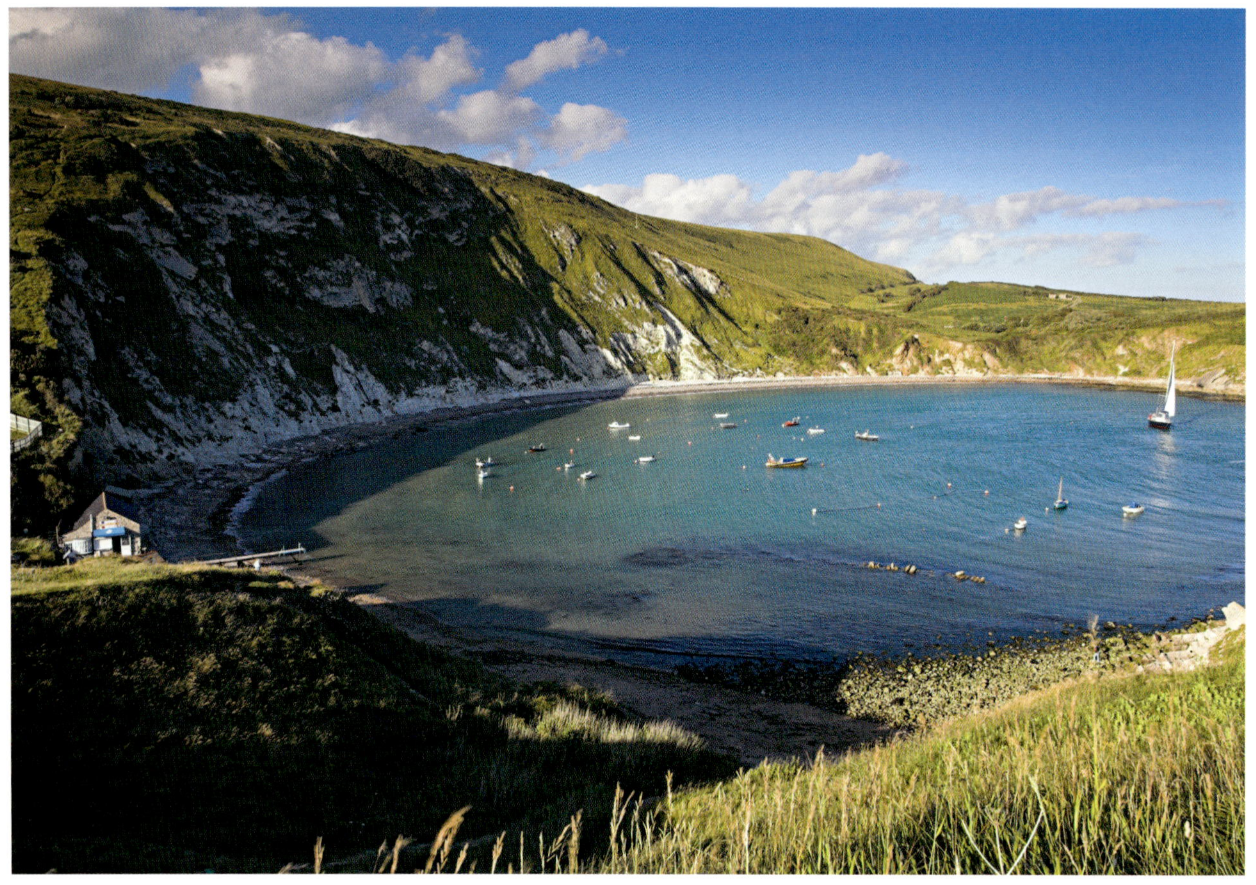

Lulworth now provides a perfect natural harbour to both fishing vessels and passing yachts. Its sheltered waters are also ideal for scuba diving and snorkelling.

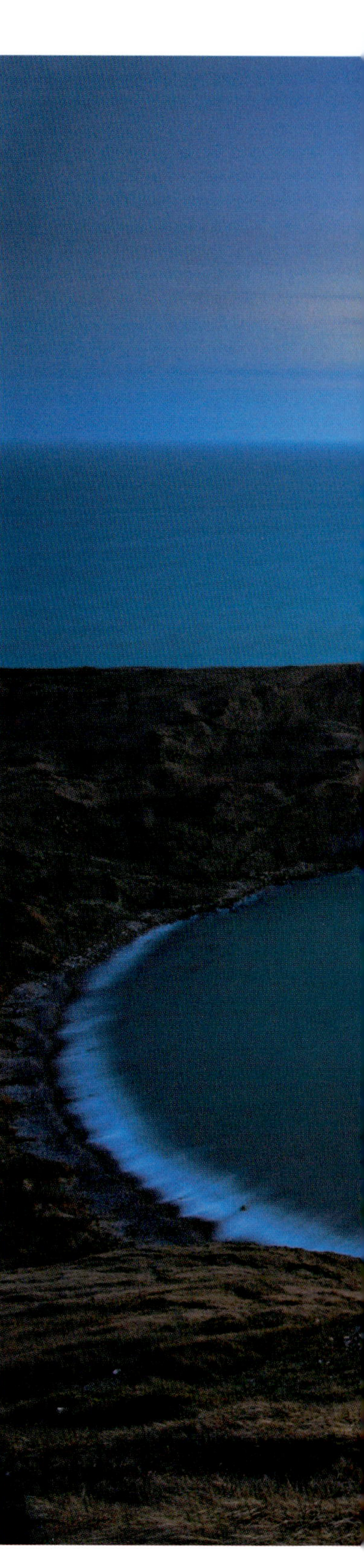

Horseshoe-shaped Lulworth Cove is
best observed from high up on the
Bindon Hill cliffside. From this
vantage point you can fully
appreciate this internationally
renowned geological wonder.

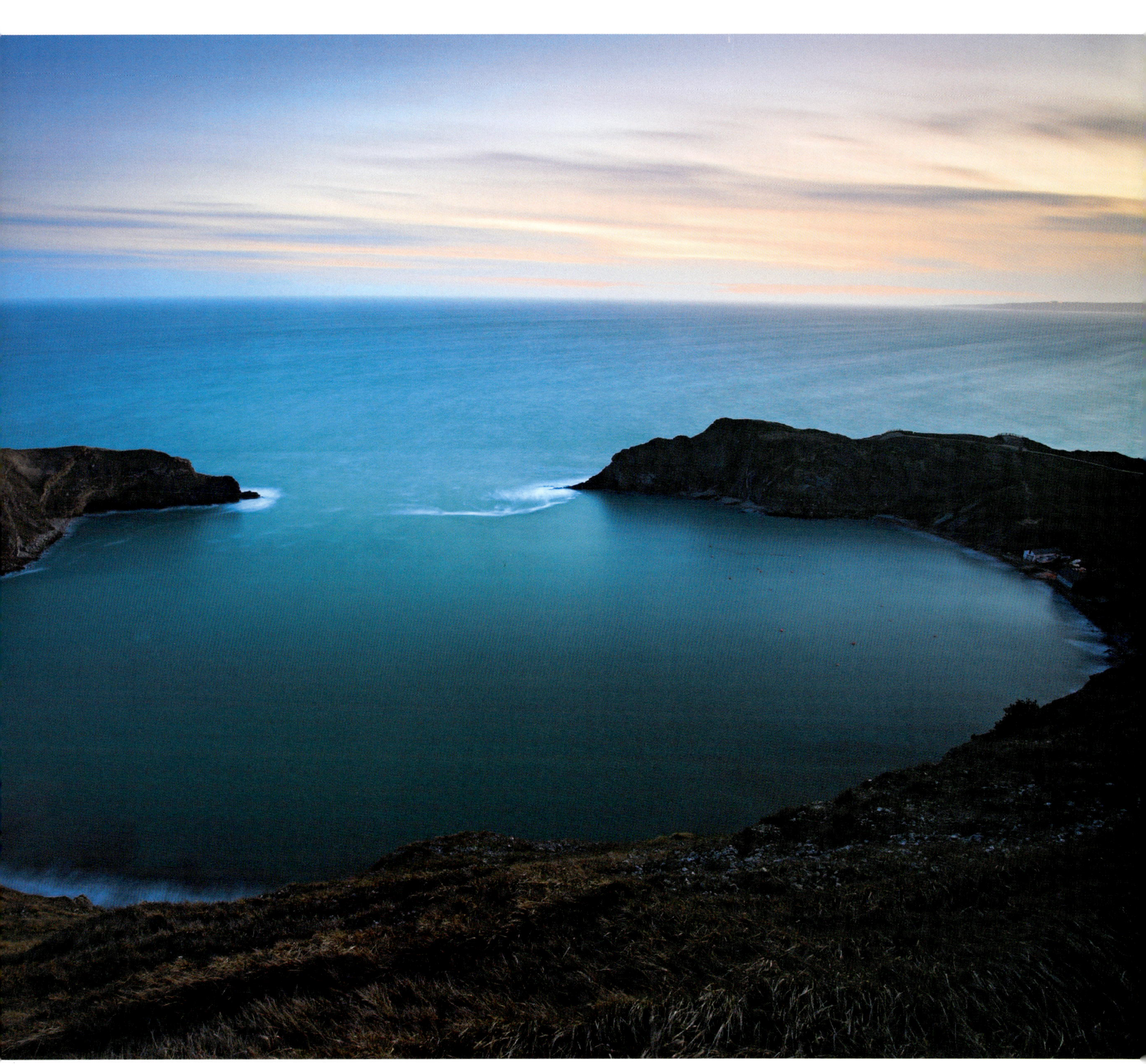

Stair Hole

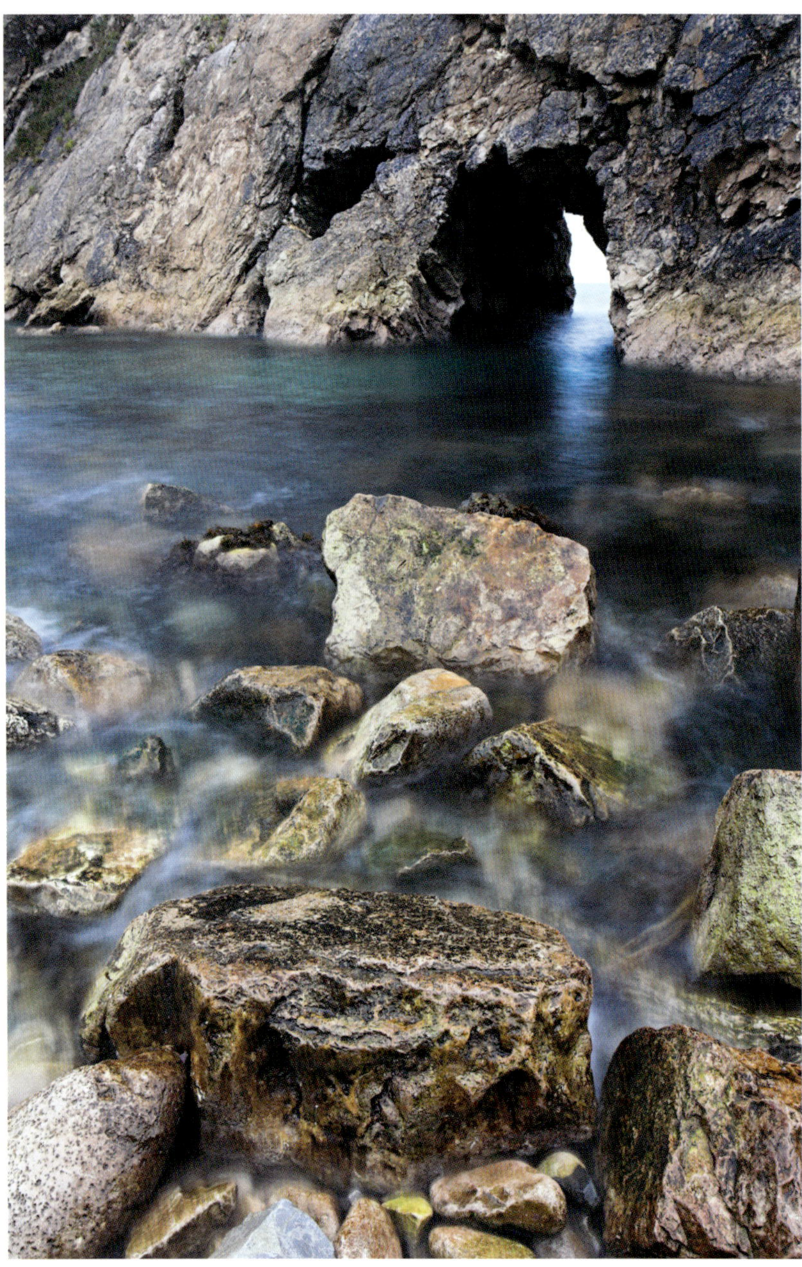

The beginnings of a new Durdle
Door are evident in this small arch
at Stair Hole.

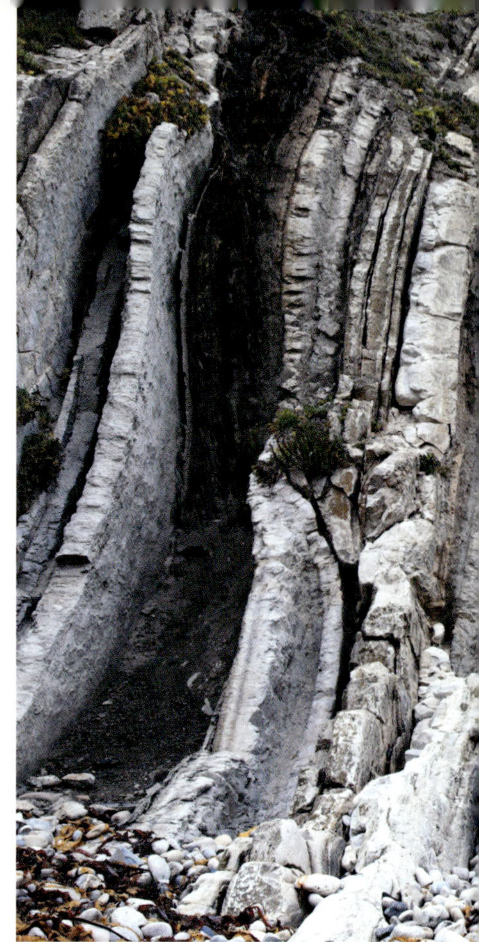

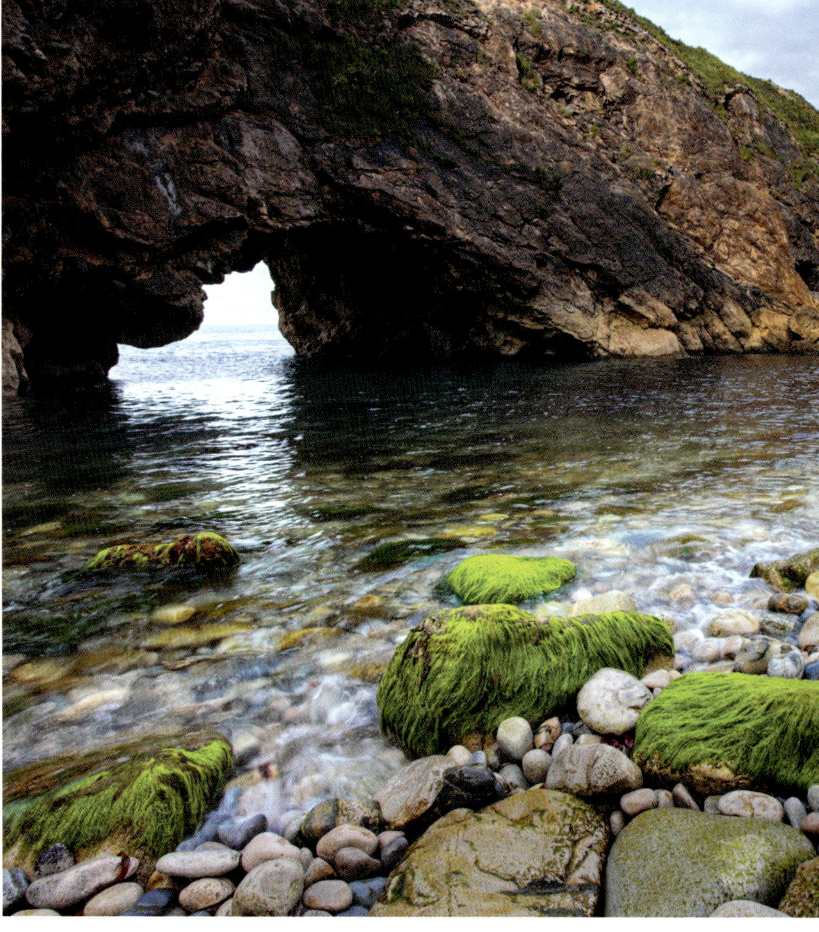

The best way to explore these
fascinating rock formations is by
kayak. Here and at Old Harry Rocks
you can easily explore in and
around the formations. As long as
you take a guide with you, even a
beginner can give it a try!

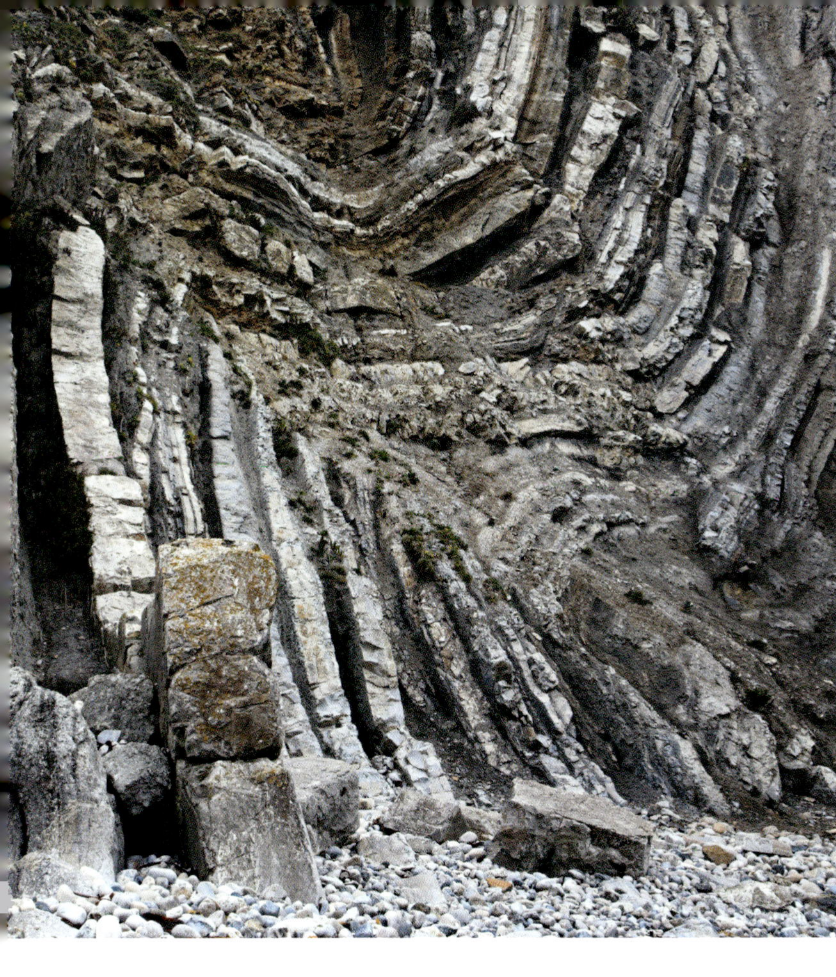

The folded layers of rock at Stair Hole are named the Lulworth Crumple. While this is the best known example of such folding, there is evidence all along the coast of such geological activity, caused when the continents of Africa and Europe collided around 30 million years ago.

Stair Hole provides a first-hand example of the endless powers of nature. The contorted rock formations on the cliff face provide living evidence of the trauma that took place millions of years ago when continents collided. In more recent times, the hard limestone cliff face has been eroded into several arches by the continual assault of sea water, providing the very beginnings of a second Lulworth Cove.

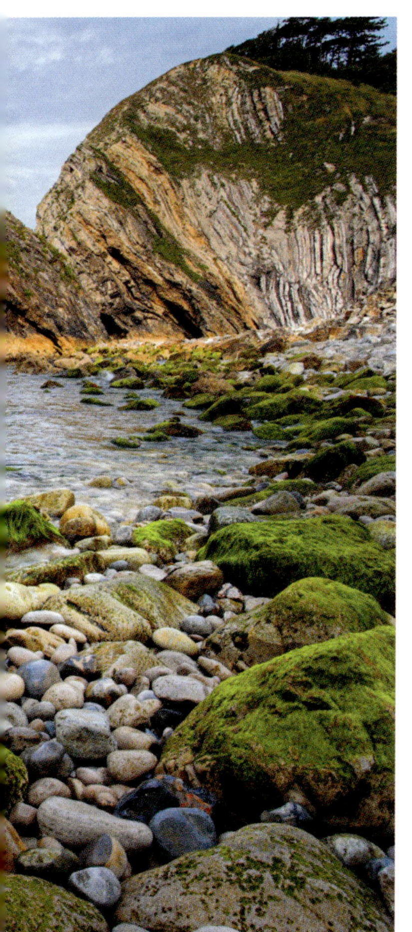

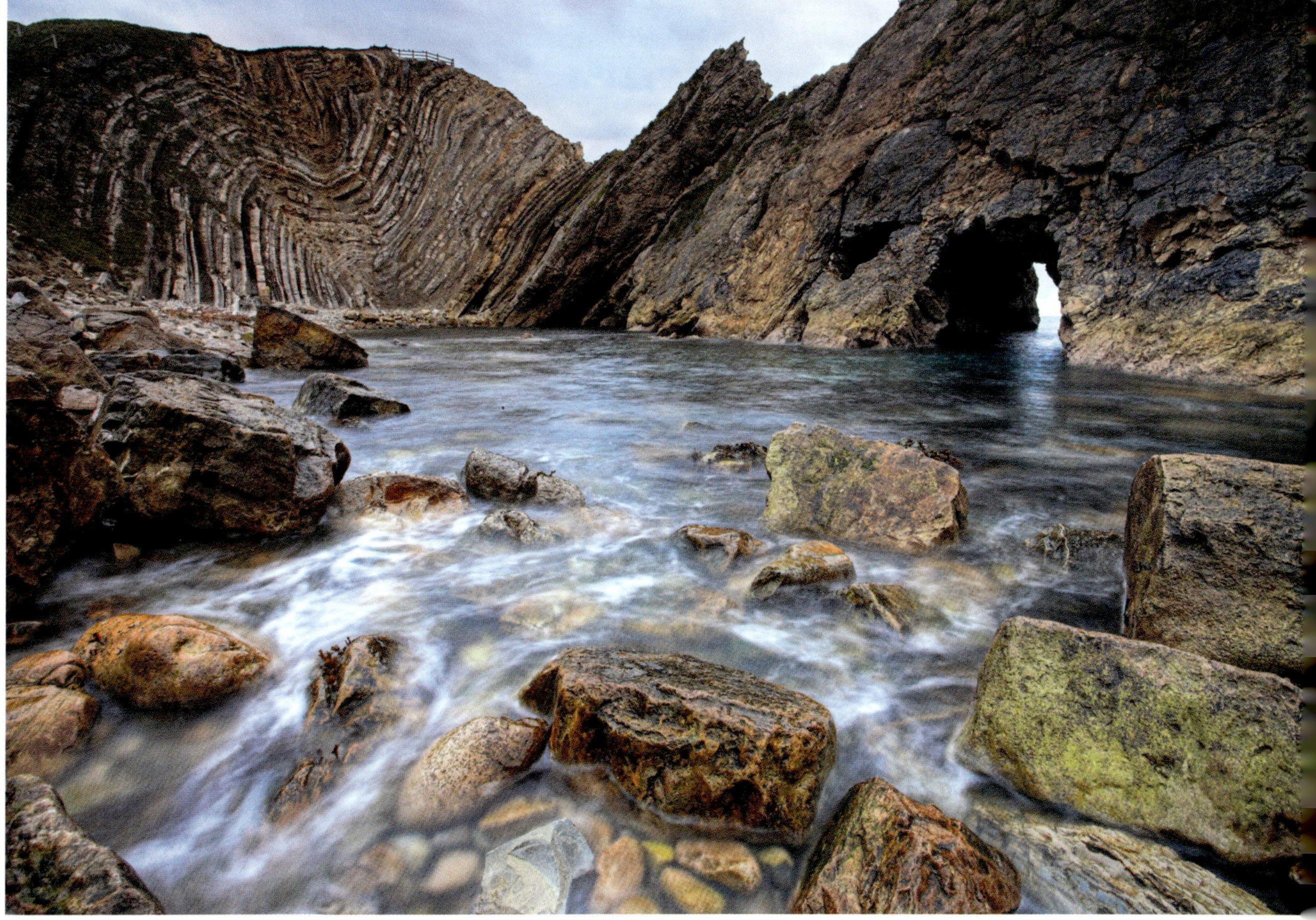

St Oswald's Bay

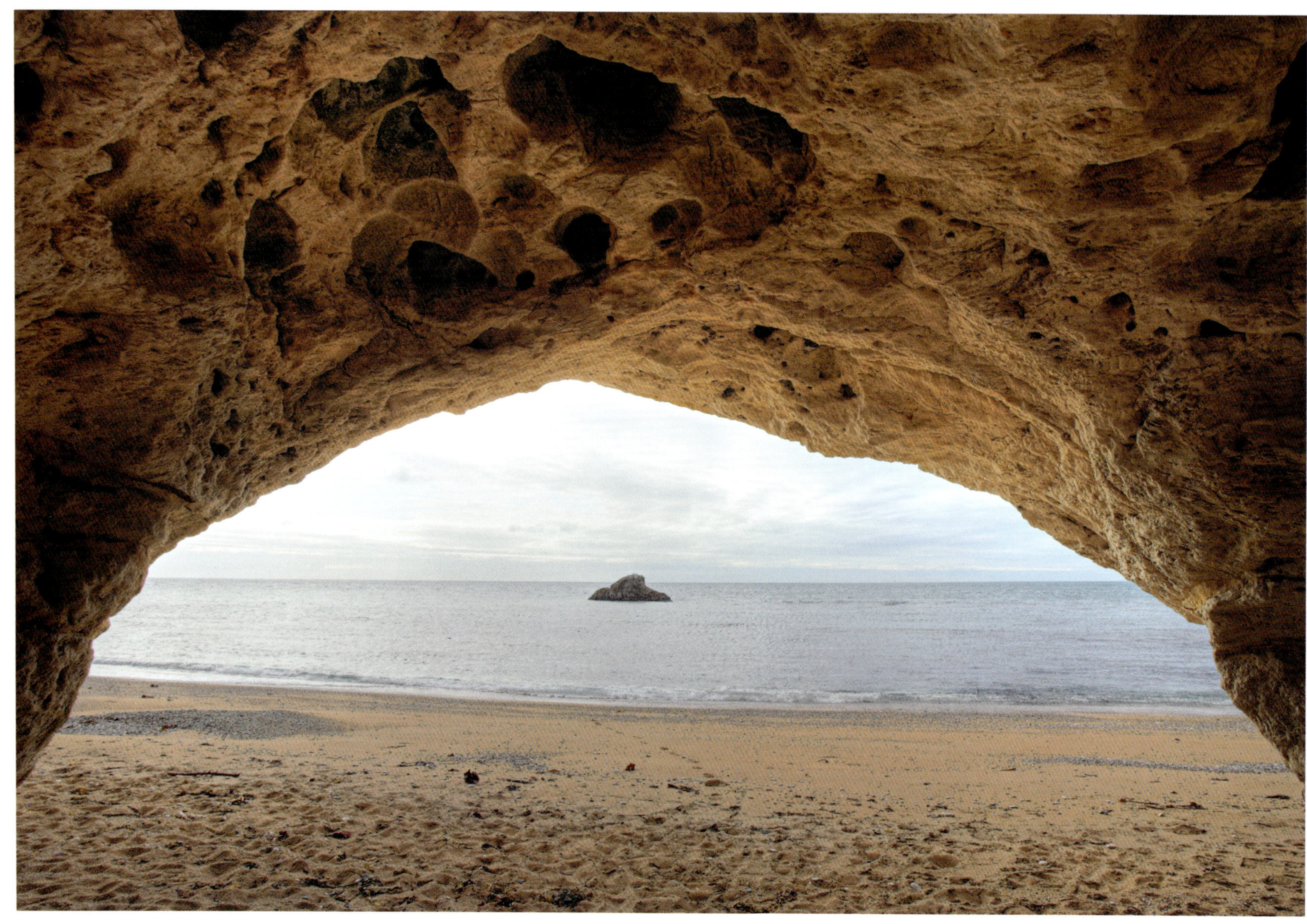

Inside one of the many small caves in the base of the cliffs in St Oswald's Bay. The small island is the highly eroded remains of the same limestone rock outcrop that forms Durdle Door just to the west.

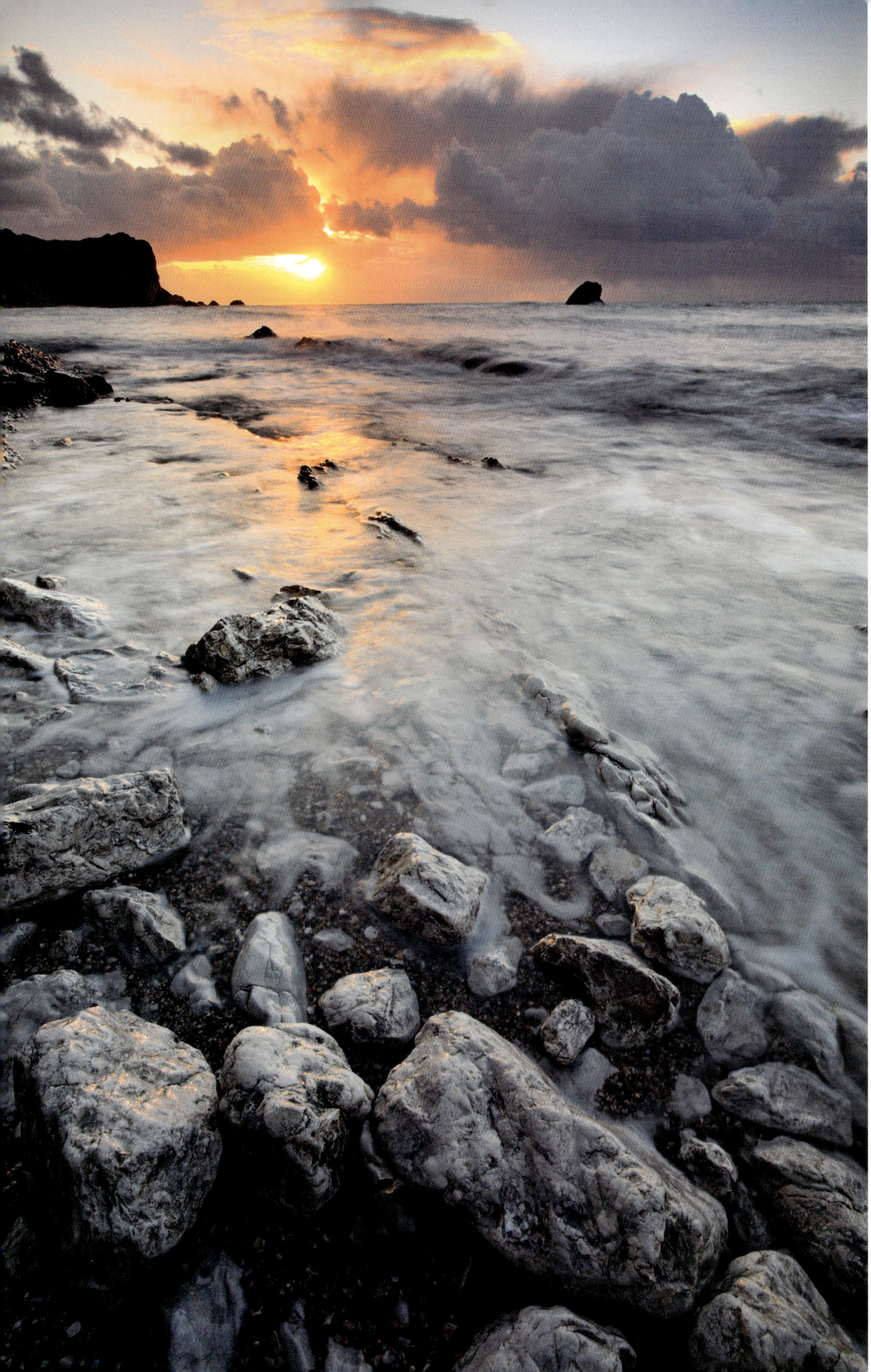

A spectacular sunrise emerges from behind the clouds near Dungy Head at St Oswald's Bay.

Man O' War Cove

High tide washes the beach clean at
Man O' War Cove.

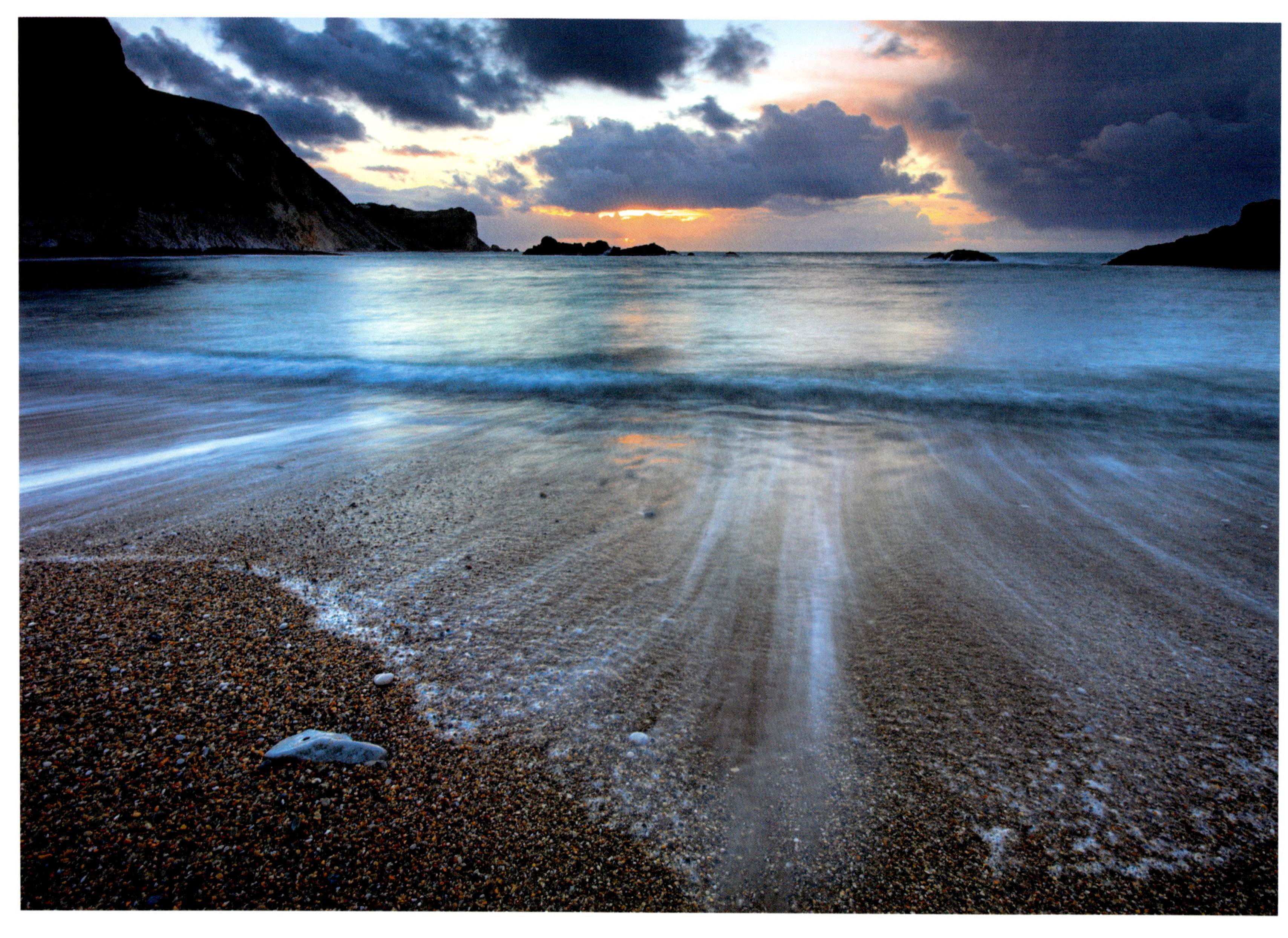

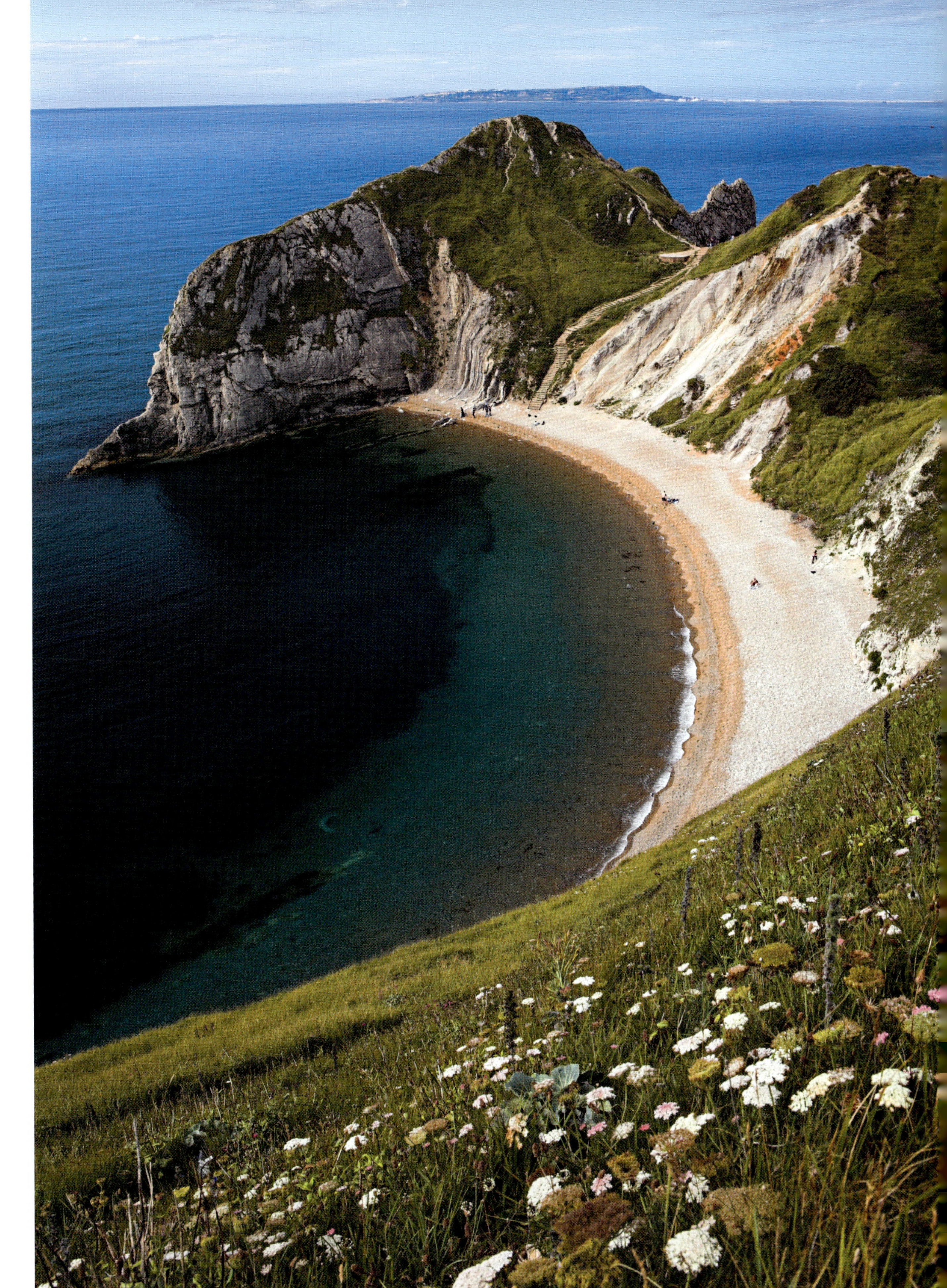

Neighbouring Durdle Door is the beautiful Man O' War Cove. The clifftop walk towards the beach provides glorious views down into the semi-circular bay. On a sunny summer's day you could be forgiven for thinking you were gazing down at a Mediterranean beach.

Durdle Door

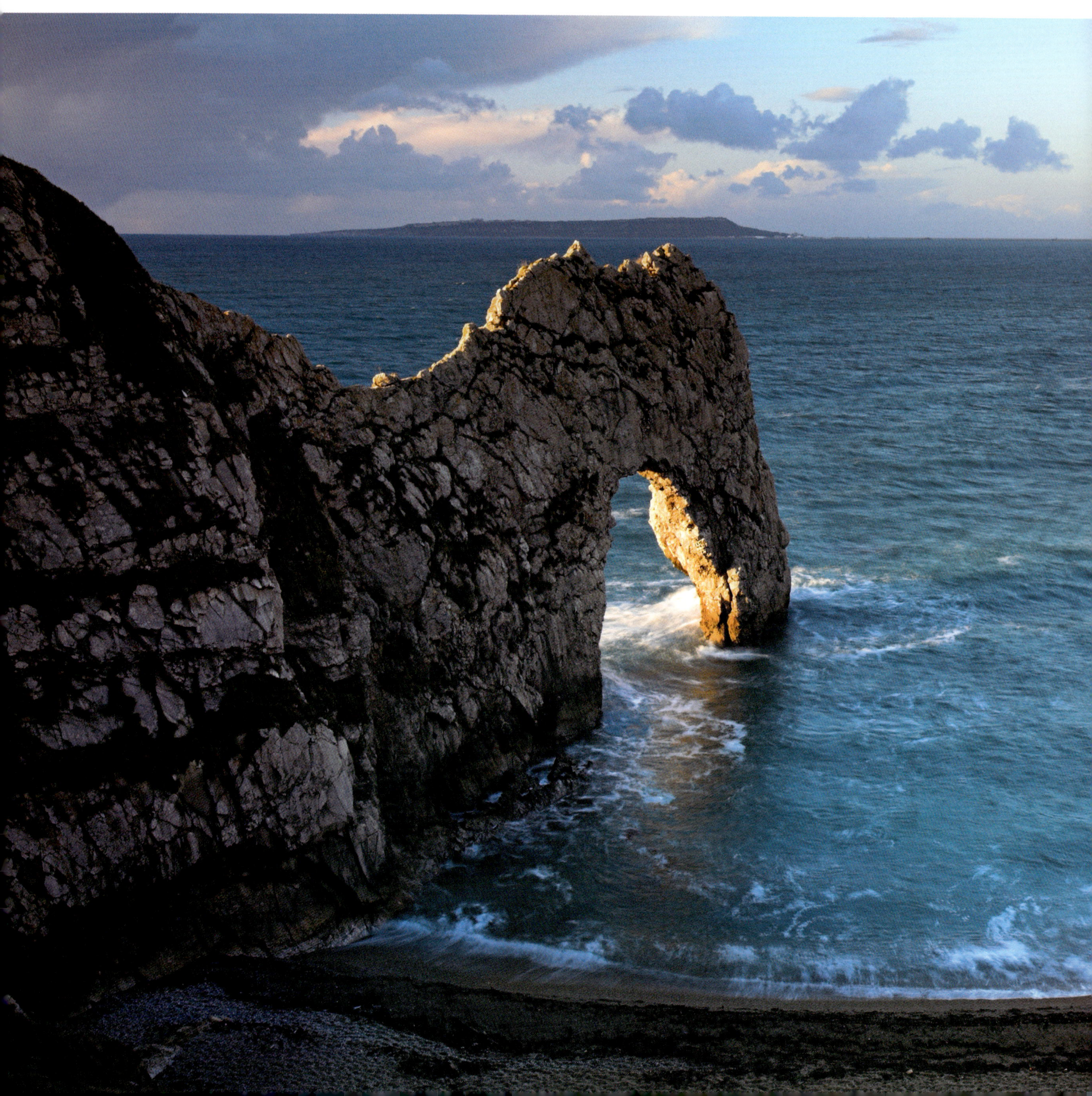

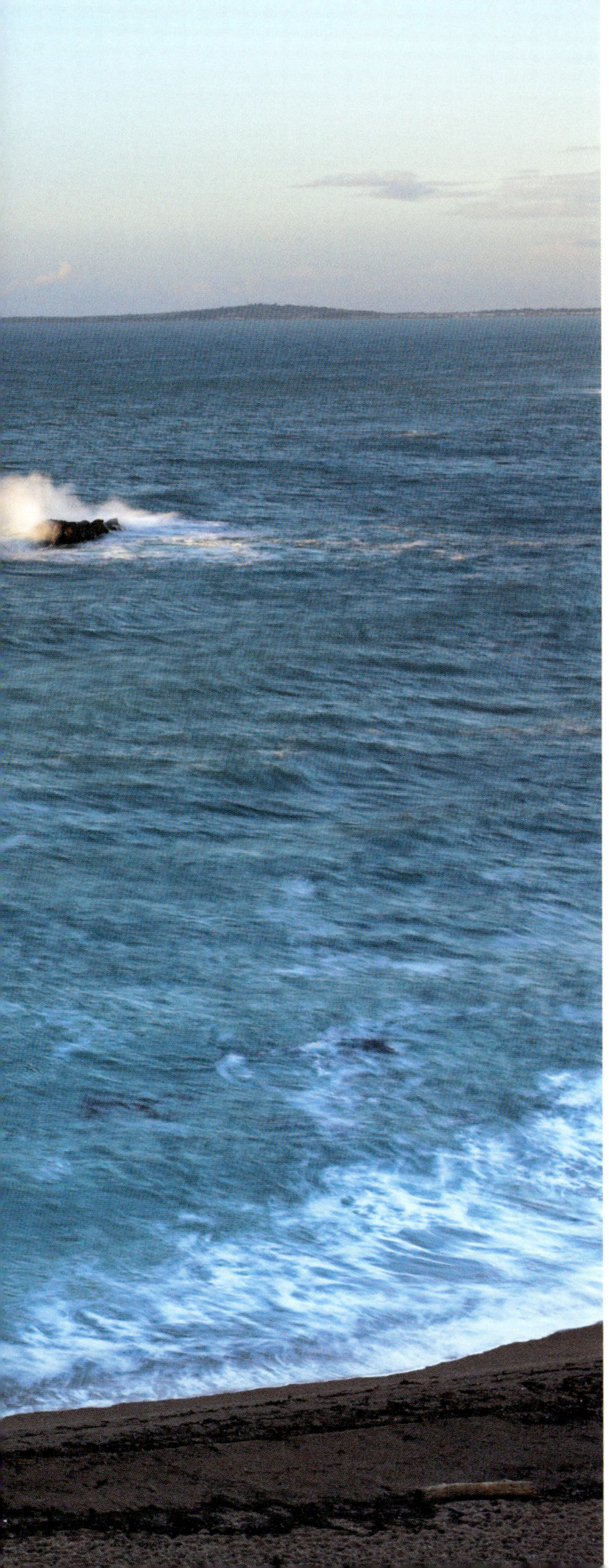

Early morning sunlight bathes the underside of Durdle Door's natural arch in golden tones.

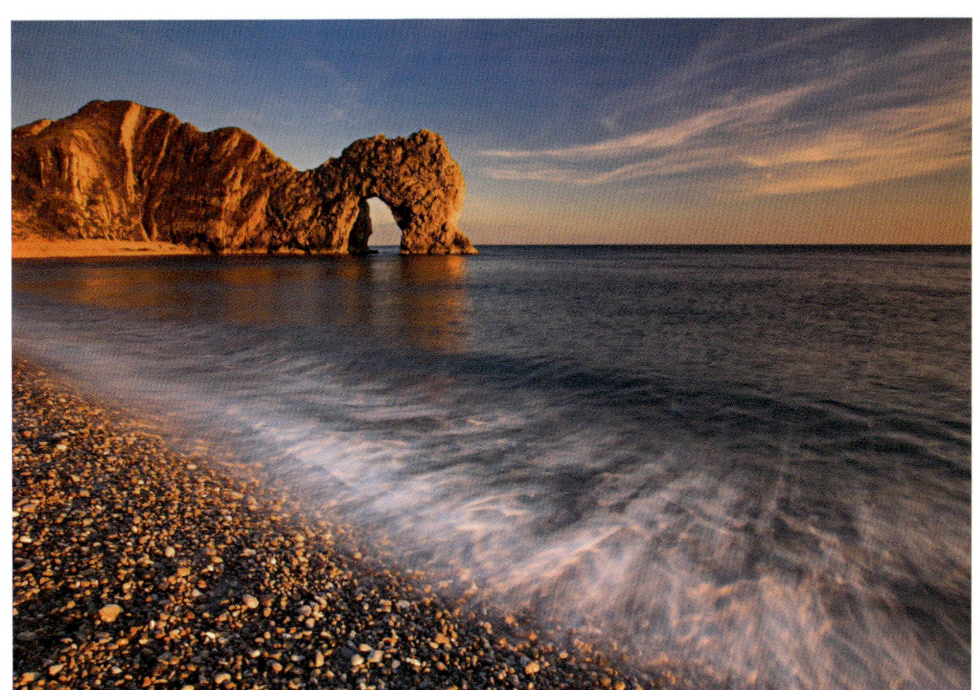

For only a brief window of opportunity each year, the position of the setting sun bathes the whole face of Durdle Door in golden sunlight.

The headland at Durdle Door consists of Portland limestone which has slowly eroded into a natural arch. Behind the arch the weaker rocks have eroded more rapidly, creating the beaches of Durdle Door and Man O' War Cove. In time, the Durdle Door headland will become an island as the non-stop erosion process merges the two beaches together.

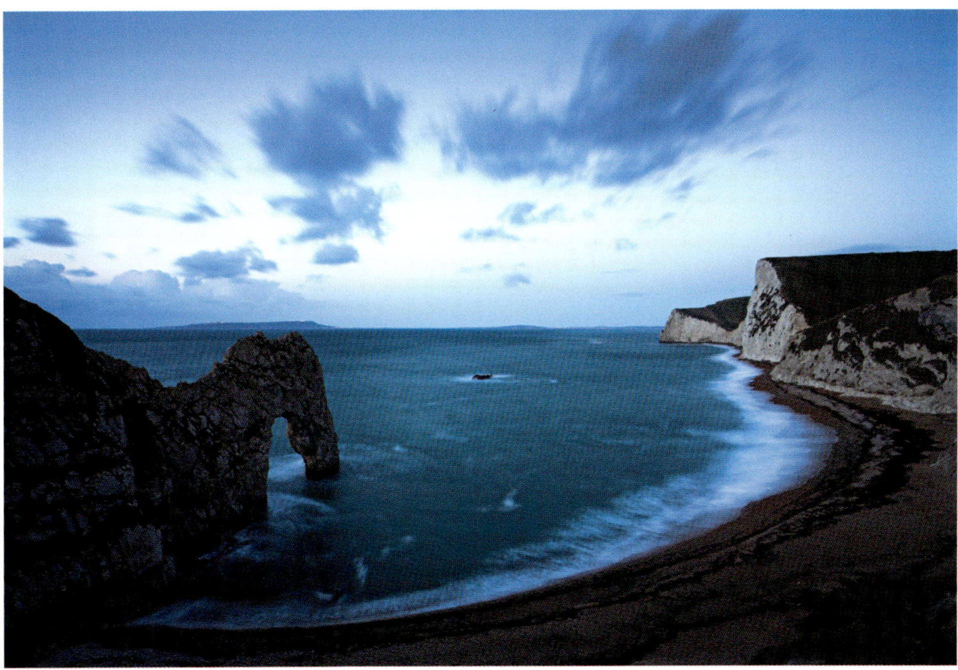

Before nightfall a pink twilight
descends over the Durdle Door
rock arch.

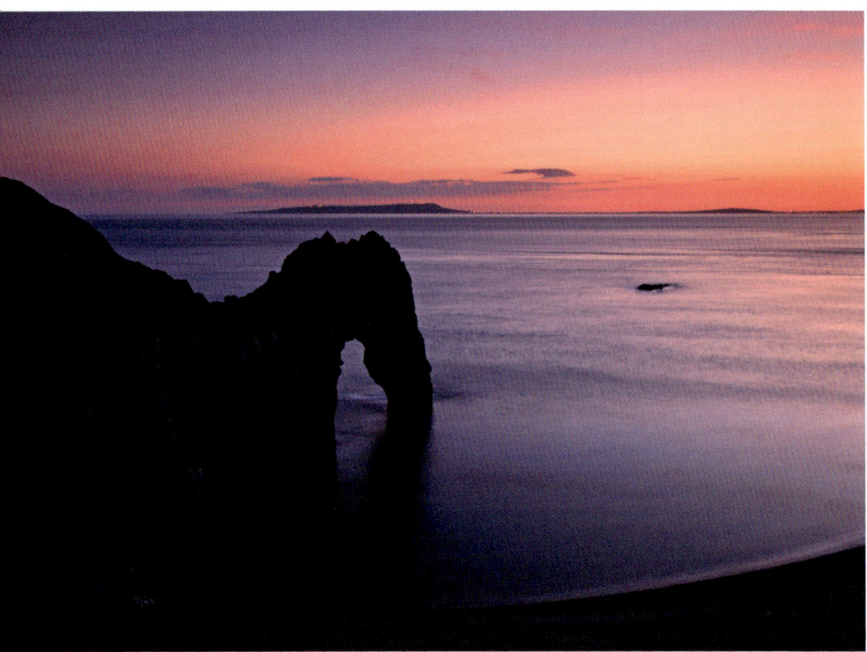

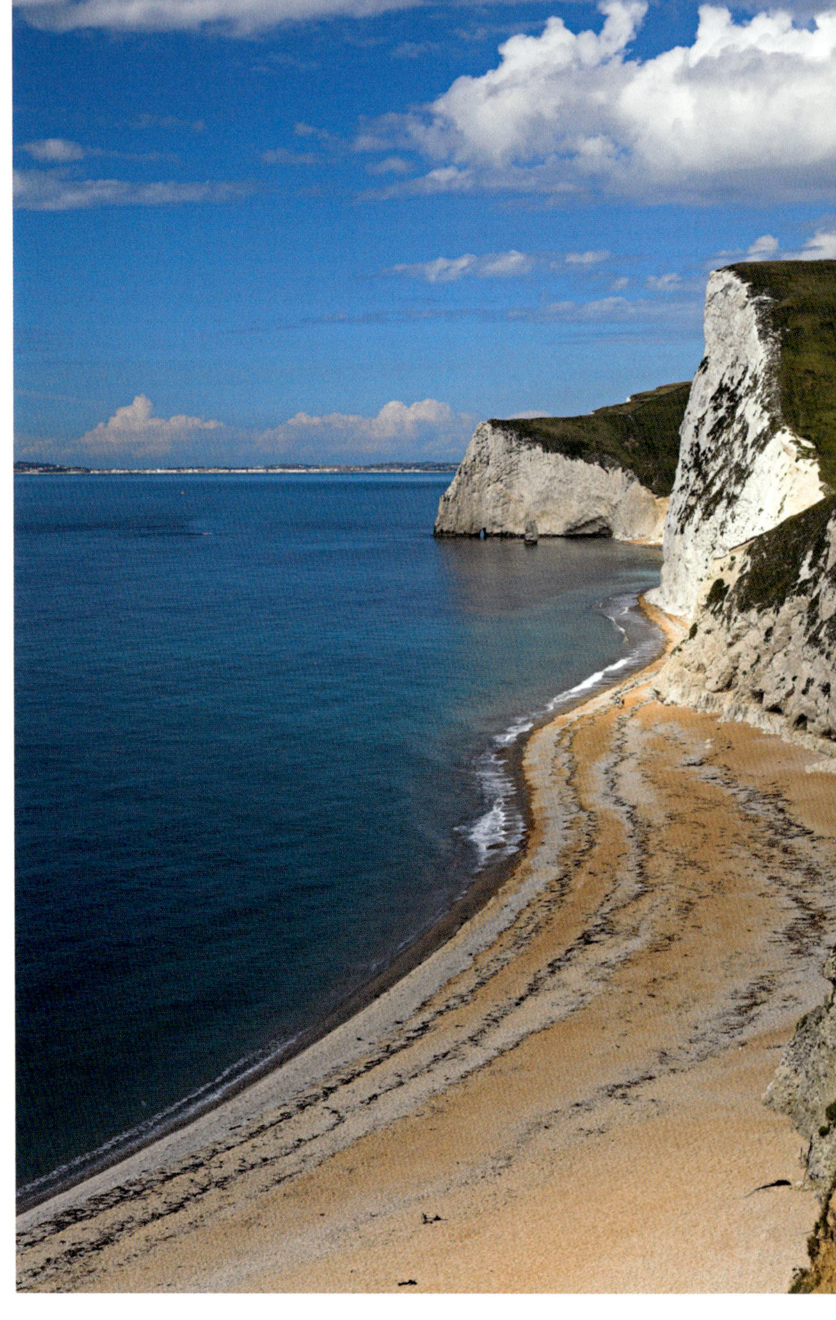

Looking westwards from the
clifftops above Durdle Door to the
chalk cliffs of Swyre Head and Bats
Head. Just visible at the base of
Bats Head is a tiny natural arch
known as Bats Hole. While
presently much smaller than the
archway at Durdle Door, the softer
chalk rock will contribute to a much
greater rate of erosion.

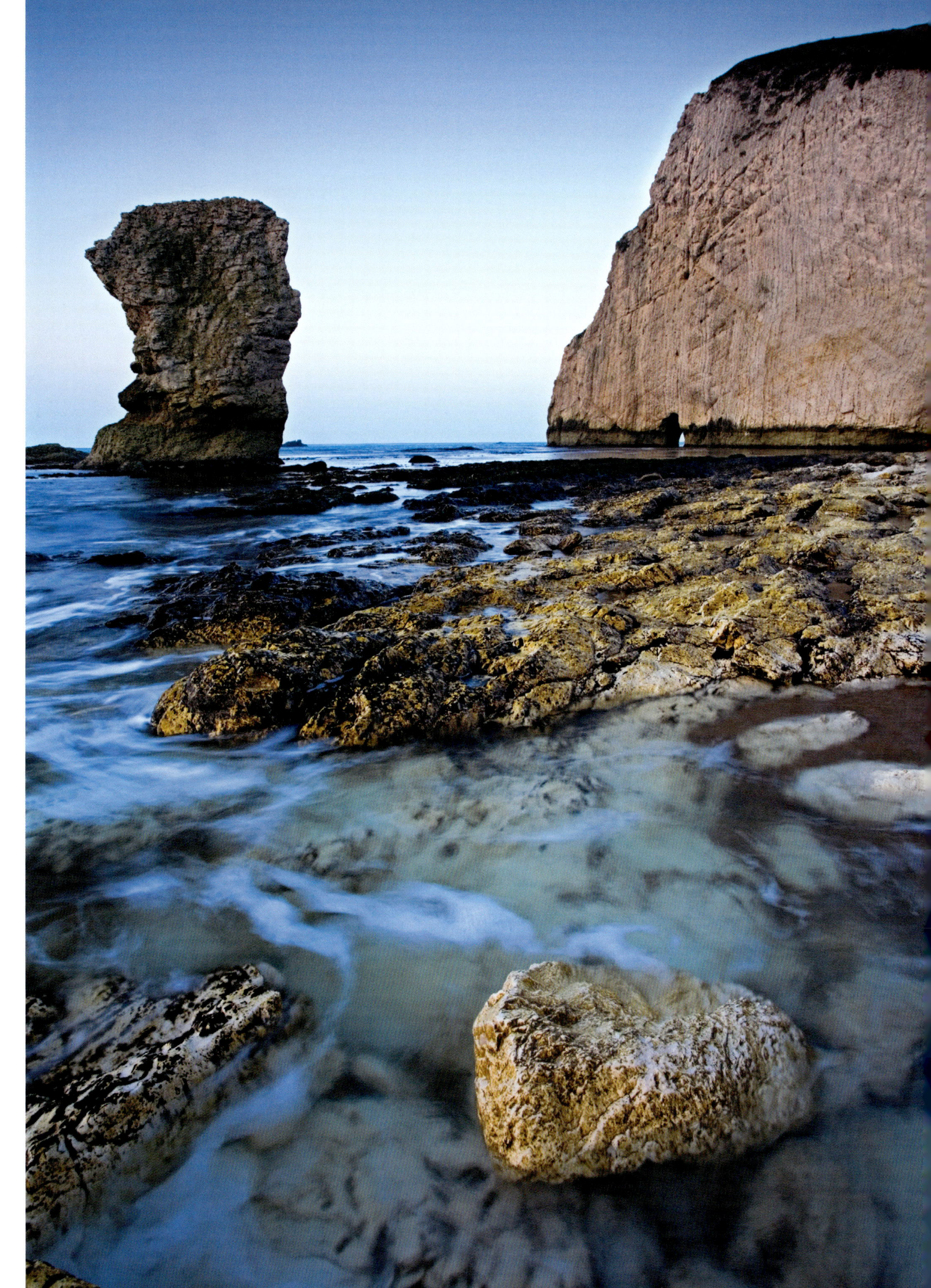

As with any rock arch, it eventually becomes eroded into a rock stack over time. This one is known as Butter Rock and is formed of chalk.

Osmington Mills

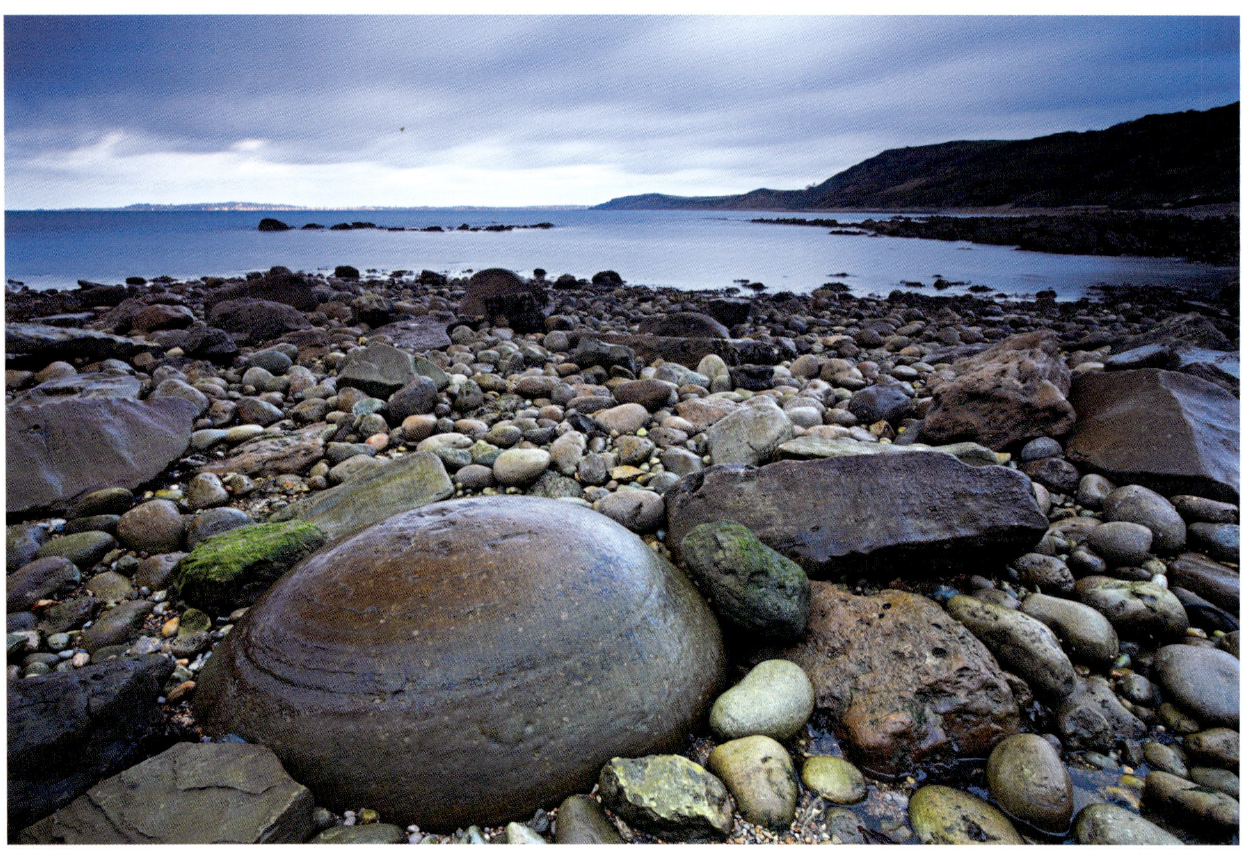

Amongst the stones on the shore at Osmington Mills, you occasionally encounter circular boulders. These spherical boulders are geologically known as septarian concretions.

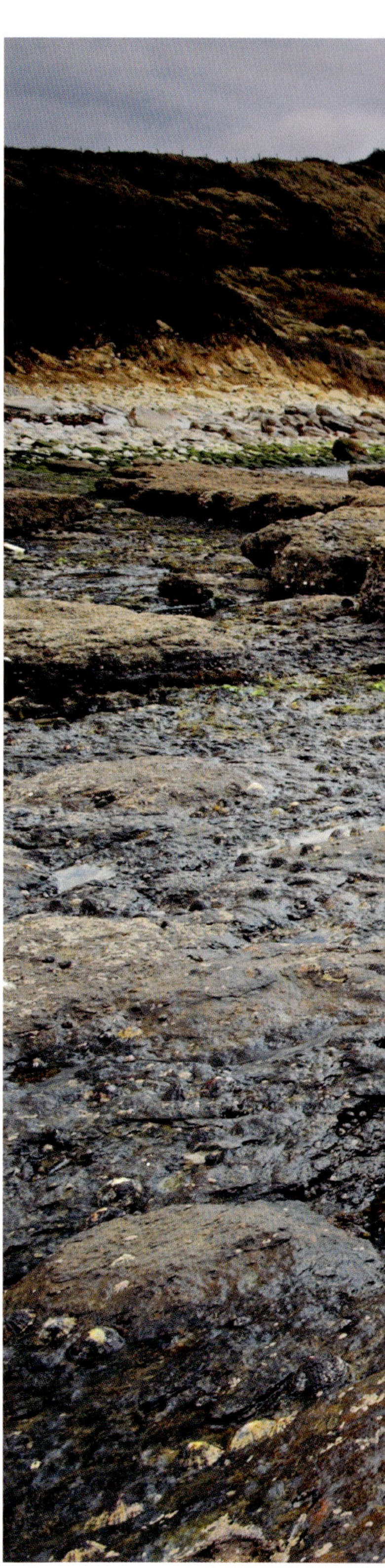

Low tide at Osmington Mills exposes a series of ledges and rockpools, perfect for exploring on a grey overcast day.

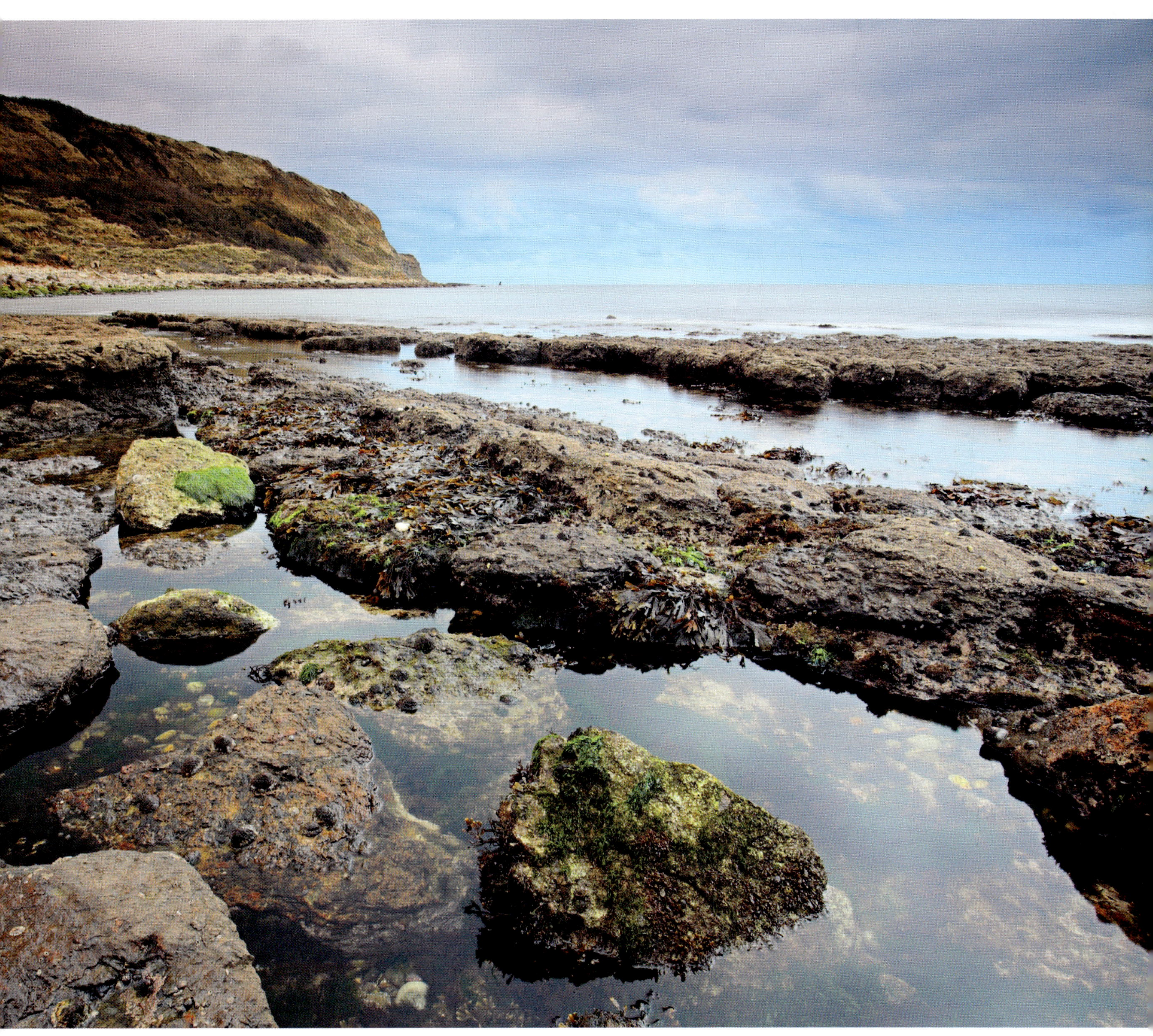

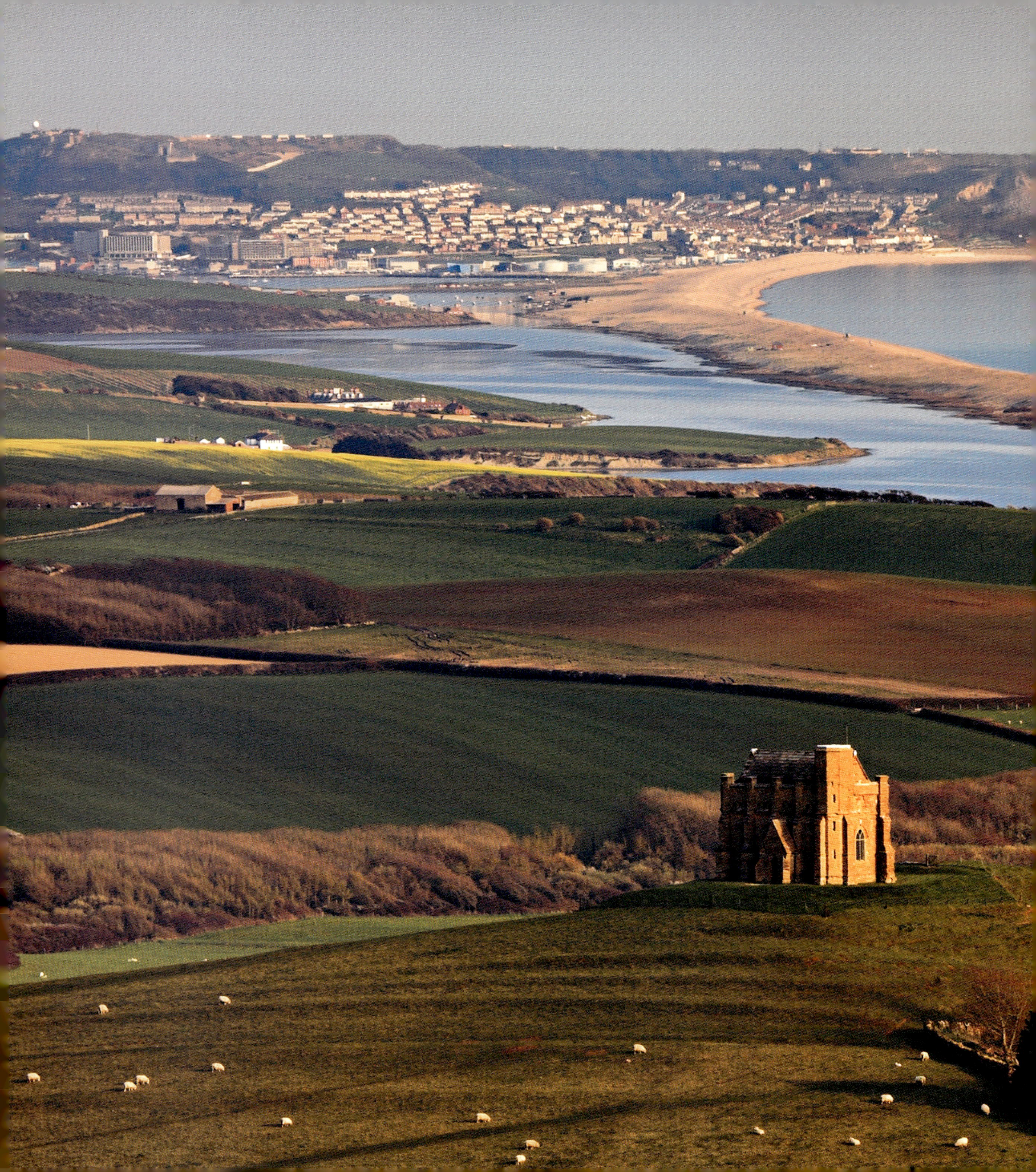

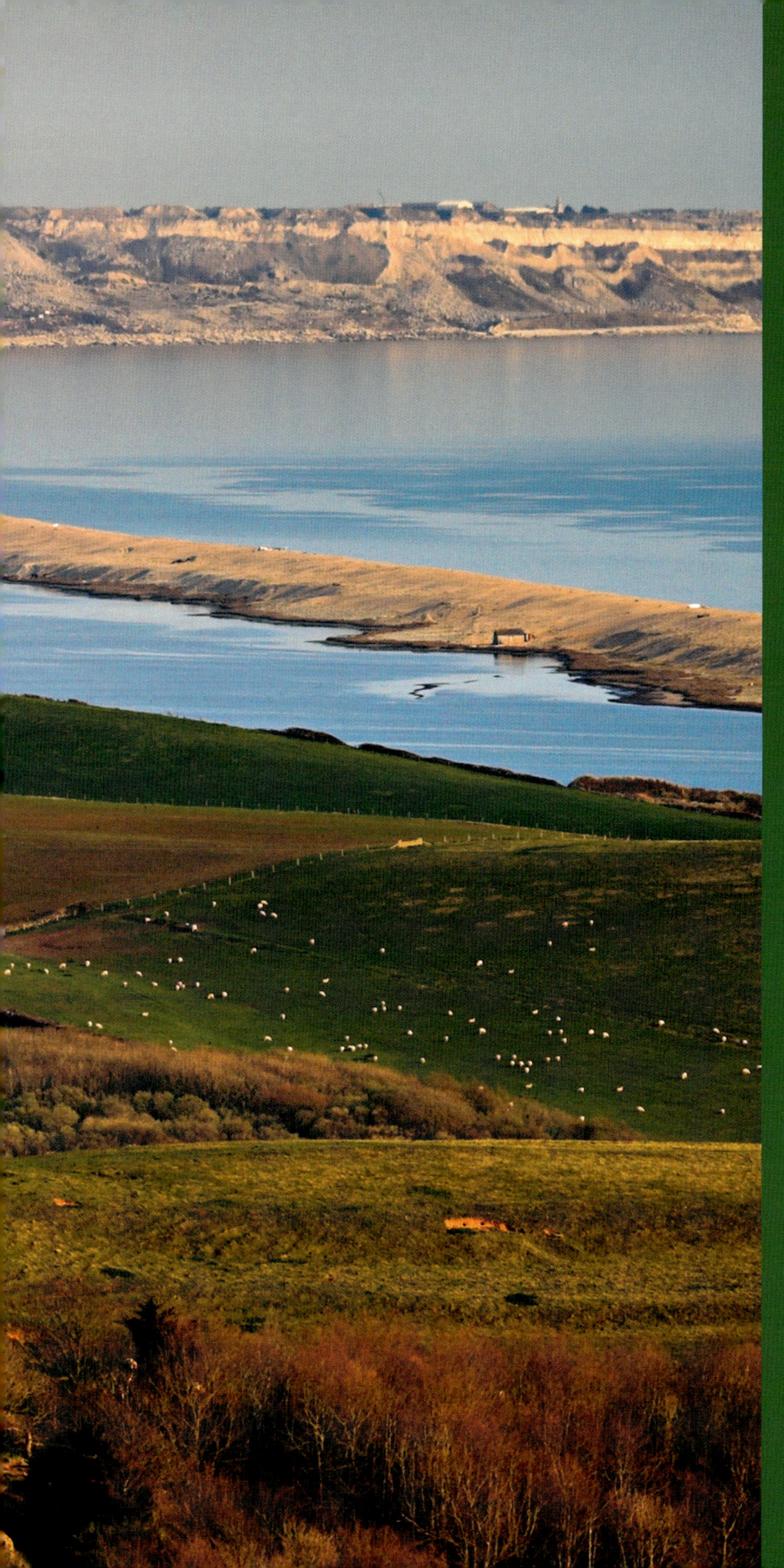

Portland and Chesil Beach

Looking eastwards from the hill above Abbotsbury towards St Catherine's Chapel and then over to Chesil Beach and Portland. In recent years voters in a national competition rated this scene as Britain's third best view.

Church Ope Cove

A small rocky inlet on Portland's east coast, Church Ope Cove was once a famous smuggling beach. Nowadays, it is a favourite location for beach huts, with many dotted around the pebbly beach.

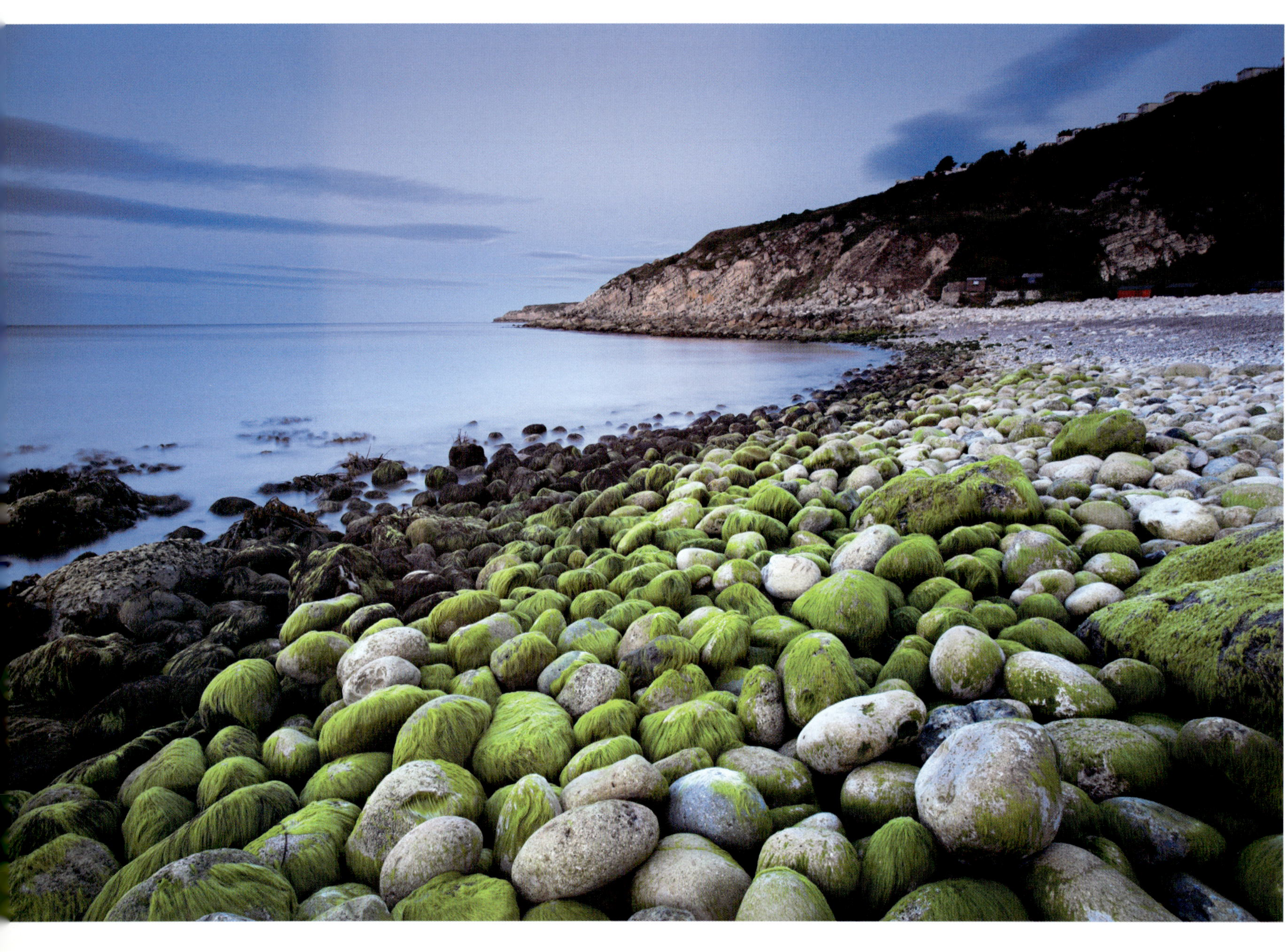

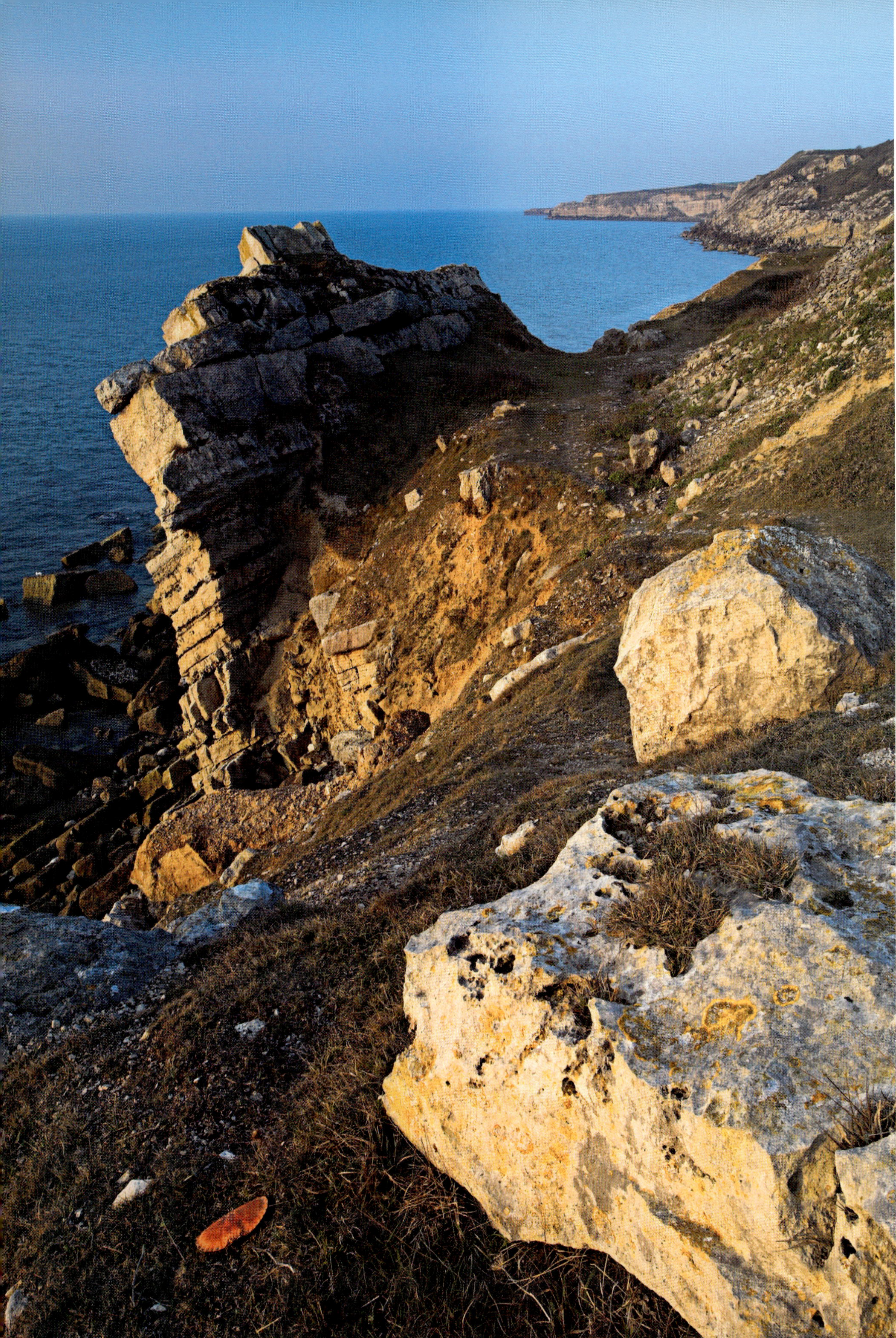

The clifftops on Portland's eastern coast are low but very jagged and crumbly. On the grass here lies the shell of a crab, no doubt discarded by a gull after eating its breakfast!

Algae-covered limestone pebbles can make a hazardous entrance to the water for bathers at Church Ope. Nevertheless, this cove can make a pleasant alternative day trip for beachgoers looking to get away from the hordes at nearby Weymouth.

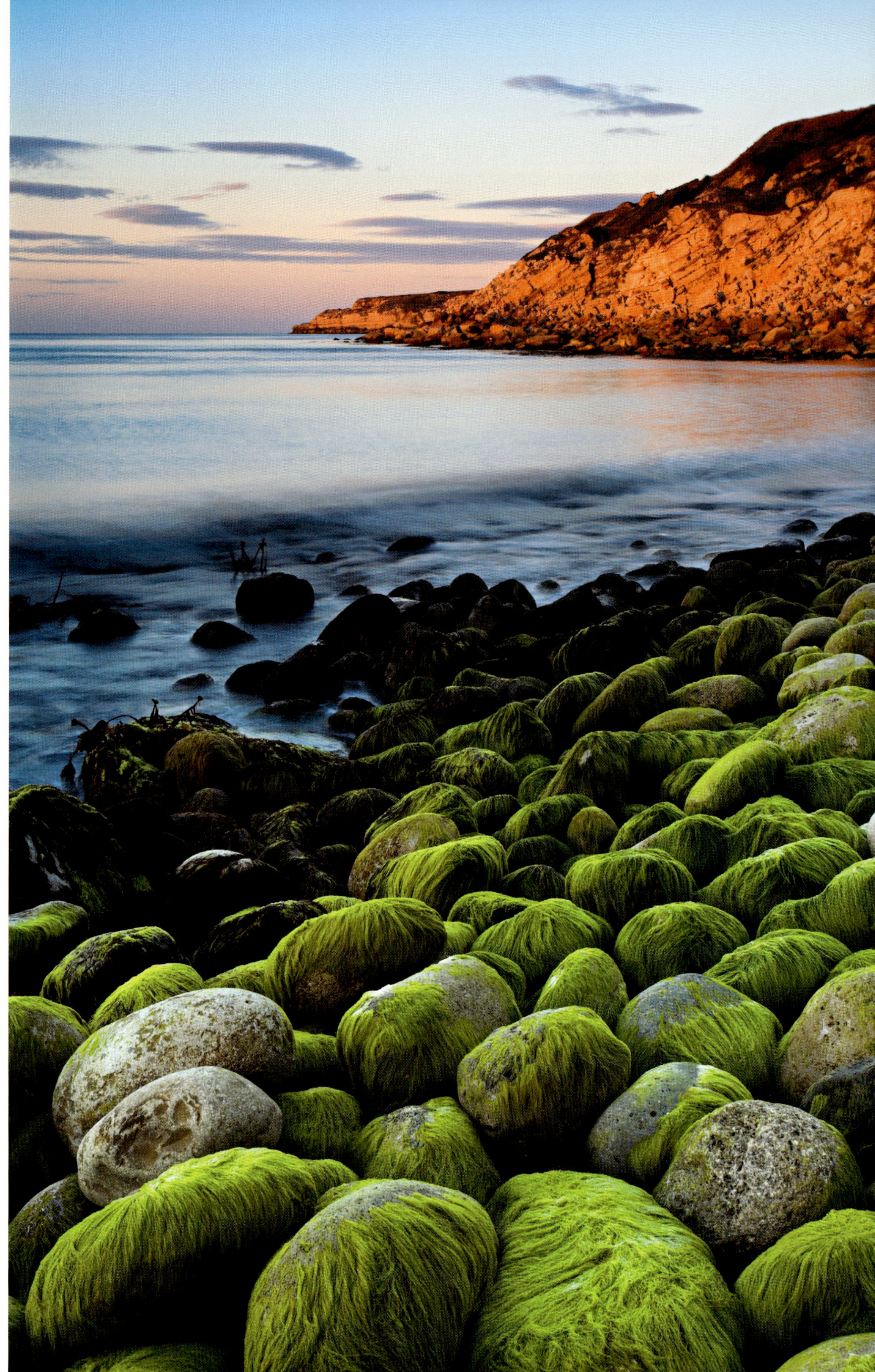

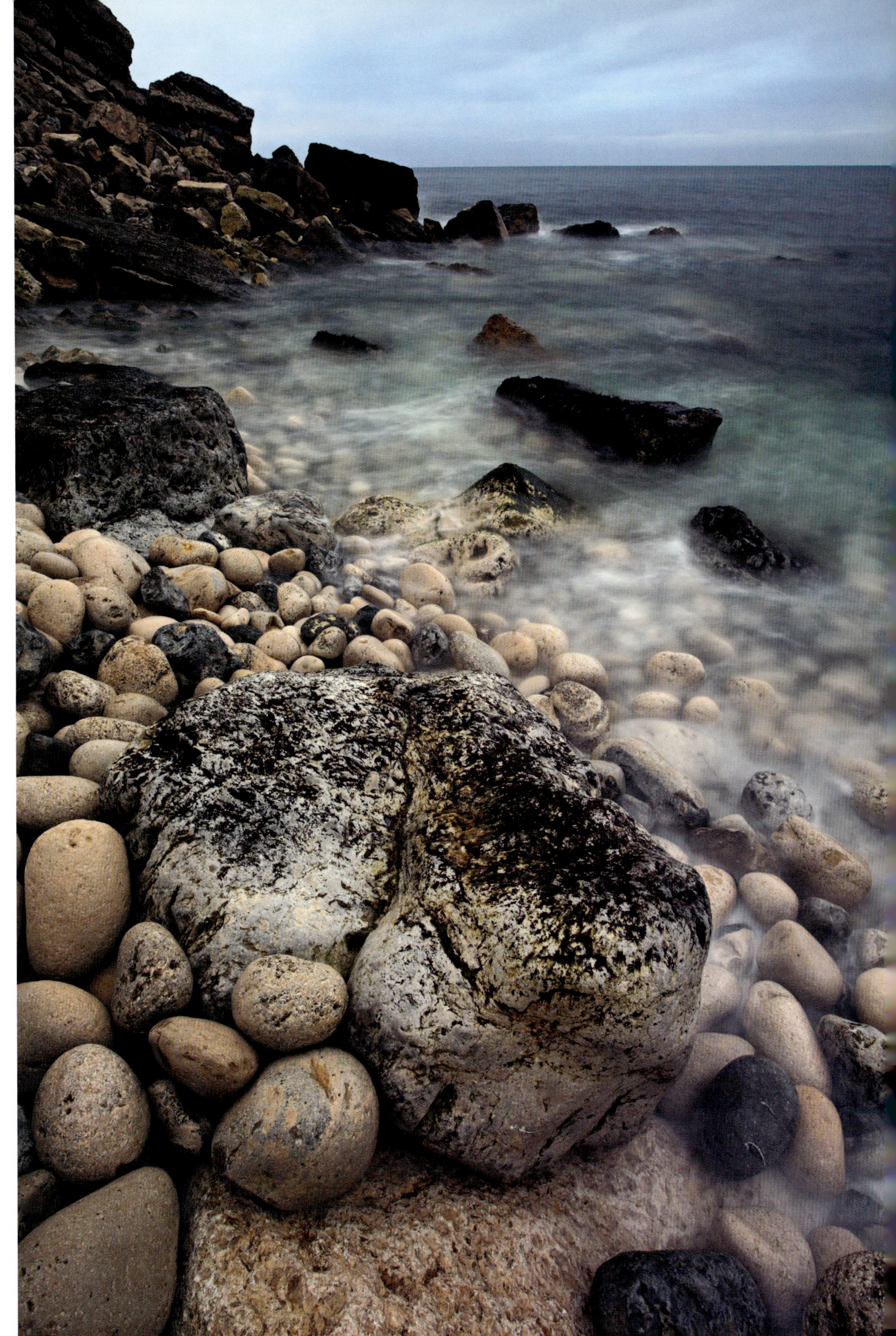

The large pebbles of Church Ope Cove are continuously sculpted by the sea into a variety of oval shapes.

Portland Bill

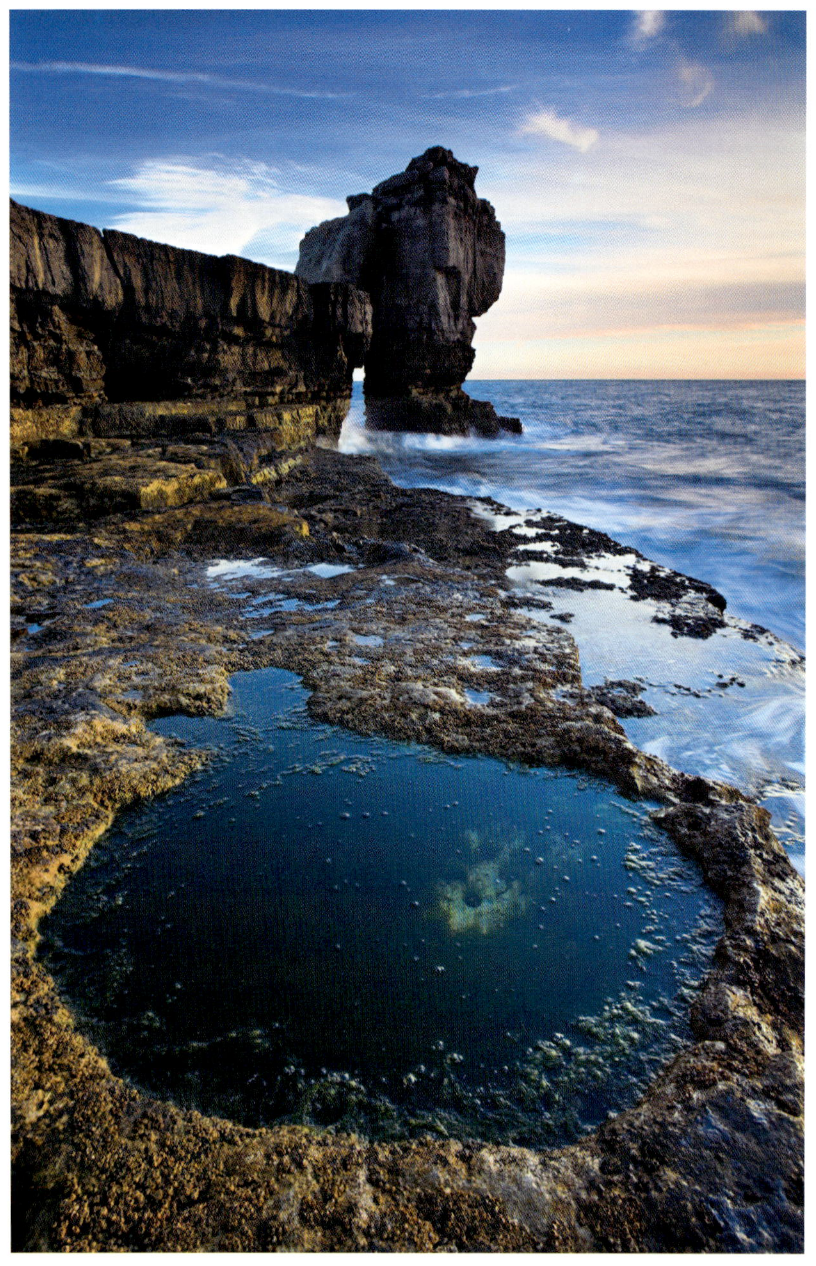

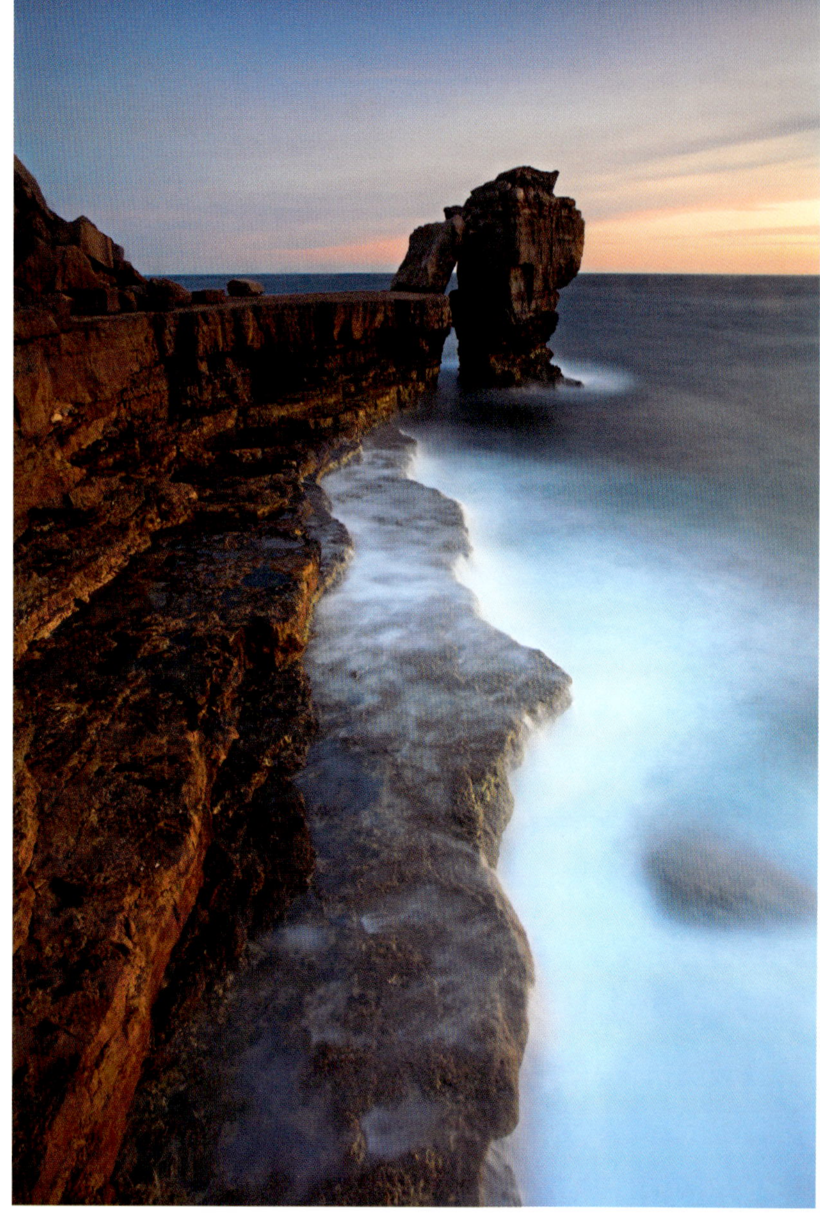

The lower ledges at Portland Bill should only be walked by the courageous or foolhardy! Due to its exposed position Portland Bill can be subjected to rough sea at any time of year. At these times lower ledge rockpools, no matter how appealing, are best avoided for the safety of the clifftops.

At first sight one could be forgiven for thinking the elements had carved the Pulpit Rock sea stack. While the sea no doubt continues to shape the rock, it was originally hewn from the nearby cliffs by men working the Beacon Quarry around 1875.

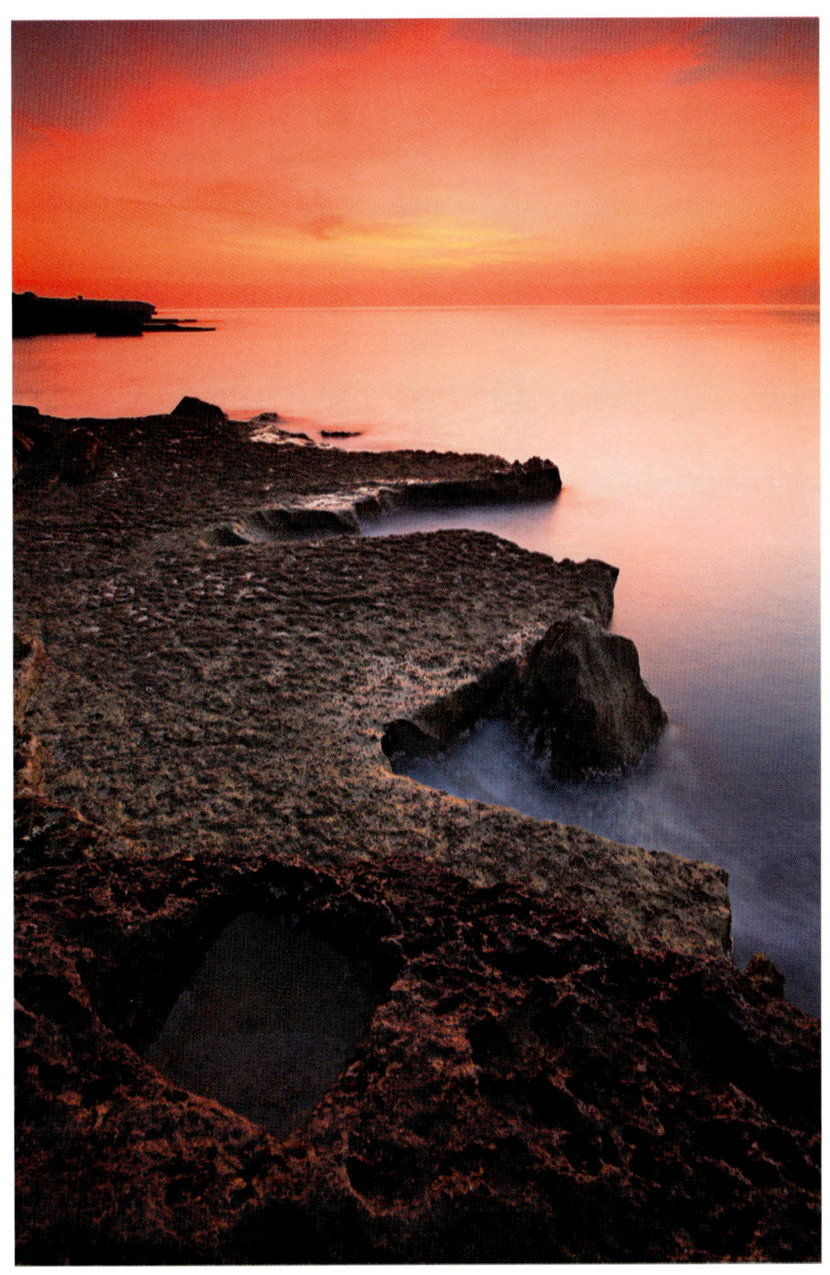 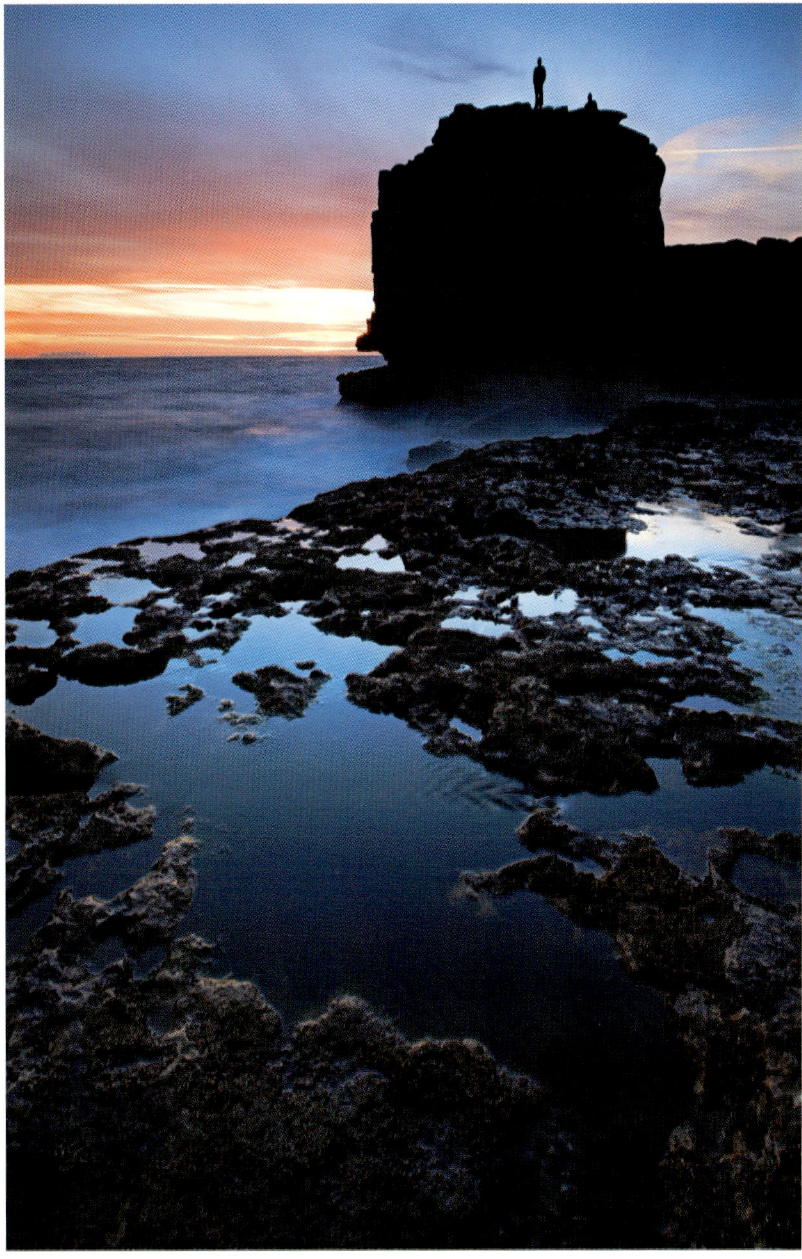

At its northern end Portland towers over the mainland with cliffs dominating over Chesil Beach far below. However, as the island stretches southward, the gradient gently decreases until at Portland Bill the clifftop ledges finally slip beneath the sea.

Portland Bill lays claim to be the most southerly part of both Dorset and the Jurassic Coast World Heritage Site. Stretching far into the English Channel, it even surpasses the most southerly tip of the Isle of Wight. At its most southerly point stands the famous landmark, Pulpit Rock.

Fishing boats lie safe from the tide on top of the low cliffs at Portland Bill. Cranes erected on the clifftops provide the only means of lowering the boats and fishermen into the water.

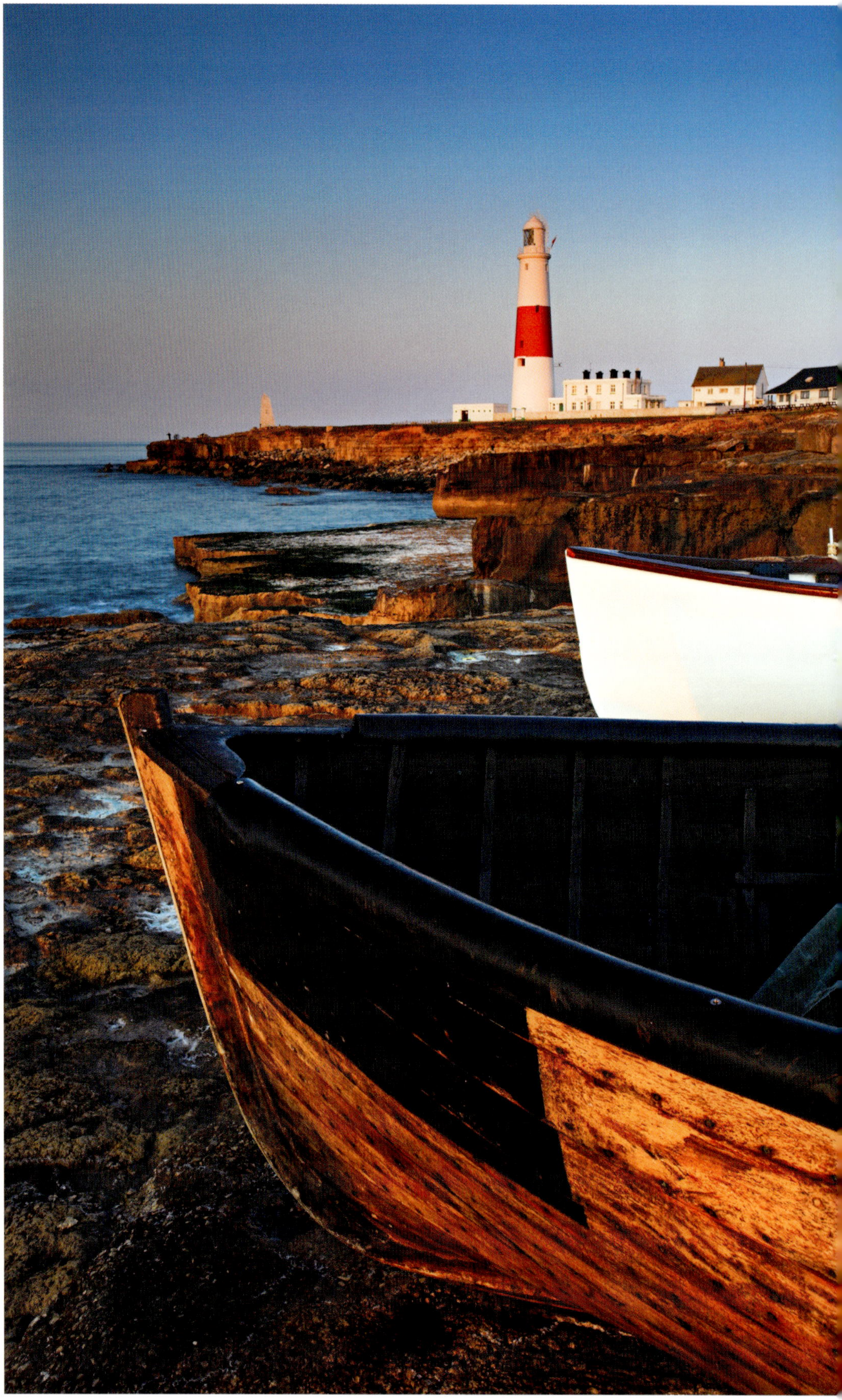

Reflections of the present Portland Bill lighthouse captured on a sunny summer's morning.

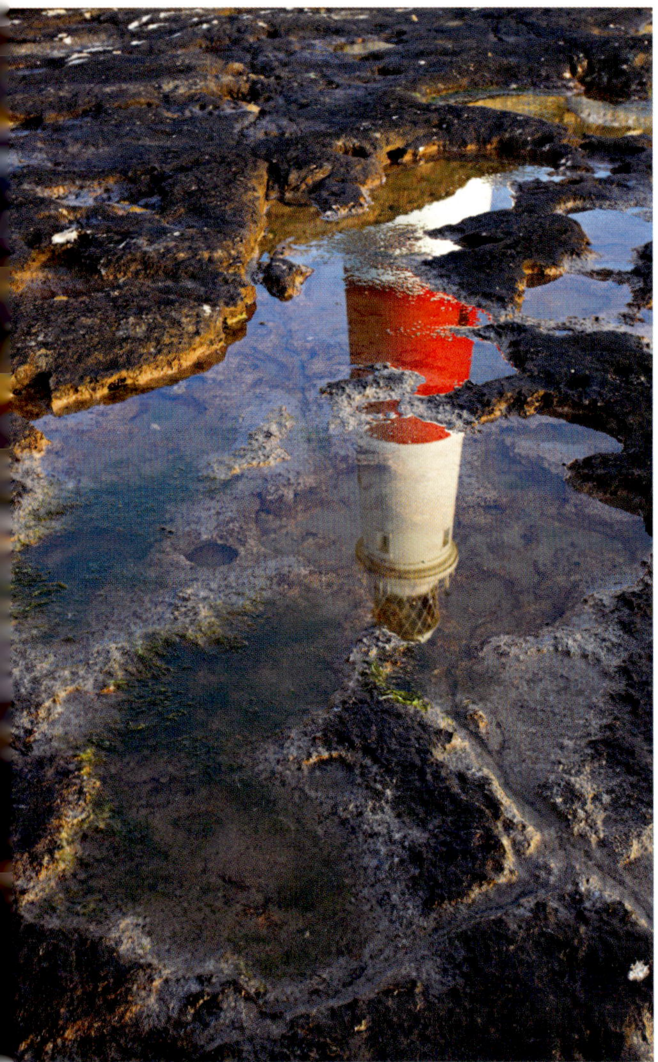

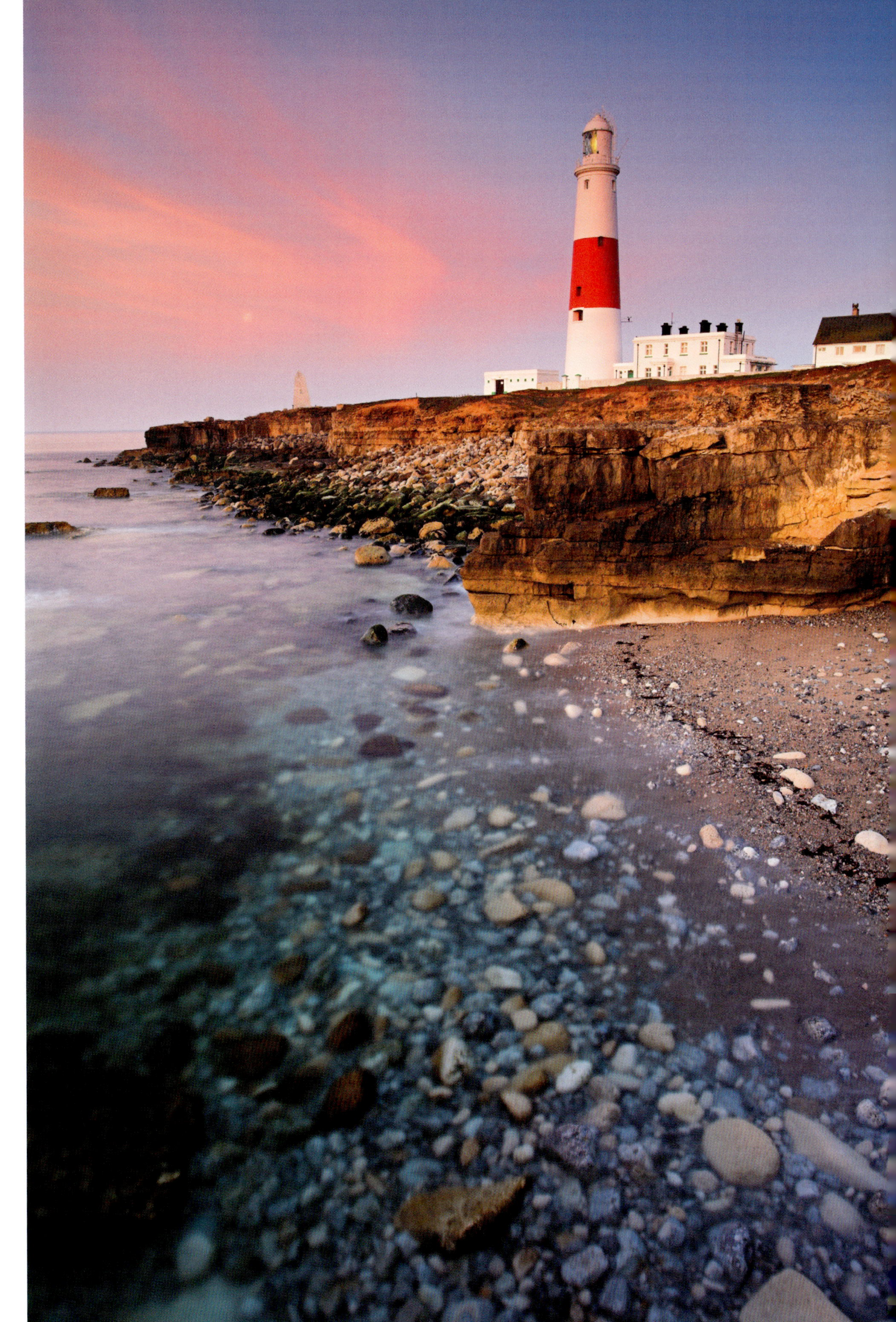

Built in 1906 and now fully automated, the red and white banded lighthouse at Portland Bill is the third of its kind to have occupied this location.

West Weares

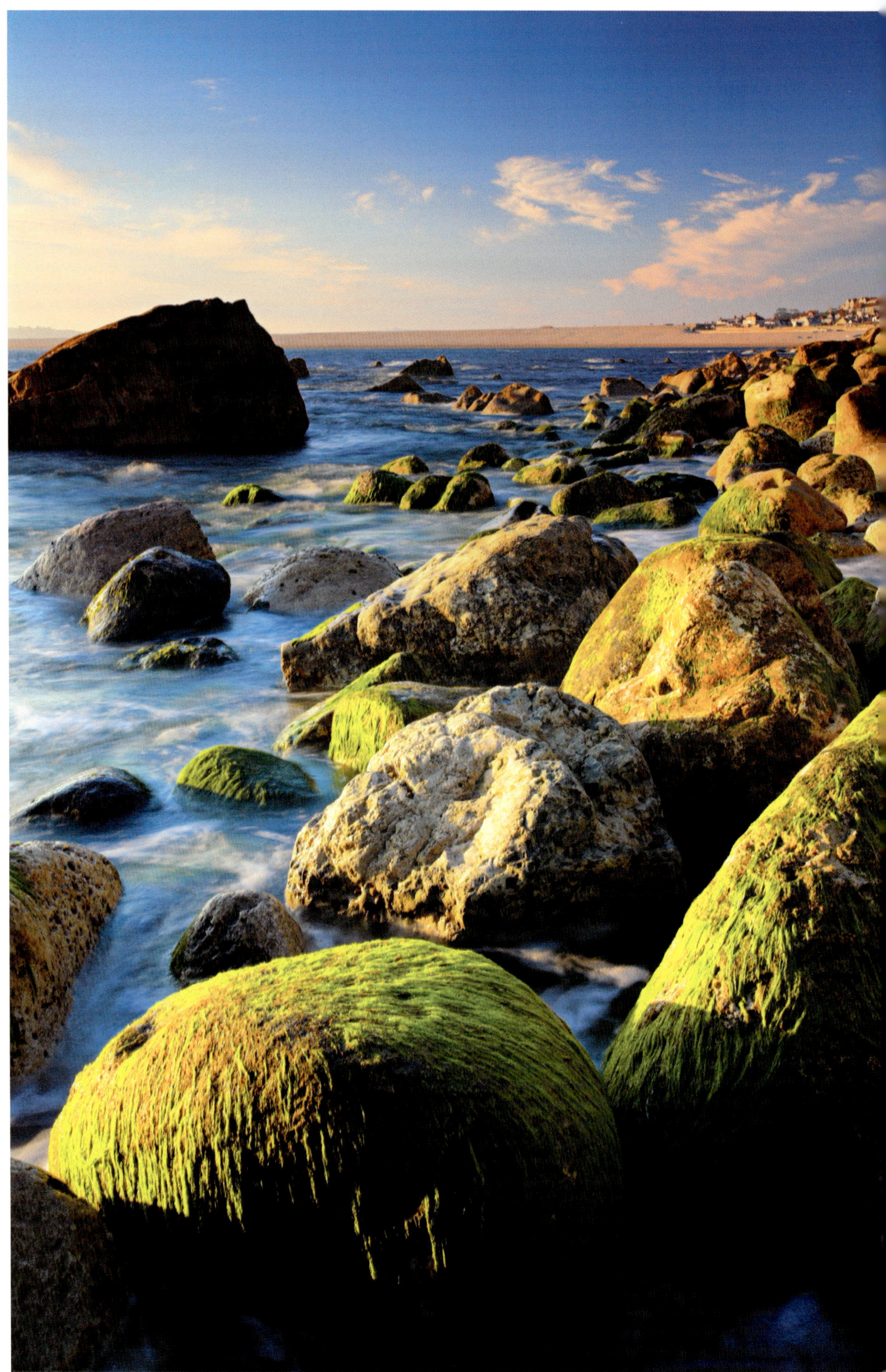

Boulder-fronted shore at the base of the cliffs at West Weares on Portland's west coast. In the distance the steep Chesil Beach begins near the town of Chiswell.

Chesil Beach

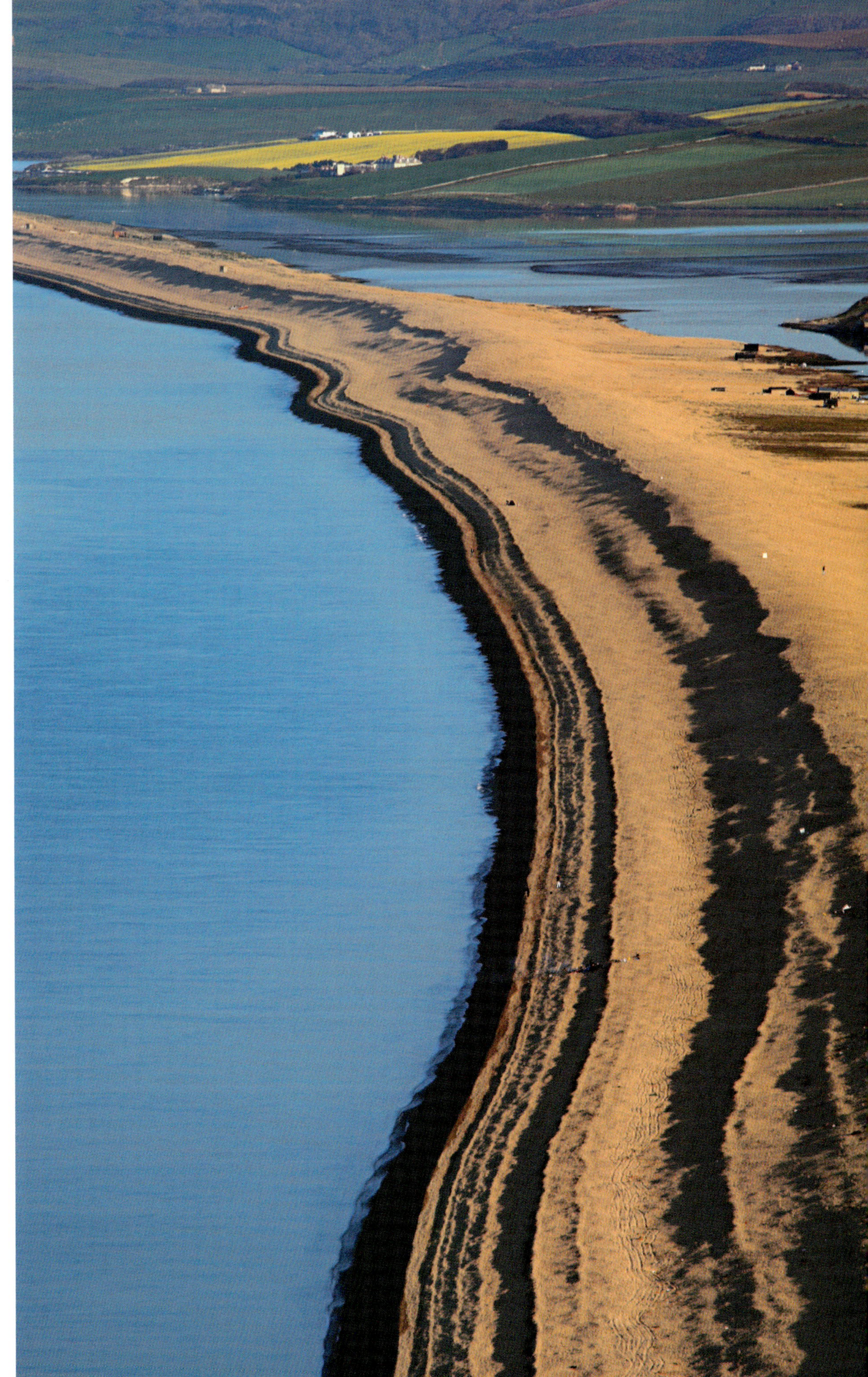

From Portland Heights, the elevated view along Chesil Beach is breathtaking. For much of its 18-mile length the shingle beach is separated from the mainland by a lagoon named The Fleet.

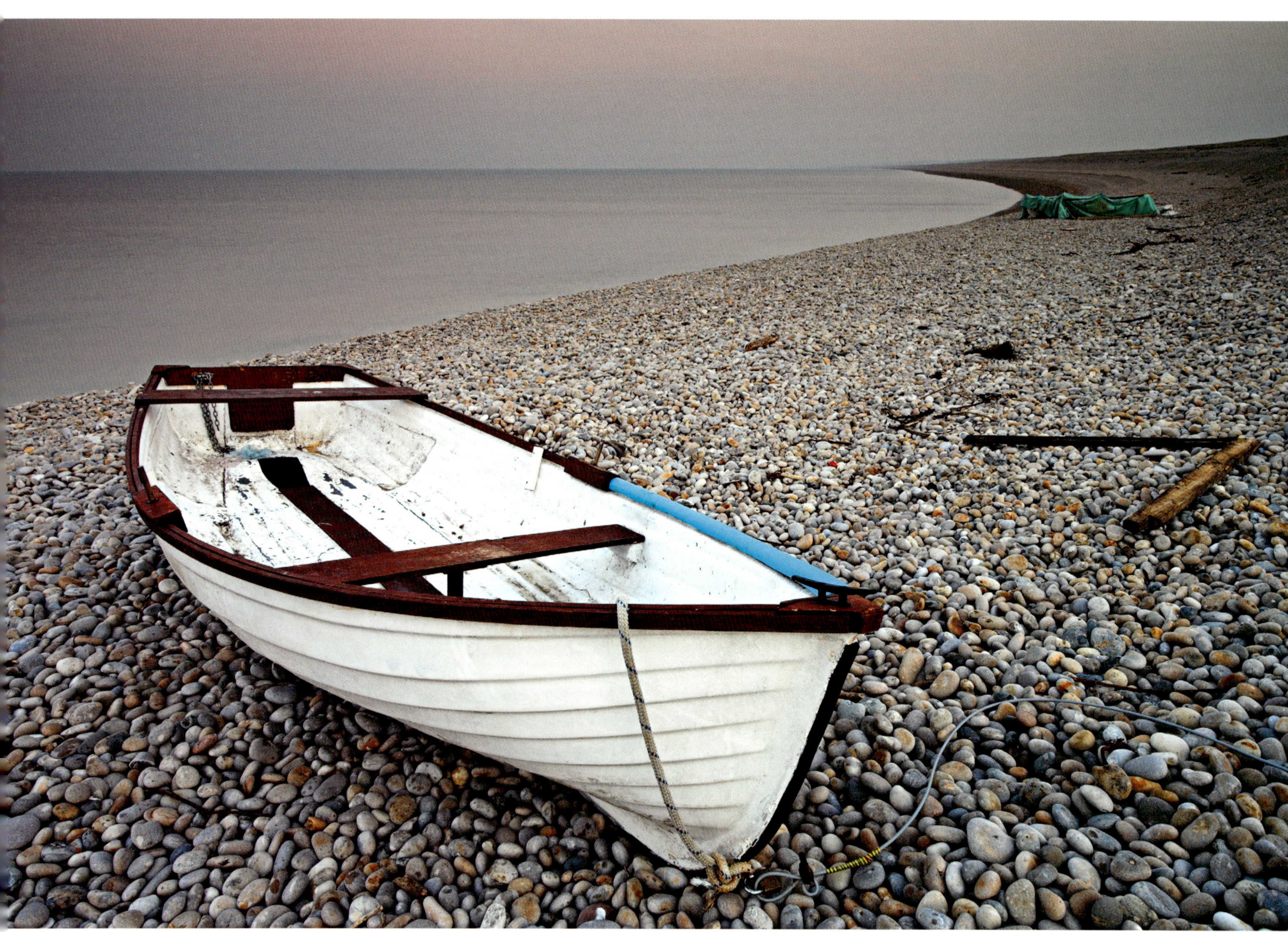

A small fishing boat safely pulled up high
on the shingle bank at Chesil Cove.

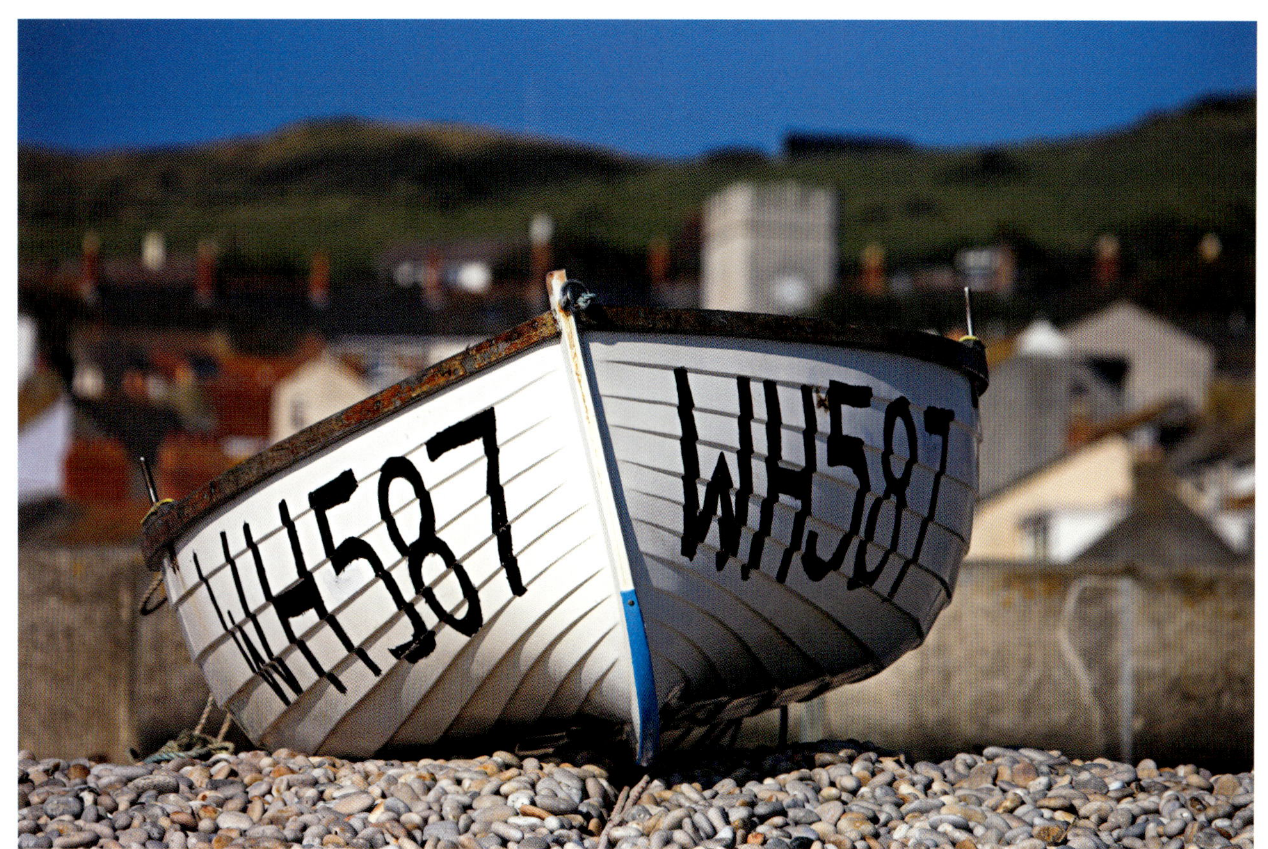

Small fishing boat safely ashore on Chesil Beach, with the town of Chiswell behind.

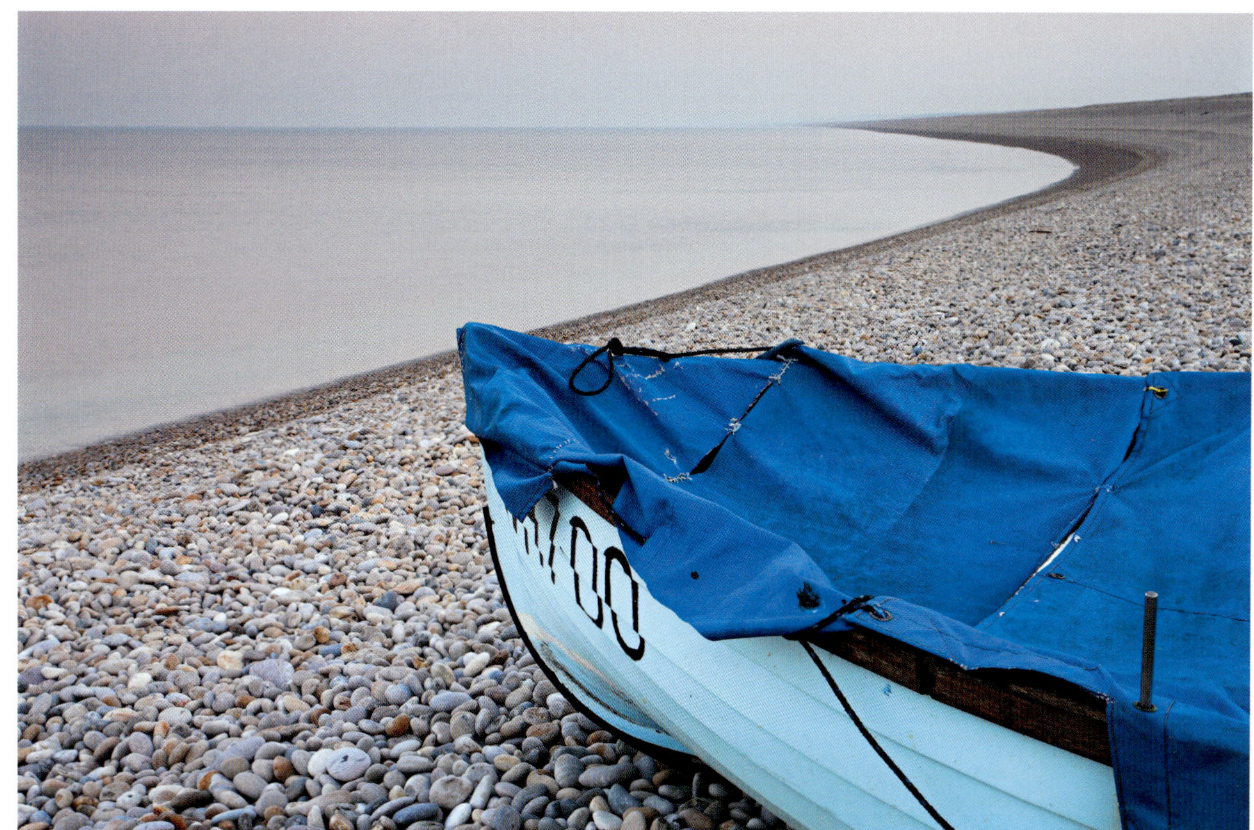

Fishing is a very popular sport in this area with fisherman busy on the edge of the shore until late into the night and others to be seen early in the morning. From these locations many species may be caught with bass, cod, eels, garfish, gurnard, mackerel, plaice, pollack, pout, smoothhounds, sole and whiting regularly found depending on the time of year.

Although jogging might prove tricky on these pebbles, the beach is enjoyed by many dog walkers, ramblers, fishermen and tourists throughout the year.

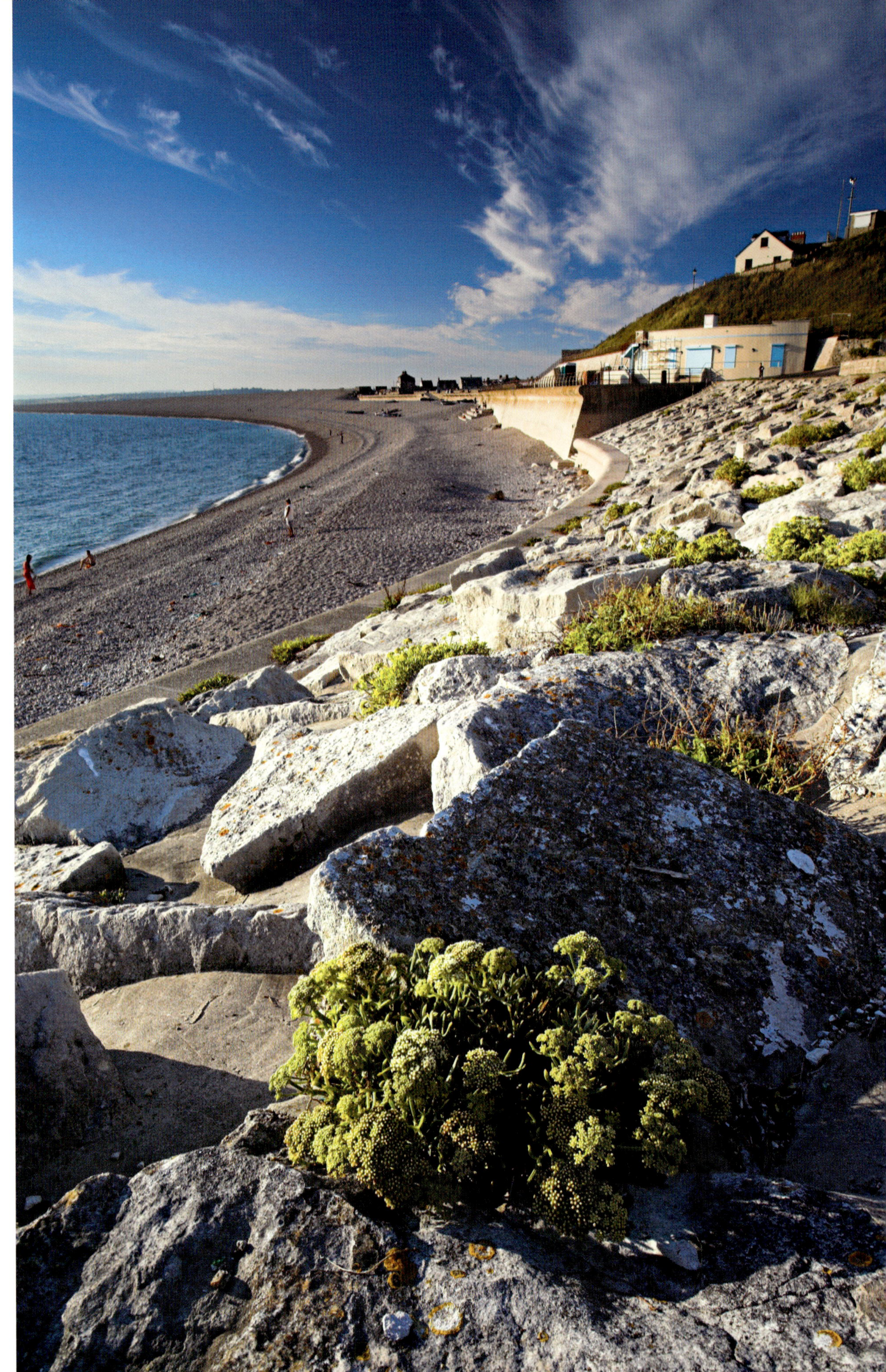

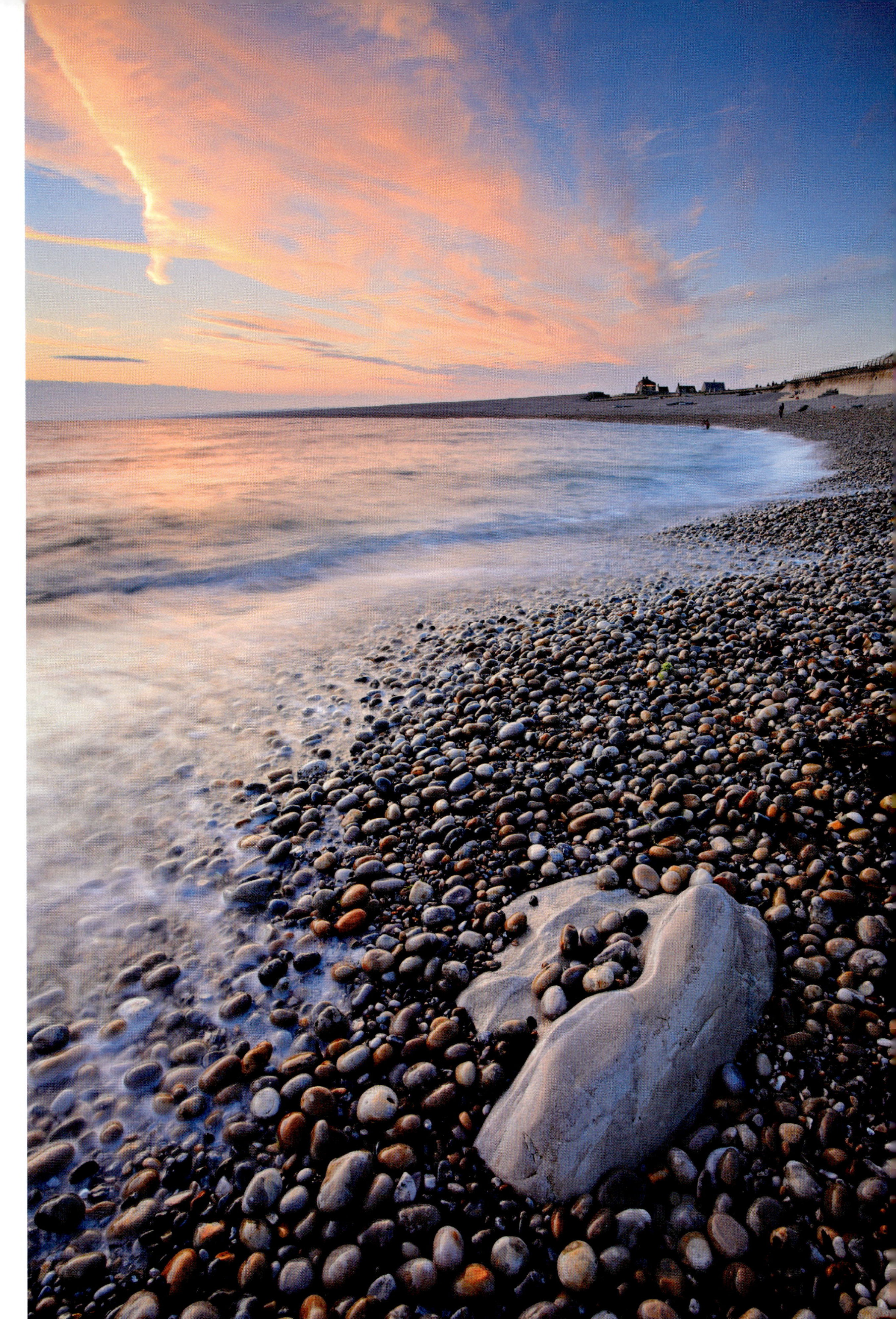

At its far eastern end, near the town of Fortuneswell, Chesil Beach bends suddenly and abruptly stops where the Portland coast begins.

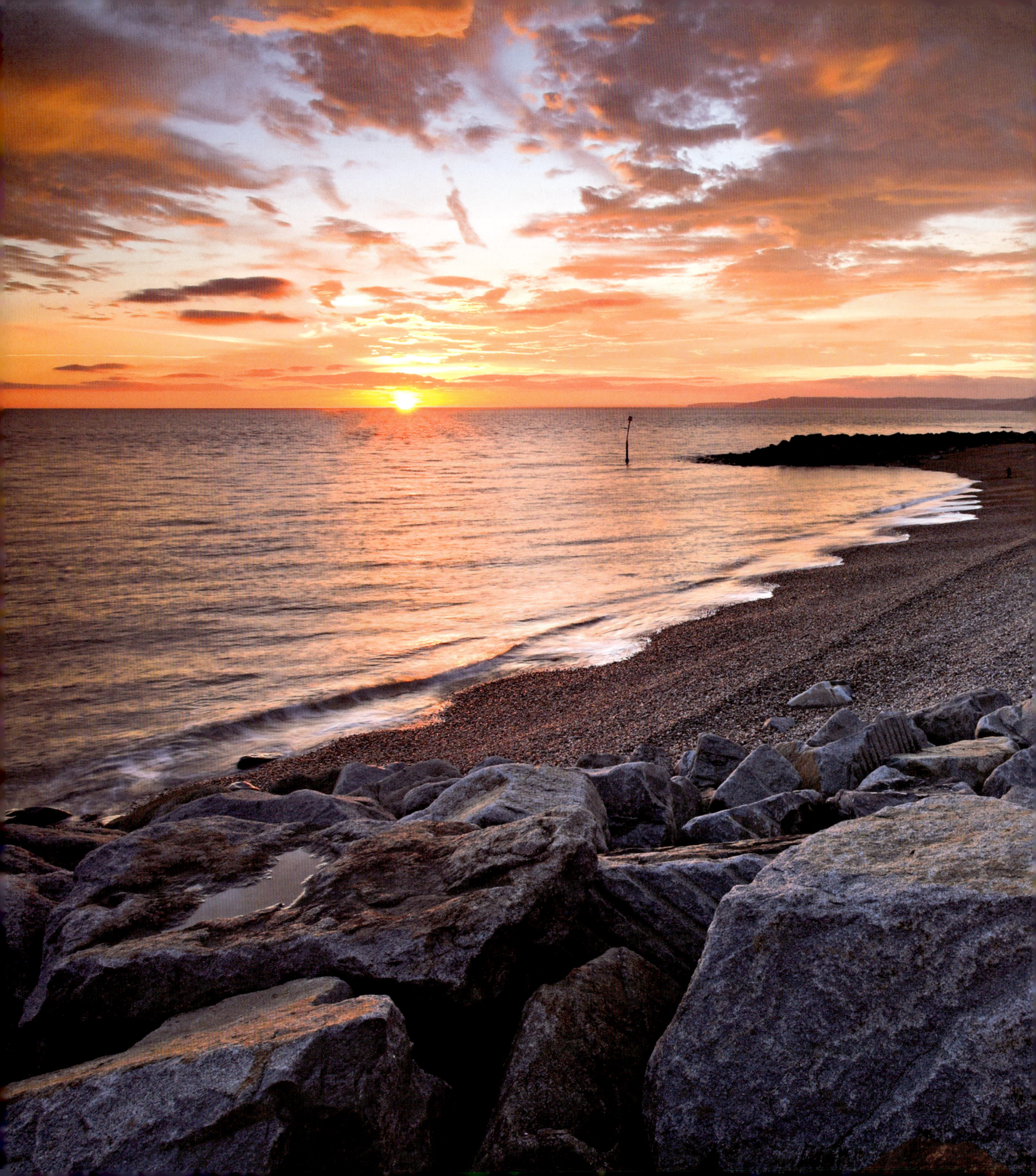

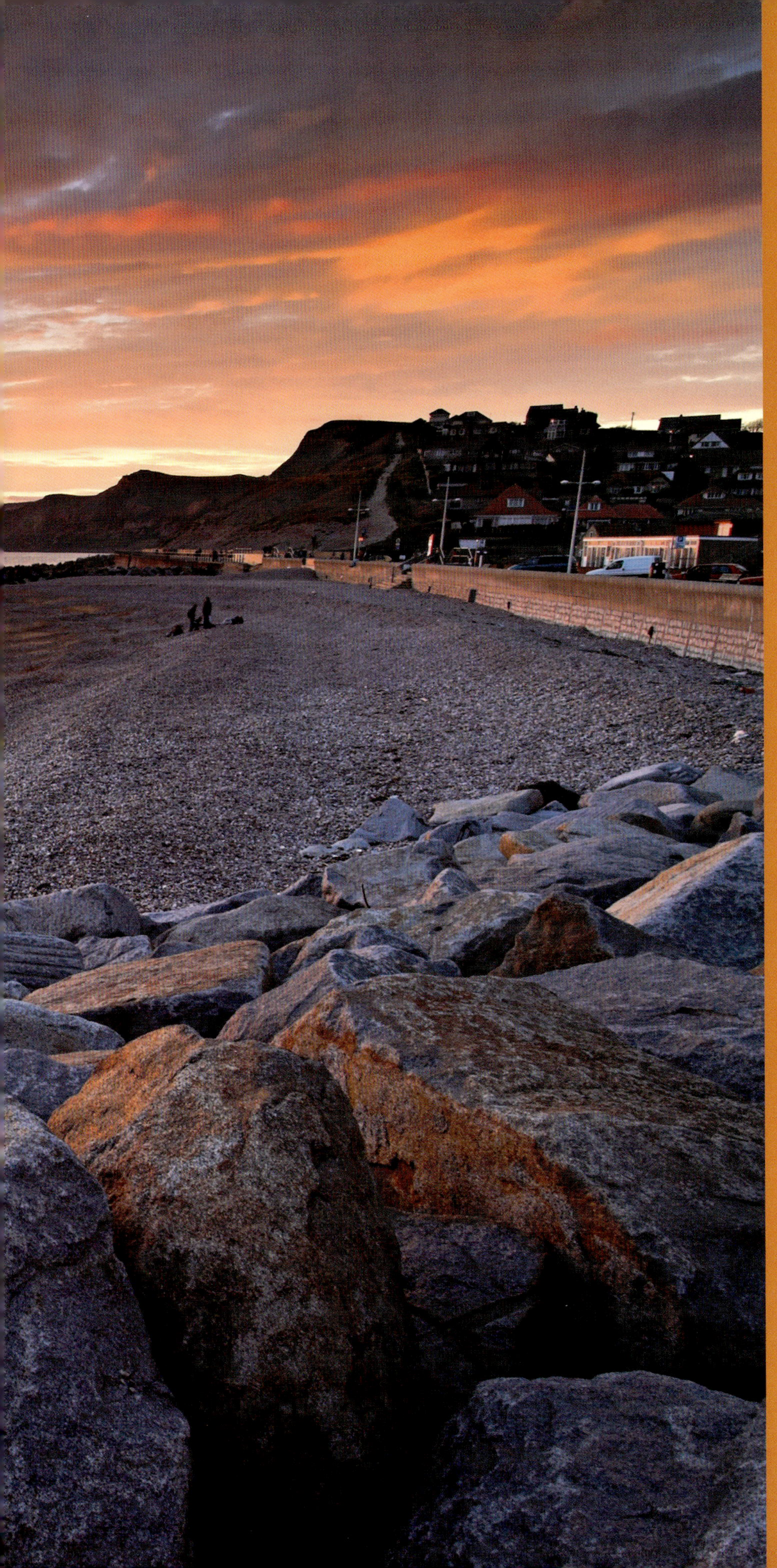

Burton Bradstock to Lyme Regis

A spectacular sunset descends over the western horizon at West Bay.

Burton Bradstock

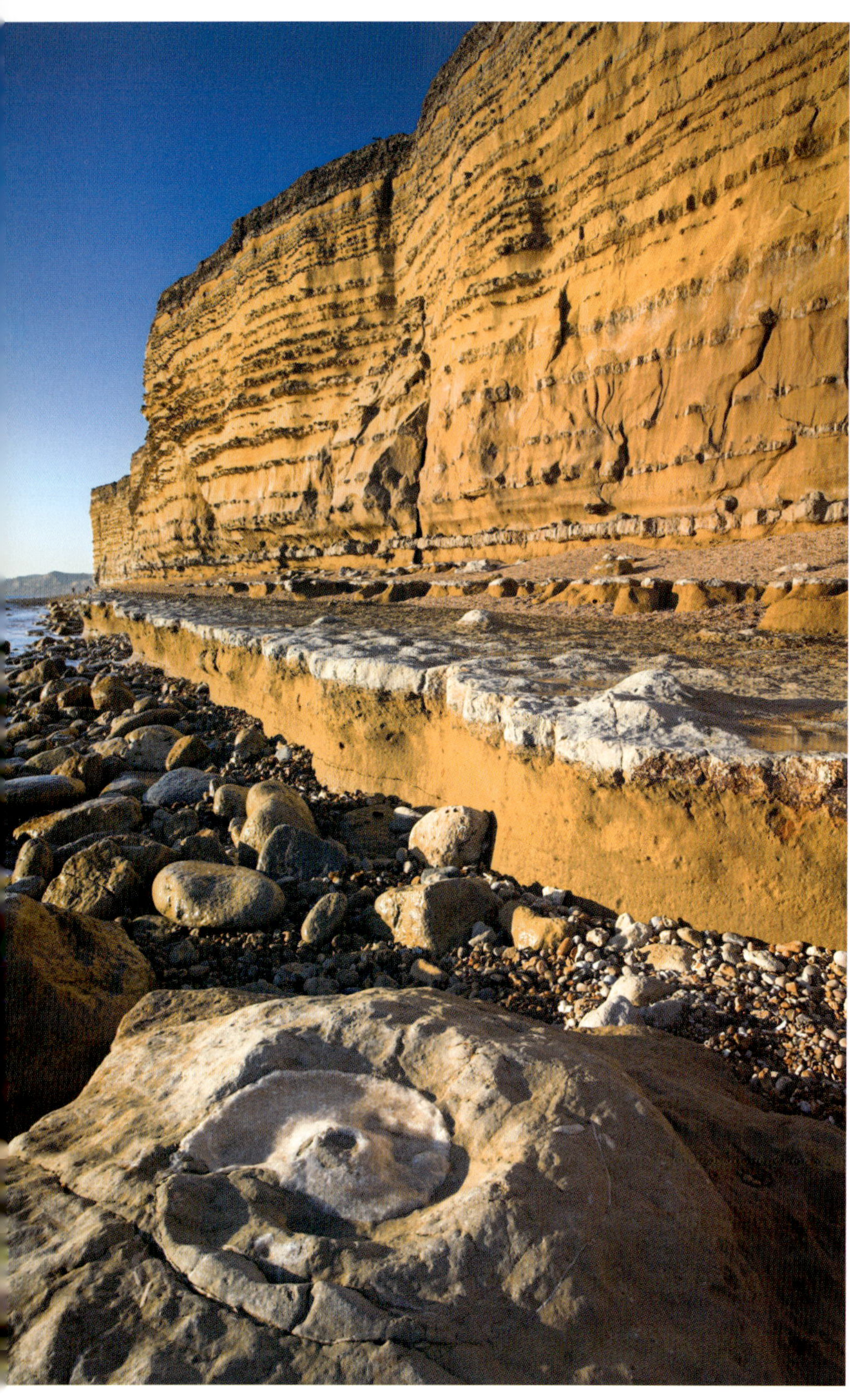

Exposed at low tide, the fossilised remains of an ammonite embedded in the rock at Burton Bradstock.

The unusual shapes on this beach are formed by pebbles becoming lodged in the rock. Over time the continual wave action causes the pebbles to create these large holes.

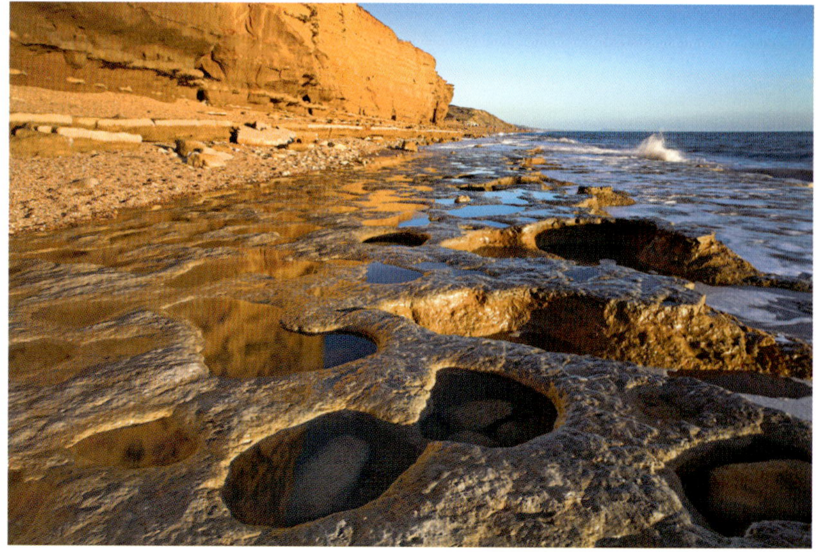

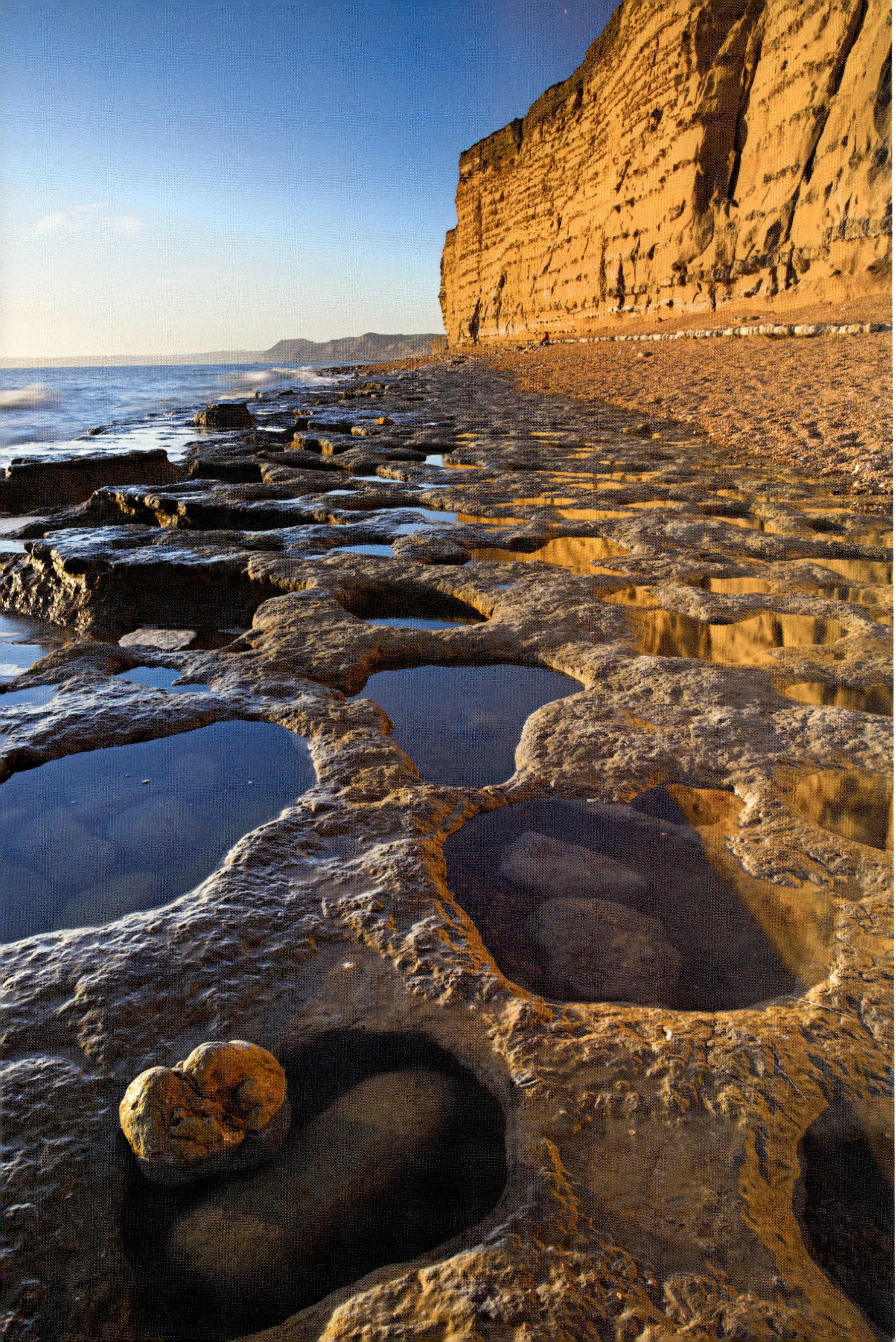

On a sunny late winter afternoon the yellow sandstone cliffs and ledges at Burton Bradstock turn golden in colour. The cliffs here and those at nearby West Bay are unlike any others on the Dorset coastline, bearing more resemblance to parts of the Australian coast than that of England.

West Bay

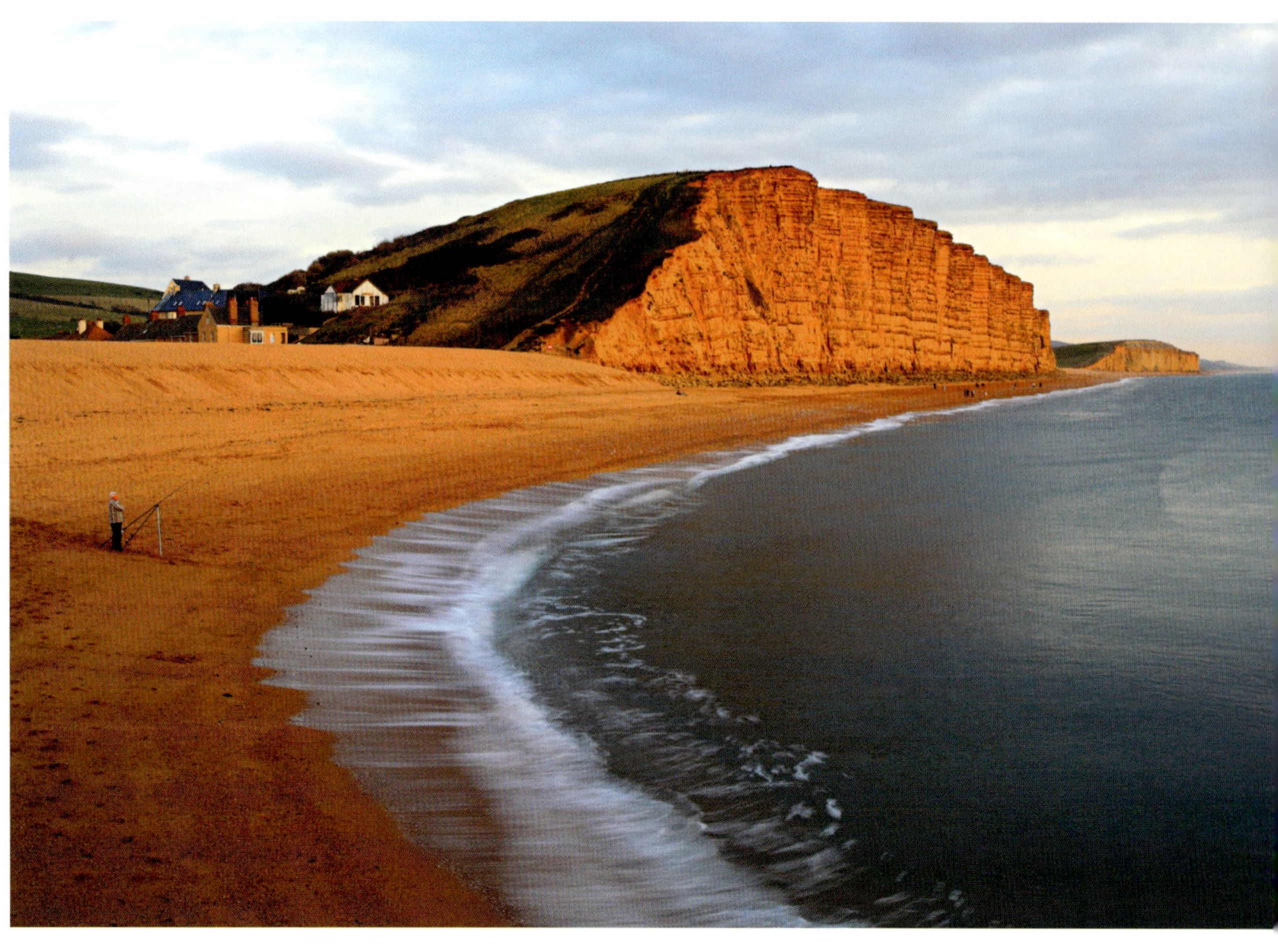

To the west of West Bay's harbour, the beach consists of small pebbles. To prevent longshore drift, several large stone groynes have been erected along the western coast.

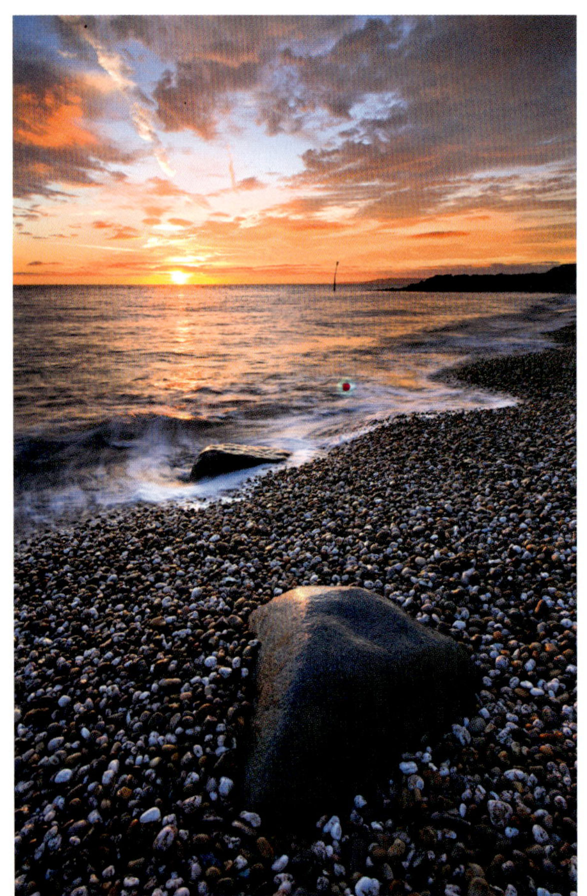

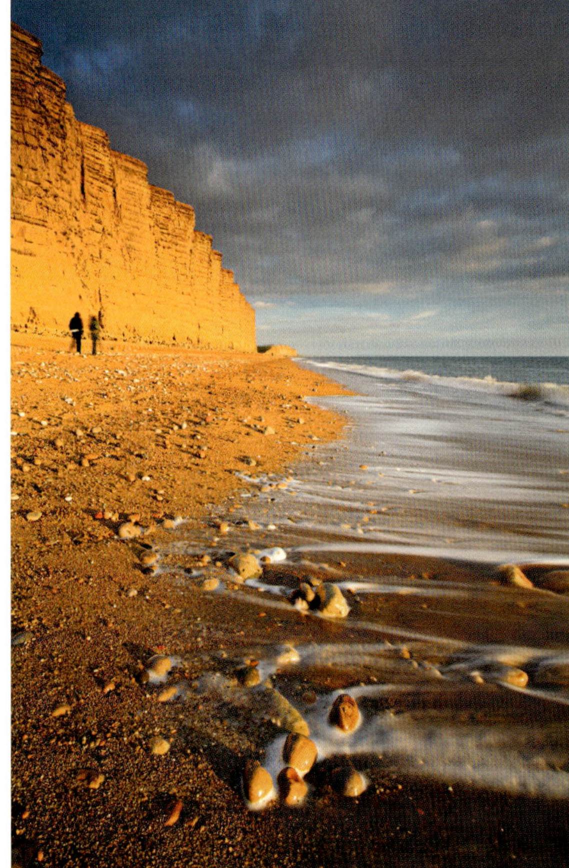

A lone fisherman contemplates his catch on the beach at West Bay. Behind, the towering vertical East Cliff stretches eastwards, and is matched in the far distance by Burton Cliff.

Walkers enjoy a stroll along the beach at the base of East Cliff.

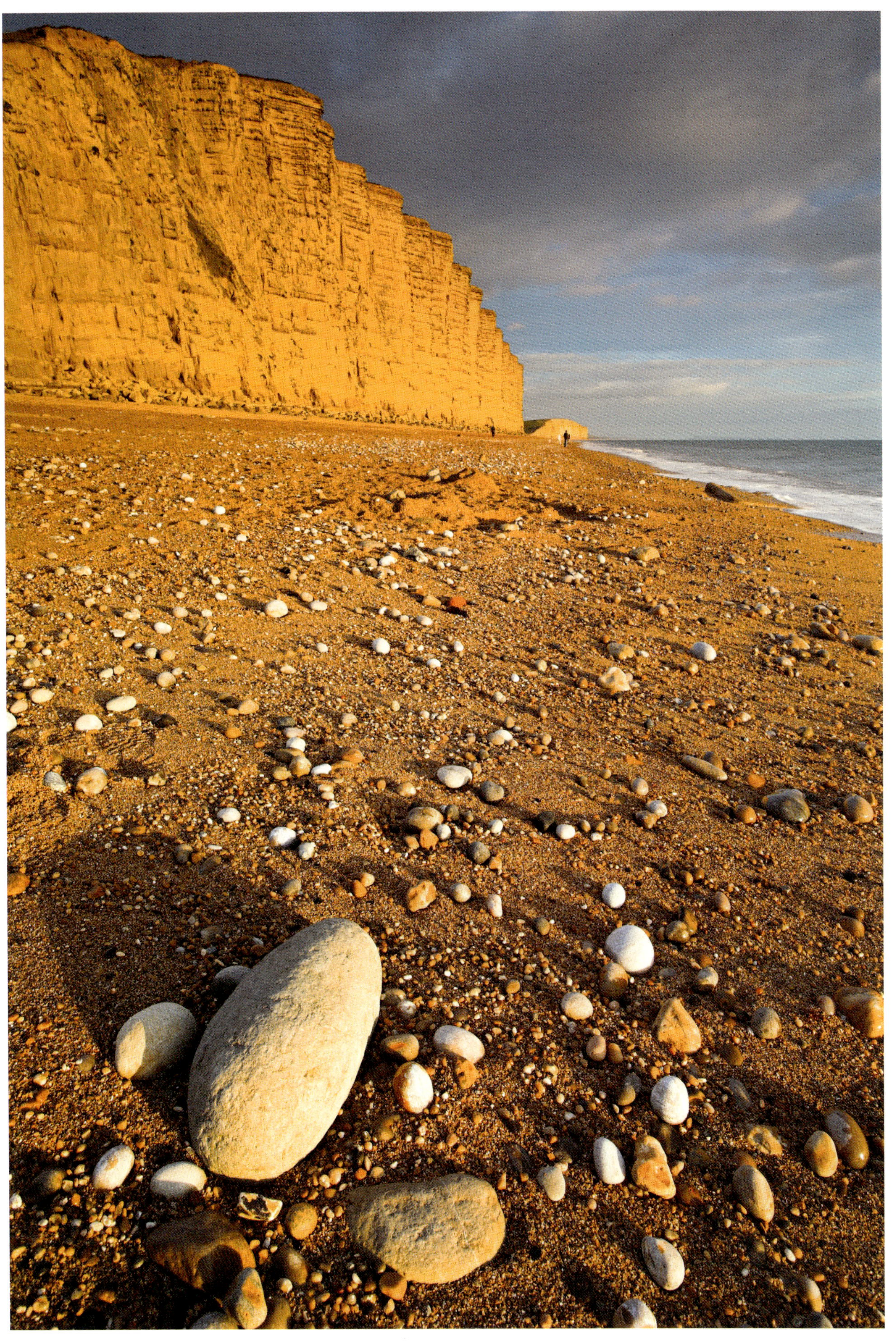

The sandstone cliffs here and at nearby Burton Cliff were used for training exercises in preparation for the Normandy D-Day landings. Troops arriving on the shore from assault landing craft scaled the vertical cliffs using rope ladders fired from rockets.

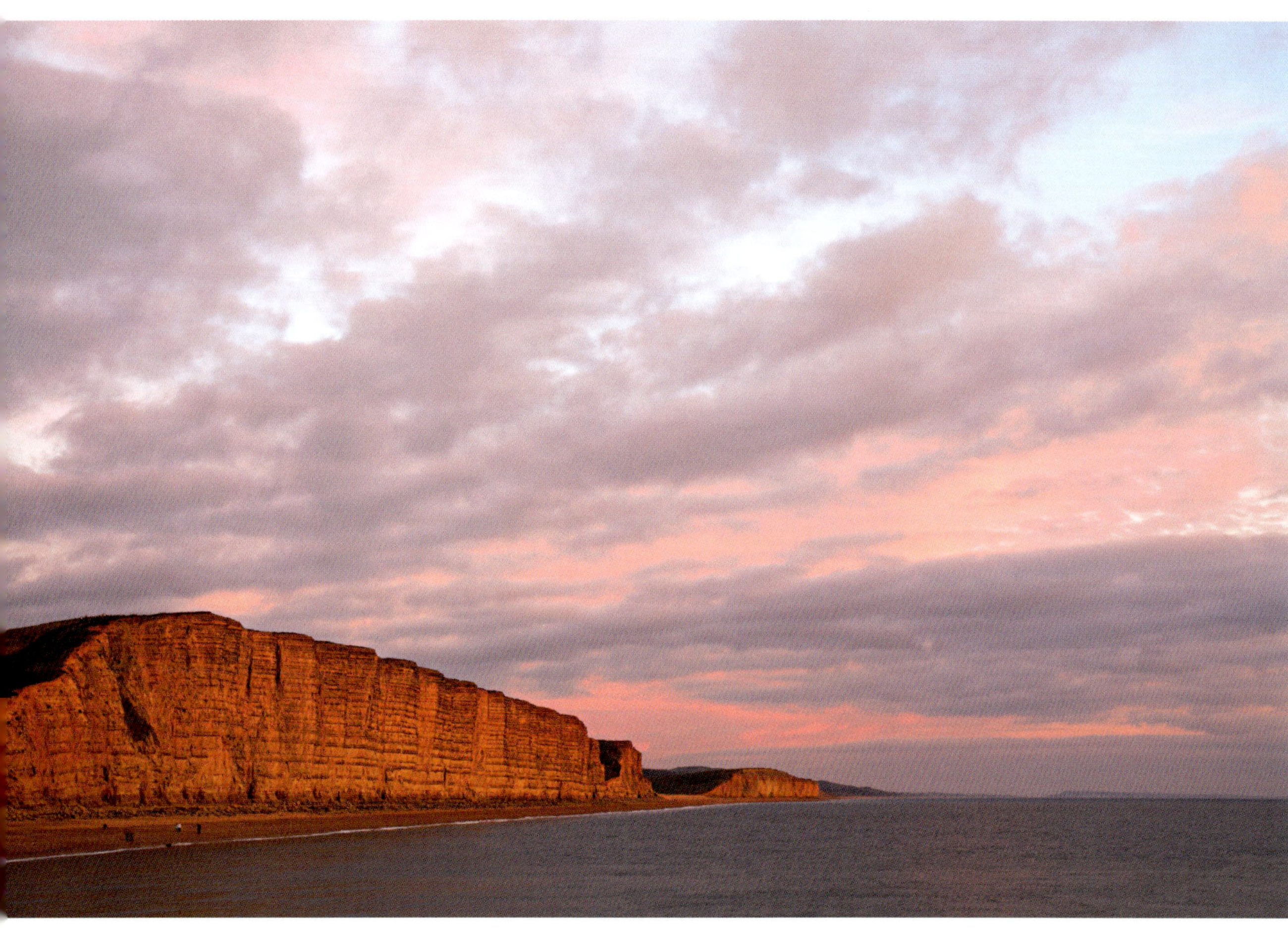

The impressive vertical East Cliff resembles a massive castle rampart wall, its strength proudly on display for all visiting this stretch of coast. Yet despite its origins as far back as the Jurassic period, in truth the yellow sandstone is soft rock which erodes very quickly.

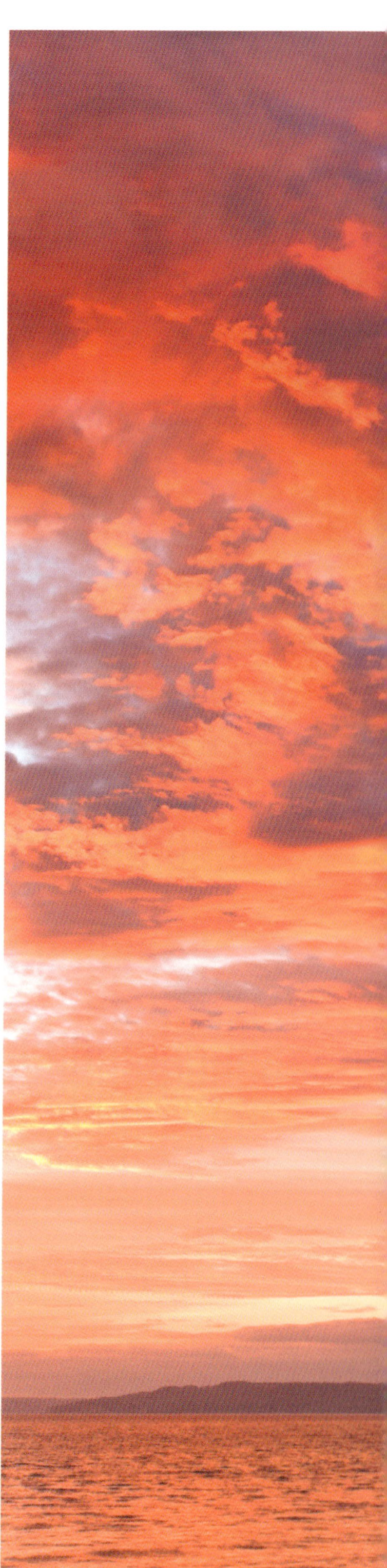

The evening skies above west Dorset put on a display of heavenly colour to the delight of tourists on West Bay's pier.

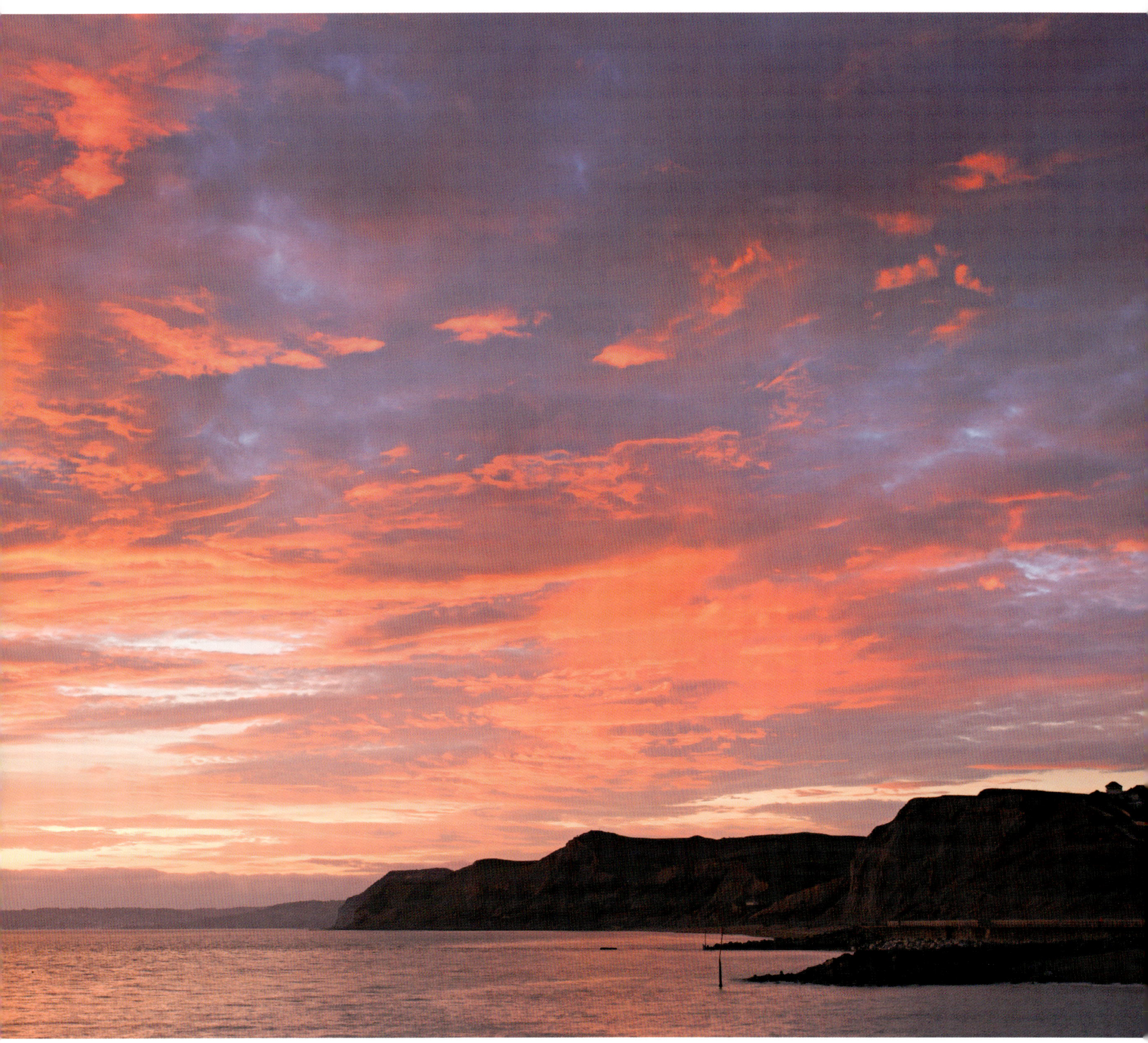

Eype

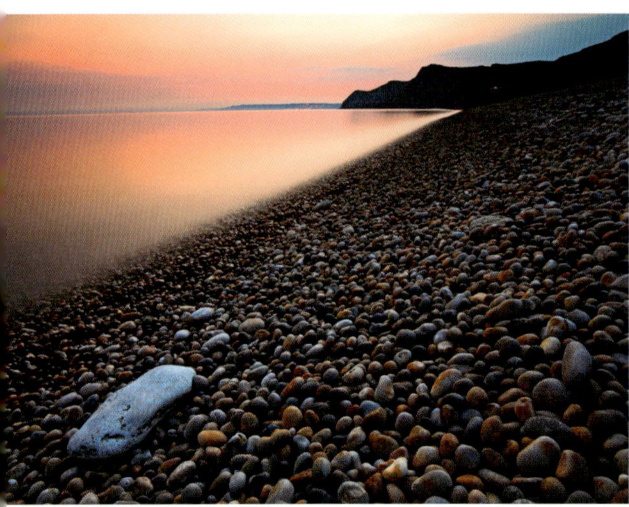

The steep pebbly beach welcomes ethereal mirror-like sea conditions on this early summer evening at Eype.

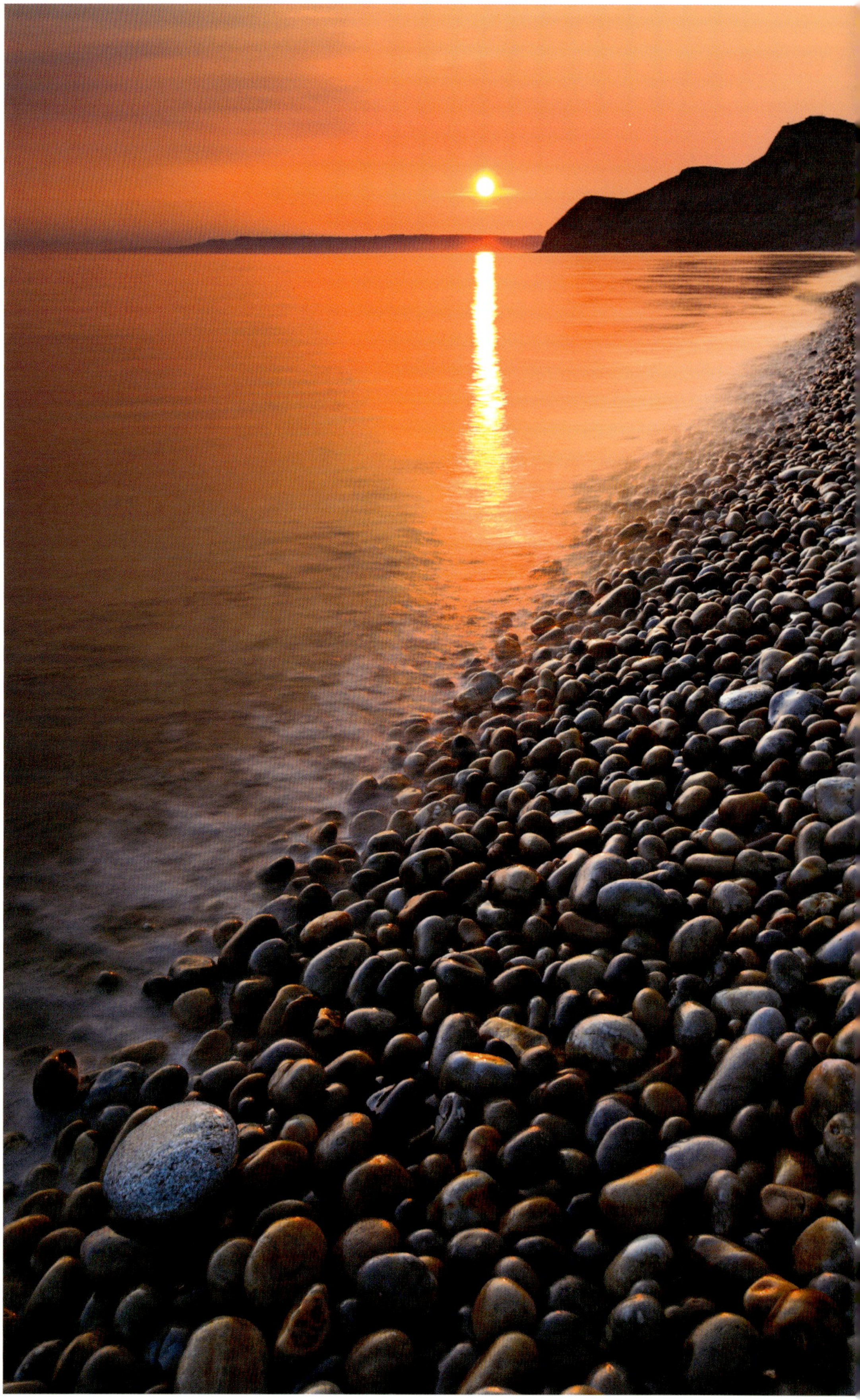

Sunset over the west Dorset coastline, captured from the pebbly Eype Beach.

Seatown

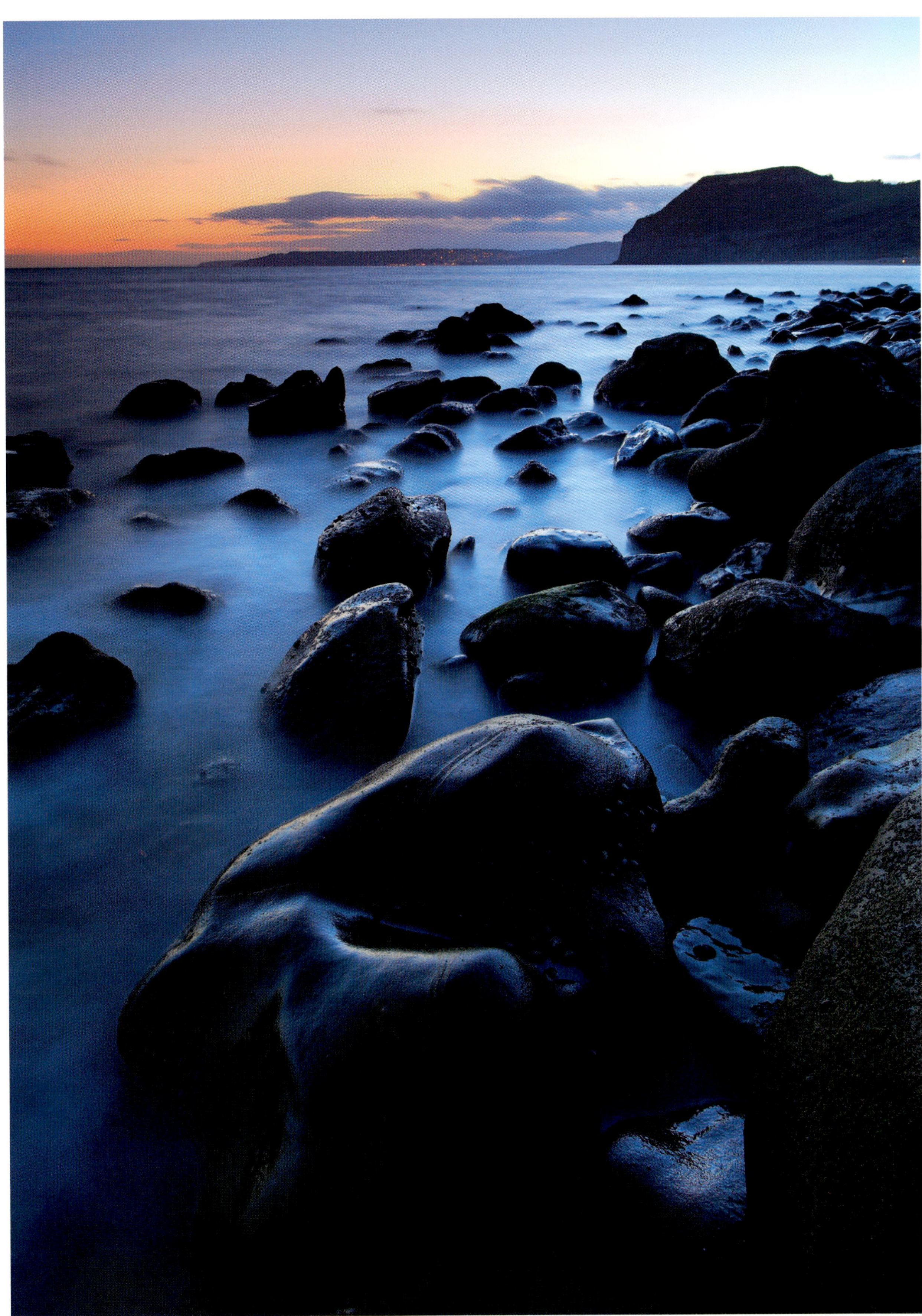

Low tide at Seatown exposes shiny black boulders, treacherous to walk upon but nevertheless fascinating to photograph. The huge cliff, Golden Cap, dominates the coastline in this part of west Dorset. At a towering 191 metres, it's the highest point anywhere along the Jurassic coast of Devon and Dorset.

Lyme Regis

Looking eastwards from the sea
defences at Lyme Regis, you may
just make out the sunlight shining
on Golden Cap in the distance.

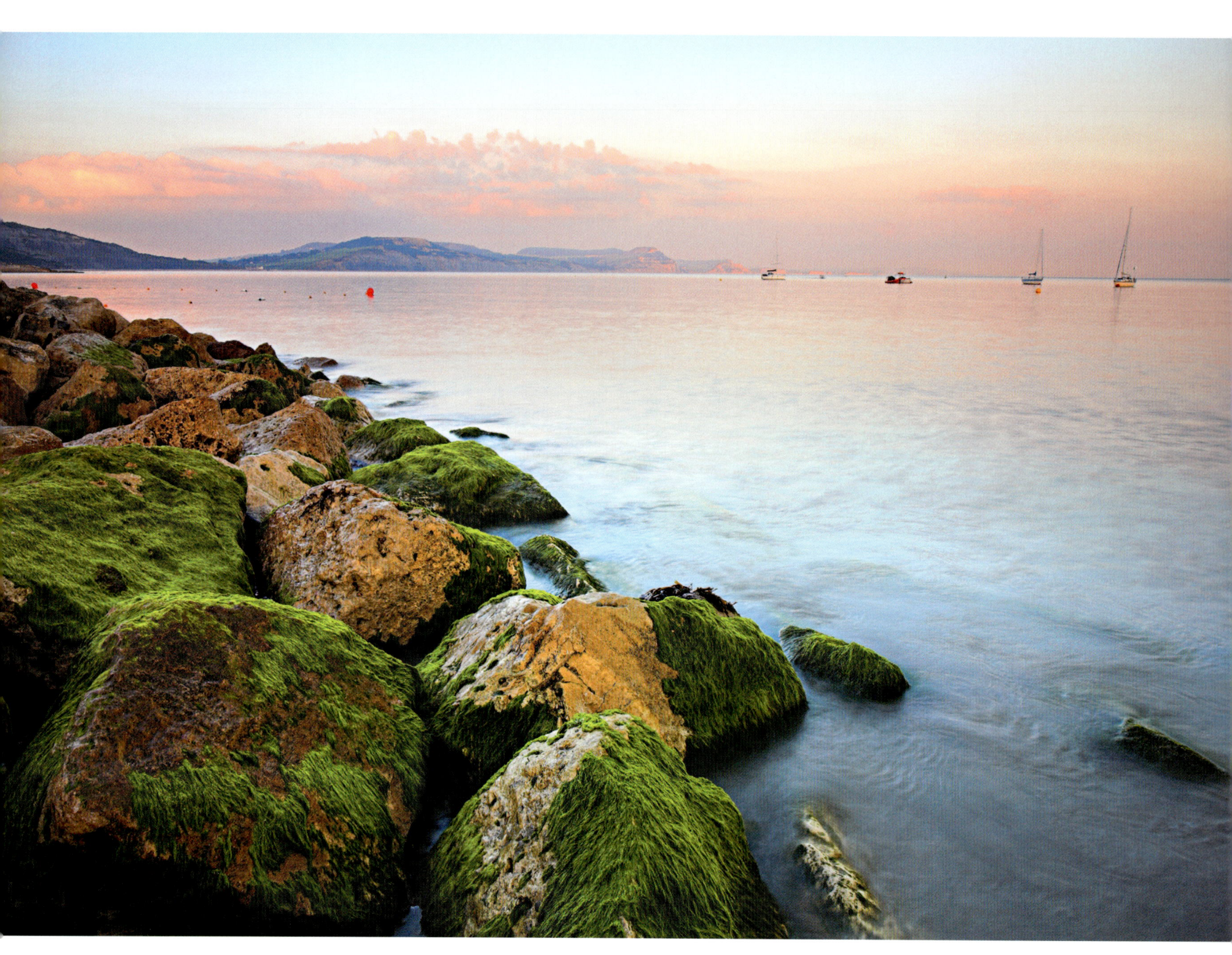

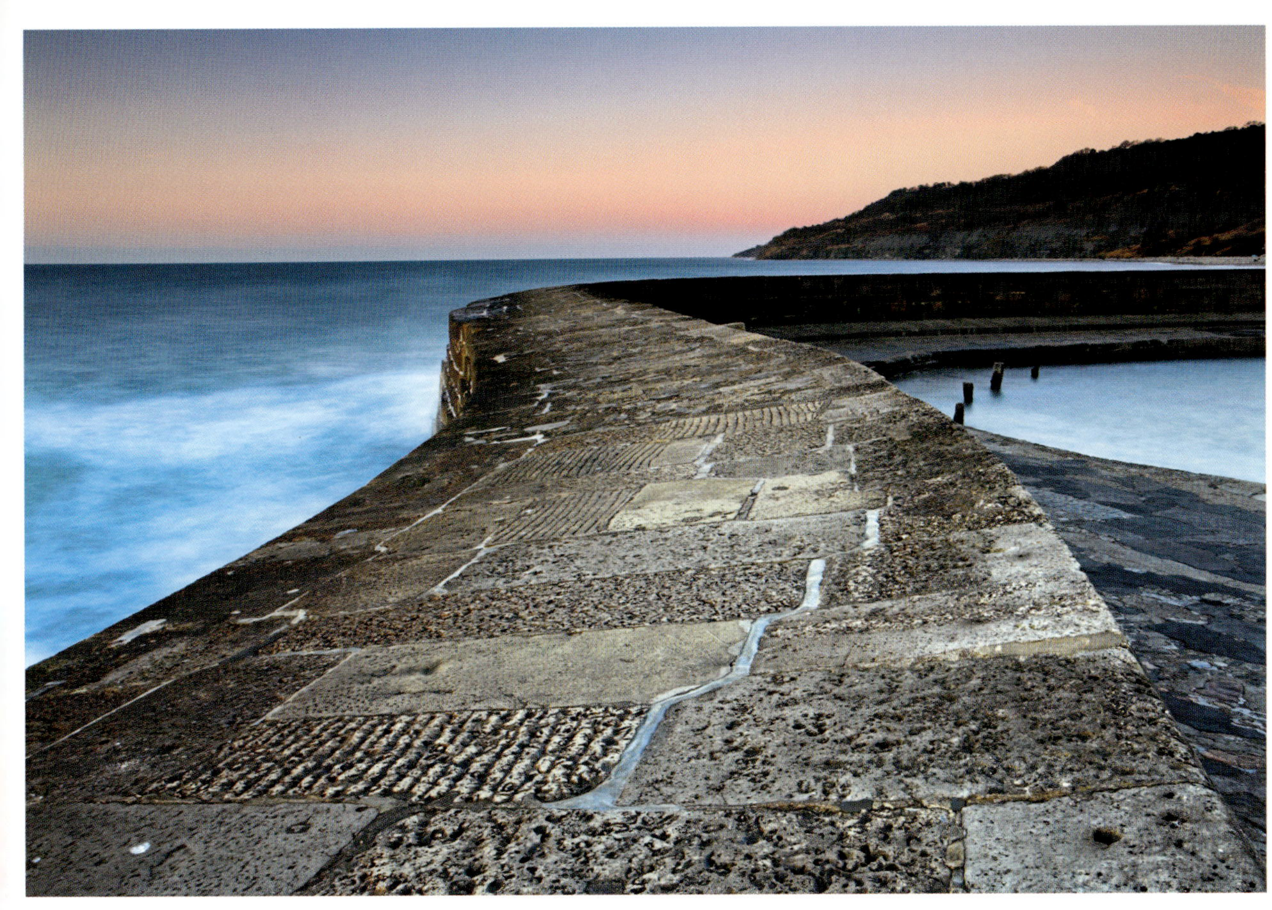

The harbour wall at Lyme Regis is known as 'The Cobb'. The original wall was created as far back as the thirteenth century to form both a breakwater and an artificial harbour for Lyme Regis. After its construction the town prospered for hundreds of years, becoming a major trading port with France.

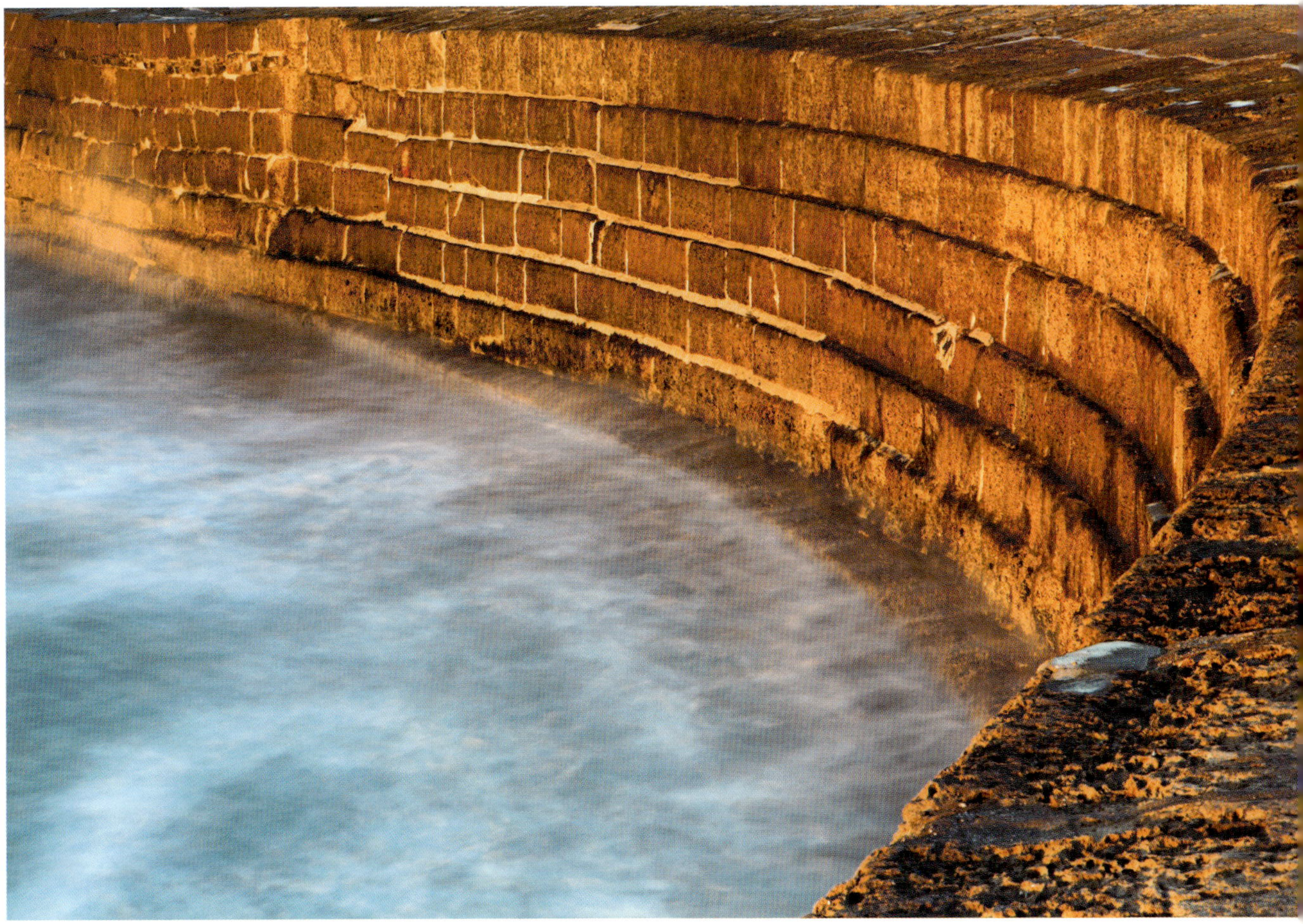

The golden light of sunset creates a peaceful atmosphere over The Cobb and transforms the grey stone of this harbour wall.

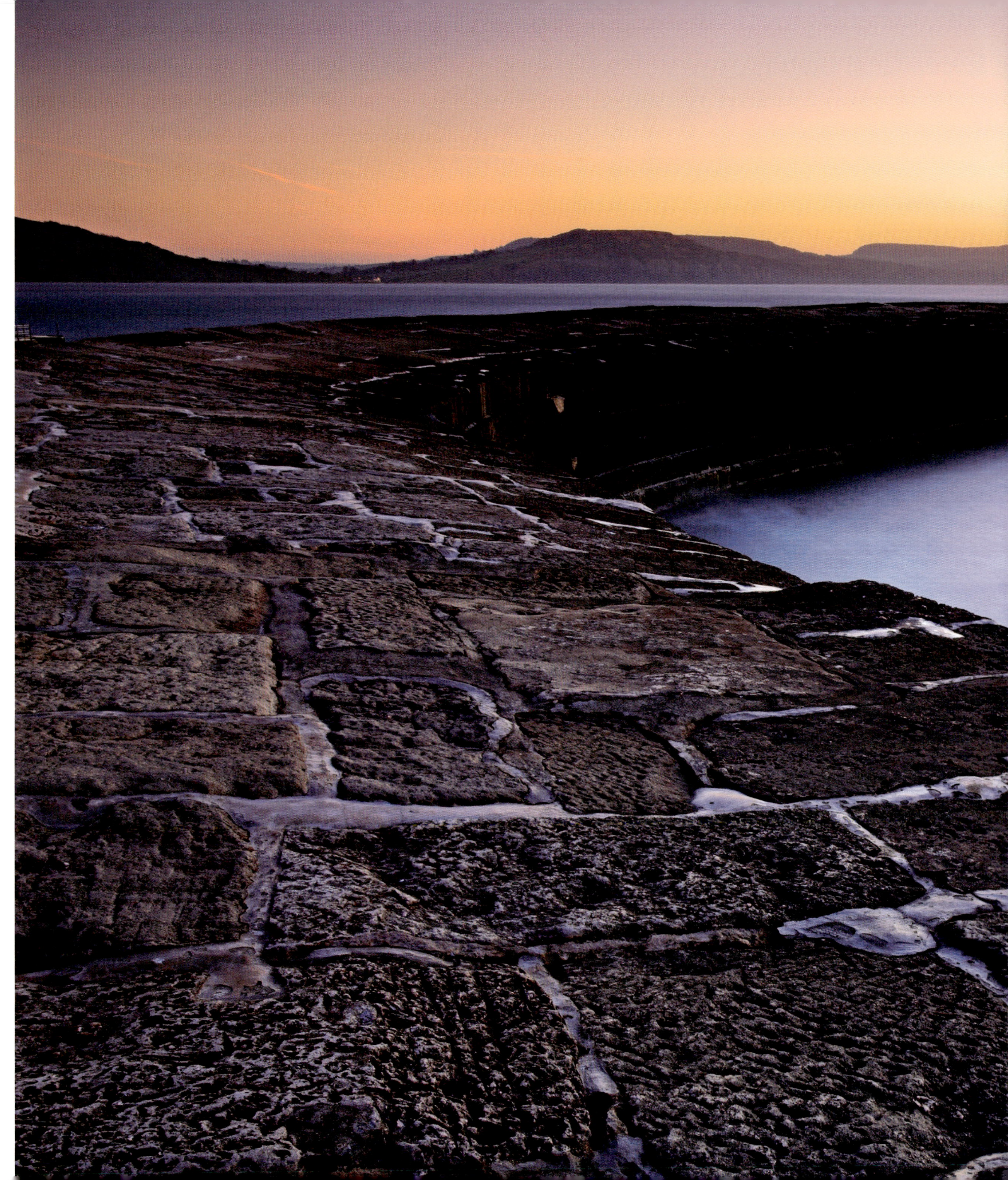

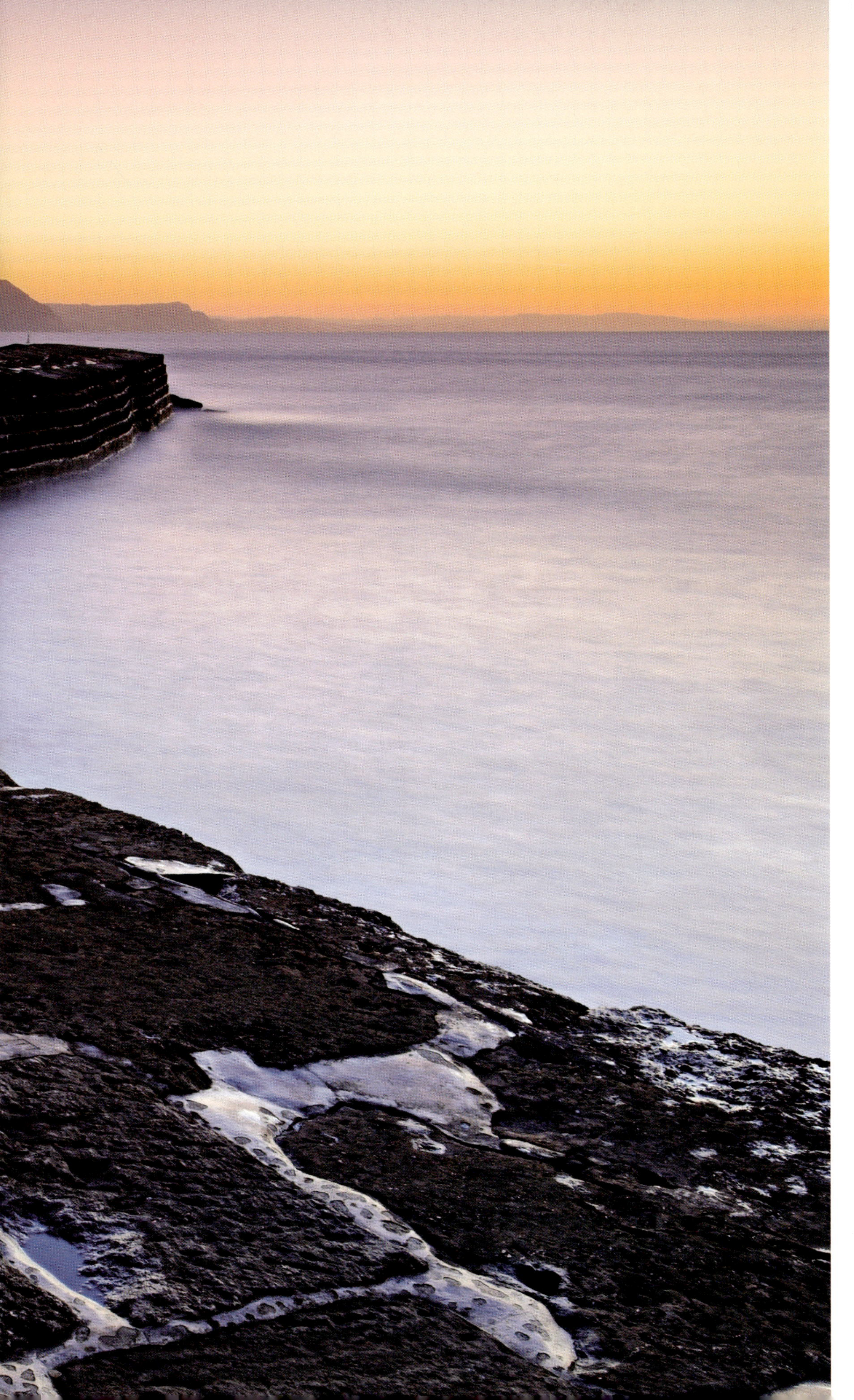

The Cobb as we see it today was constructed in 1820 using Portland stone. This curving wall boasting tremendous character has featured prominently in history, most recently rising to Hollywood stardom in the film The French Lieutenant's Woman with Meryl Streep and Jeremy Irons.

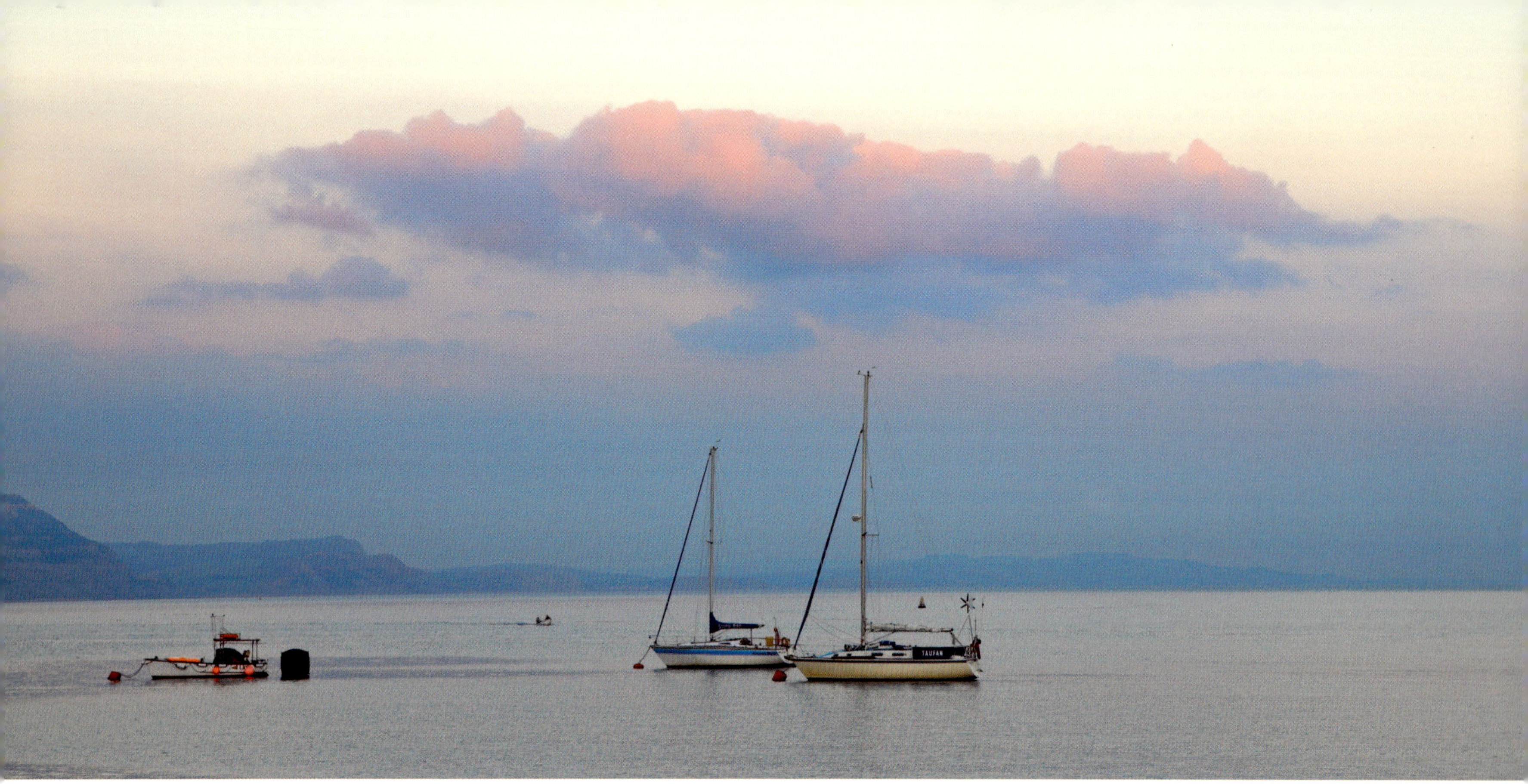

Together with some much loved
fish and chips, this Lyme Regis
scene makes for the perfect English
summer holiday!

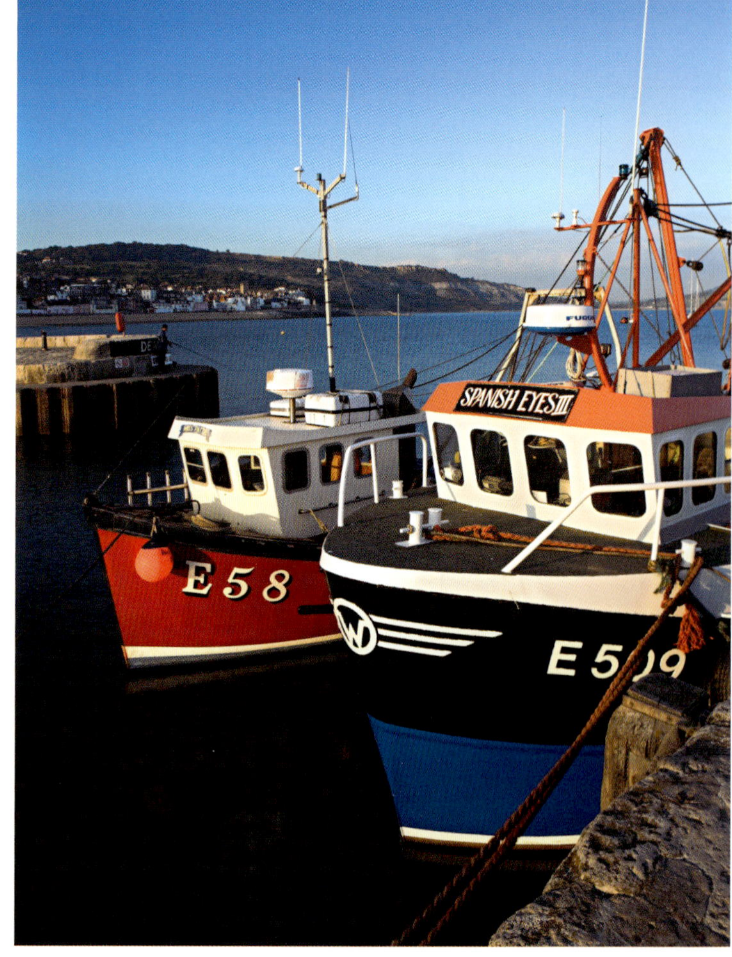

Fishing vessels safely moored within
Lyme Regis' strong harbour walls.